IMAGES
of America

THE NEW JERSEY TURNPIKE

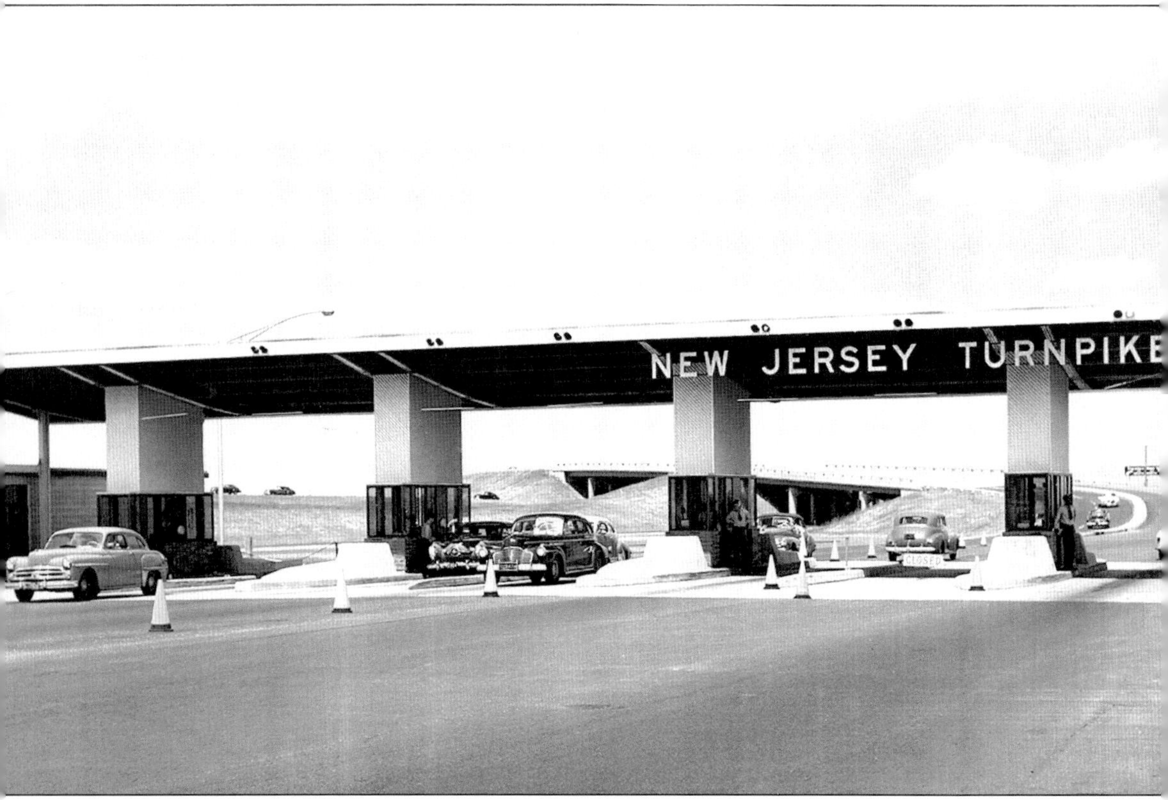

Even though traffic looks light in this early-1950s photograph of Interchange 11 in Woodbridge, traffic on the turnpike in 1952—the first full year of operation—exceeded traffic and revenue volumes that experts predicted would be attained in 1968—some 16 years in the future. In 1952 almost 18 million revenue vehicles, averaging 20,765 vehicles per day, paid over $16 million in tolls, a daily average of $44,386. Truck traffic exceeded the original estimates of the engineers, running 231 percent ahead in volume and 76 percent ahead in tolls. These accomplishments, while exceeding the most optimistic expectations, posed a problem for the Turnpike Authority in providing for immediate enlargement of certain parts of the turnpike's facilities. The problems were solved in a short time, and the unusually heavy travel during summer and fall, at times averaging four times the engineers' estimates, was handled throughout the 118 miles of the turnpike without delay.

IMAGES
of America

THE NEW JERSEY TURNPIKE

Michael Lapolla and Thomas A. Suszka

ARCADIA
PUBLISHING

ISBN 978-0-7385-3577-7

Published by Arcadia Publishing
Charleston, South Carolina

Printed in the Unites States of America

Library of Congress Catalog Card Number: 2004102349

For all general information contact Arcadia Publishing at:
Telephone 843-853-2070
Fax 843-853-0044
E-mail sales@arcadiapublishing.com
For customer service and orders:
Toll-Free 1-888-313-2665

Visit us on the Internet at www.arcadiapublishing.com

The authors' proceeds from the sale of this book will be given to the Harry Laderman Scholarship.

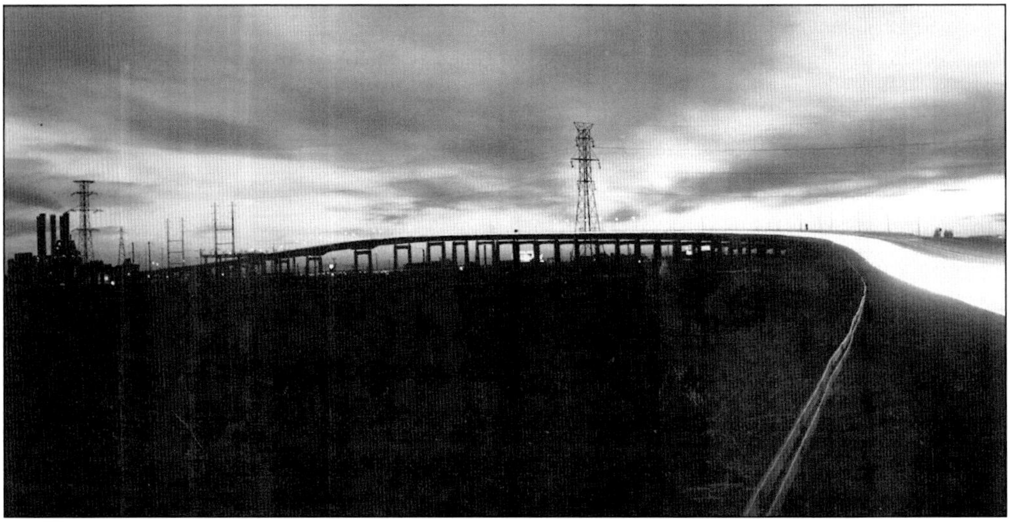

This dramatic night view of the Passaic River Bridge in Newark was prominently featured in the 1952 New Jersey Turnpike Authority Annual Report. The bridge, located at the northern end of the turnpike, is the section most people identify with the New Jersey Turnpike: car and truck lanes, oil refineries, and skyline views of Newark, New York City, and the Jersey Meadows. This visually interesting section has been the inspiration for artists and is immortalized in countless songs, poems, and paintings.

CONTENTS

ACKNOWLEDGMENTS

Thanks to the following people for their help in the completion of this book: the New Jersey Room of the Jersey City Library, the New Jersey Room of the Newark Library, the Alexandria Library at Rutgers University, Joe Keenan of the Elizabeth City Library, Betty Epstein of the State of New Jersey Archives, New Jersey County Government magazine, and Rachel Swayze. Special thanks to B. R. Rapacki and family, Teresa Hale, Charlene Sanders, Mitchell E. Dakelman, Joe Viola Jr., Richard Walley, and Homer R. Hill for use of their turnpike photographs, former turnpike photographers Martin Ostergaard, Al Oleck, and Joe Ferrigine for their timeless photographs; John Keller, turnpike engineer, for the section on Potter's Field; Joe Orlando and Mary Lou Einhorn for their help in the completion of this book; George Meyer of HNTB for his photographs and knowledge of turnpike engineering history; and Michael Costello for being a huge help in research, layout, and text preparation for this book.

Growing up in Elizabeth, I could see the old Exit 13 from my bedroom window. Now, 40 years later, the fact that I am in charge of the world's greatest highway means that the gods definitely have a sense of humor.

I would like to dedicate this book to my wife, Sue, for her love and unending support; to my children, Michael and Maggie Mei, who I hope won't be too disappointed when they finally realize that their Dad doesn't own the turnpike, he just works there; and to my nephew, John, whose strength and courage (and appreciation of a good turnpike joke), while facing one of life's greatest challenges, never ceases to amaze me.

—Michael Lapolla

At a 1984 Bruce Springsteen concert in New Jersey, before playing "Open All Night," Bruce said, "This is a song about the Golden Roadway of the East, the New Jersey Turnpike." For me, it's not the roadway, but the people I have worked with here at the turnpike, my "Turnpike family," especially Diane Scaccetti and Michael Lapolla, who have made working on the highway golden. To my friends and family, especially my sister Wanda, you have made my life pure gold. And to my wife, Mary, and children, Thomas, Matthew, and Elise, to whom I dedicate this book, you have given me more love, understanding, and joy than heaven will allow. Thank you and I love you.

—Thomas A. Suszka

INTRODUCTION

Why write a book about the New Jersey Turnpike? Surely you have heard about it somewhere—a late-night comedian's joke, a story on the news, a reference in a book, maybe even in a cartoon. It has been in all those places.

Having lived in the very shadow of the New Jersey Turnpike for my entire life, I, like most people, tended to take it for granted. It is there. As far as most of us are concerned, it has always been there and always will be there. It is just an amazing concoction of pop culture and functionality in your backyard.

Still, you may tell yourself that it is just a road, so what is the big deal? Well, you would be very surprised to find out.

Just over two years ago I had the privilege of being named executive director of the New Jersey Turnpike Authority. Shortly after walking through the front doors of the administration building, I could just sense something was different. To understand the people and the place, you have to know the history. And once you understand the history of the New Jersey Turnpike, you understand that anything is possible and anything can and will happen.

It was the road that had to be done. Not just done, but done in what would be considered an impossible time frame by today's standards. The very thought of the expedience necessary to complete the original New Jersey Turnpike is enough to cause an administrator panic in this day and age. By comparison, an ongoing project one-sixth the scale of the New Jersey Turnpike has been on the drawing board for more than 10 years.

But the times called for the project, and so it had to be. And like most initiatives of such great scale, leaders create the vision, but it falls to the people to get it done. And in this case, the difference turned out to be the people.

The original New Jersey Turnpike employees had an inordinate sense of pride in what they were accomplishing. It is a rare experience to be able to get involved on the ground level of something as enormous as the construction of the New Jersey Turnpike, but a handful of people had just such an opportunity. They made history and a difference in the lives of billions of people, all the while probably never realizing just how much of an impact they were making. From the engineers designing the road to the construction workers building it and the clerks and administrative personnel helping to organize it, there was a pride of ownership that was immeasurable. I am convinced that this is where all the great things of the following half-century have emanated from.

But being a relatively young roadway at 53 years old, there has been an amazing intermingling of the original employees with the current ones. Just about everyone here today seems to know someone from the first days of the turnpike, including myself, despite my late arrival. The pride that each employee has had for his or her job has carried forward from one era to the next.

We recently said goodbye to one of our longstanding employees who retired after serving the Turnpike Authority with distinction for more than 50 years. And while there never may be another 50-year employee, there will most certainly be the legacy of one.

When the television news crews focus their attentions on impending snowstorms and the ongoing efforts to keep the roads clear, there are New Jersey Turnpike employees driving those trucks with plows.

When the national media lauds the success of Express E-ZPass for reducing congestion on the roadways, there are New Jersey Turnpike employees working behind the scenes to make it run.

When accidents happen and a television reporter says, "Delays are minimal and the roadway has been cleared," it is because New Jersey Turnpike employees got it done.

Just about everything that you see, hear, and read about when it comes to the New Jersey Turnpike stems from the employees who do their jobs every day with the same conviction and pride of the people who set the whole operation in motion in 1951.

Pride has stood the test of time, and so many of us have reason to be grateful—commuters, people just passing through, and yes, comedians, too.

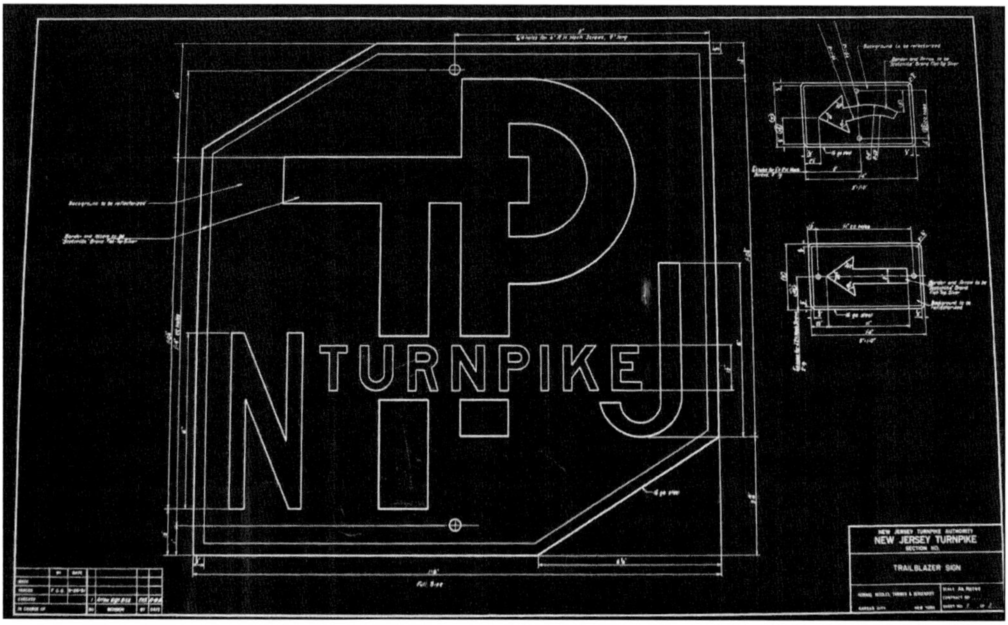

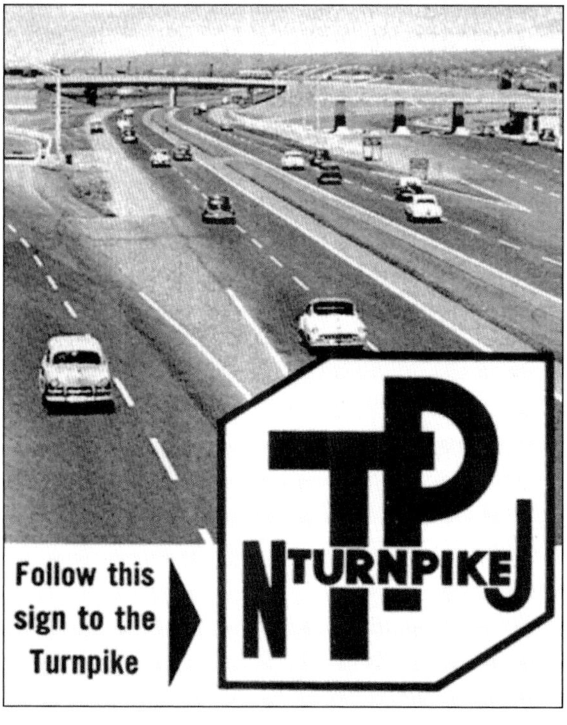

"Many names have been suggested for the new turnpike. The one that will serve the state best in all parts of our land is undoubtedly the one that was instinctively selected at the time the Authority was created, namely, New Jersey Turnpike," Gov. Alfred E. Driscoll stated in July 1950. The New Jersey Turnpike trailblazer sign was created prior to the opening of the turnpike in 1951. Placed in hundreds of locations throughout the tri-state region, as well as in newspaper advertisements and turnpike brochures, the Authority wanted motorists to recognize this sign and travel on the new toll road. Toll revenues were needed to repay $225 million in bond debt for original construction. At the end of the turnpike's 51st year of operation (2002), more than 6.2 billion revenue vehicles had followed this trailblazer sign and traveled on the New Jersey Turnpike.

One

The Vision, the Building and the Opening 1948–1952

Fifty-three years after the first cars traveled along it, the New Jersey Turnpike remains a marvel of engineering and operations, but the greatest marvel of all is how it came to be.

In the mid-1940s, New Jersey was stuck firmly in the middle of things—firmly between Delaware and New York to be exact. As a major conduit between the mid-Atlantic and New England regions, New Jersey lacked a major artery to connect these two popular areas, as well as to handle growing interstate commerce. Although traffic volumes were nowhere near today's levels, planners recognized the handwriting on the wall, and it was spelling logjam.

All too often it is the case that by the time you realize there is going to be a problem, it is usually too late to prevent it. That was more or less the situation that transportation officials found themselves facing in June 1948. Delaware officials had started construction of the massive Delaware Memorial Bridge that replaced the New Castle—Pennsville Ferry, which served as a connector between the two states. With its completion an influx of new traffic to New Jersey was sure to come, putting a strain on existing infrastructure and leaving motorists without options other than to lengthen the duration of their trips.

A year into the construction of the Delaware Memorial Bridge, New Jersey transportation officials put in motion the plan to build the New Jersey Turnpike, and they did so in record time. By governmental standards, the decision to approve construction and the target completion date were beyond ambitious. In fact, if proposed today, the plan would be called outrageous. Officials said the New Jersey Turnpike would open to traffic in 1951, and there would be no debate.

Planned as a 118-mile direct route between the Delaware Memorial Bridge and the George Washington Bridge in New York City, the New Jersey Turnpike was billed and marketed as the "roadway of the future," complete with technological innovations to improve motorist safety. Previously unheard-of methods of communicating with drivers to warn them about road conditions through changeable roadway signs and weather reporting stations along the road became the standard on the turnpike. Technology allowed for roadway speeds to be adjusted according to weather conditions in different sections of the state.

But more impressive than its technological advancements was the manner in which the turnpike was paid for—privately and without state assistance. The entire estimated cost of more than $230 million was funded through private bonding that was repaid by toll revenue.

Private funding. Advanced technology. Short deadline. New Jersey Turnpike planners had found nearly every wrinkle to make their efforts more difficult.

In January 1950, the first contract was awarded for construction of the roadway. From that point on, the project was in the hands of contractors and engineers to make the dream of the roadway of tomorrow a reality.

Over the course of the next year, construction moved at a breakneck pace. At the same time, the New Jersey legislature added some new features to the roadway's final design that provided connectors to the Pennsylvania Turnpike and across Newark Bay to Hudson County and ultimately New York City. Regardless of the challenges, officials were unmoved from their self-imposed construction deadline.

On November 5, 1951, three weeks ahead of schedule, the first 53 miles of completed roadway were opened to the public. Doing so opened up a new era of transportation in New Jersey, as motorists were able to travel from Deepwater to Bordentown. Over the next few weeks, the remainder of the roadway was opened to traffic, culminating in the completion of the New Jersey Turnpike's mainline roadway of 118 miles, from Deepwater to the George Washington Bridge, on January 15, 1952.

At a final cost of $230 million, New Jersey finally had an answer to the future needs of travelers and commuters.

In its first year of operation, the New Jersey Turnpike handled 787,195 vehicles. Now, 53 years later, more than 230 million cars travel the roadway annually thanks to the foresight and determination of a handful of men and women who had a vision half a century ago.

It now falls to another group of men and women to ensure that the future of the New Jersey Turnpike is as much an achievement as its past.

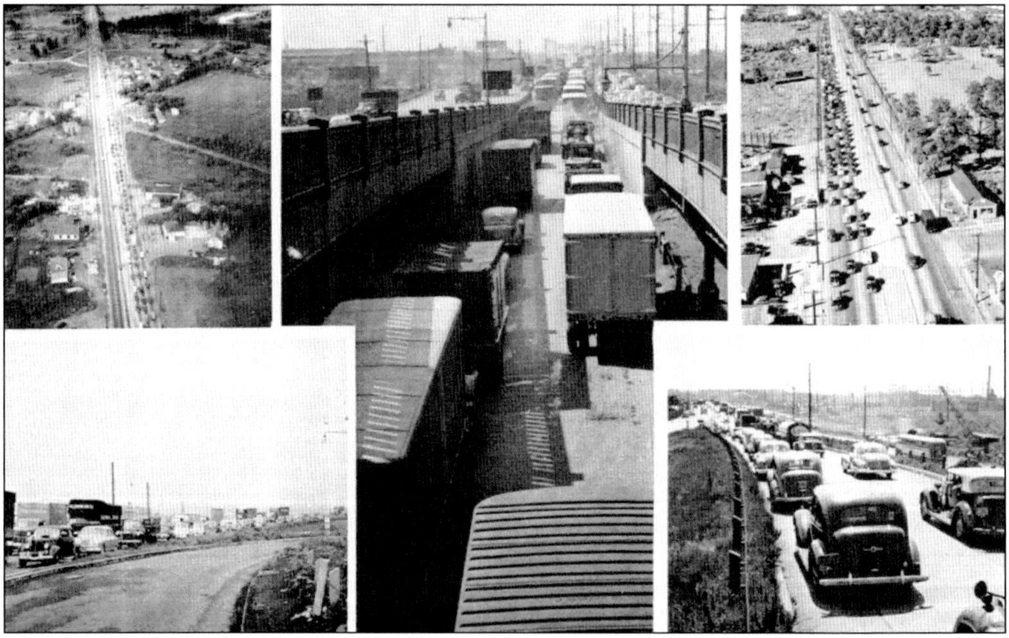

This collage of photographs showing traffic congestion on New Jersey Route 25 was part of a study done by Howard, Needles, Tammen, and Bergendoff, consulting engineers to the New Jersey Turnpike Authority. In the *Revenue and Engineering Costs Estimates Consolidated Report* dated September 15, 1949, E. R. Needles stated, "The need for the New Jersey Turnpike is so great and so obvious, and its financial soundness appears to be so clear, based on estimated costs and anticipated traffic and revenue from tolls, that the building of this Turnpike will prove to be a most notable accomplishment in serving highway transportation within the state of New Jersey and throughout the eastern states." (Courtesy of the *Newark News*.)

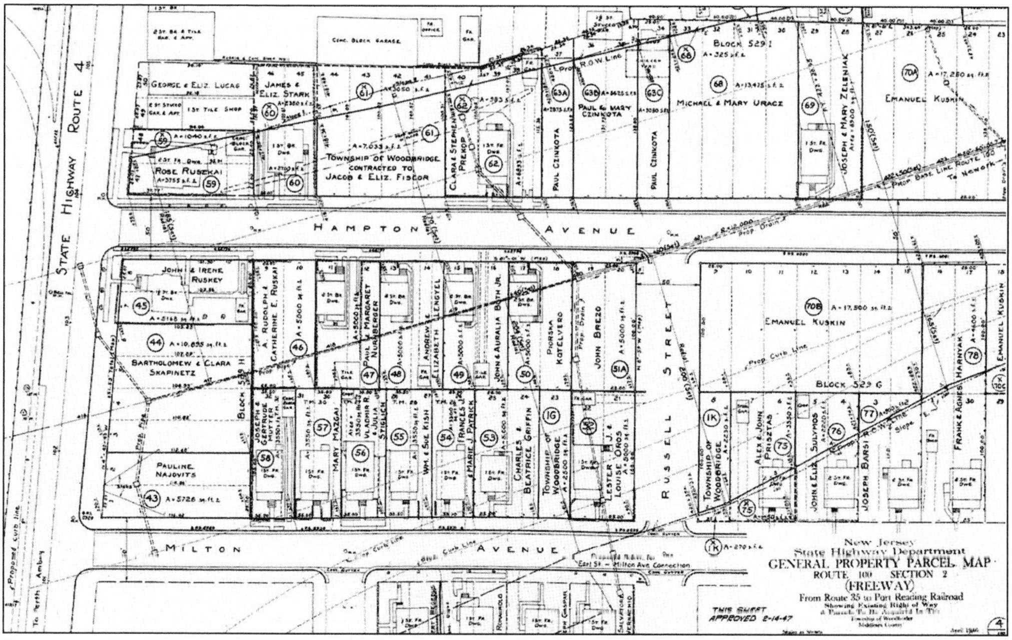

For several years prior to 1949, New Jersey highway officials realized the need for bold planning regarding major traffic arteries to solve the highway problems of the state. Route 100 was conceived as an expressway connecting the New Castle–Pennsville Ferry on the Delaware River, in the southern part of the state, with the George Washington Bridge over the Hudson River in the northern part. In June 1948, the State of Delaware began building the $45 million Delaware Memorial Bridge to replace the New Castle–Pennsville Ferry. After construction of the Delaware Memorial Bridge had started, New Jersey governor Alfred E. Driscoll realized the imperative need for a new artery in the state, and in 1949 steps were taken to determine the desirability and practicability of suggested Routes 100 and 300 as the state's backbone highway—the New Jersey Turnpike. It was then that the New Jersey Turnpike took the place of the proposed Route 100.

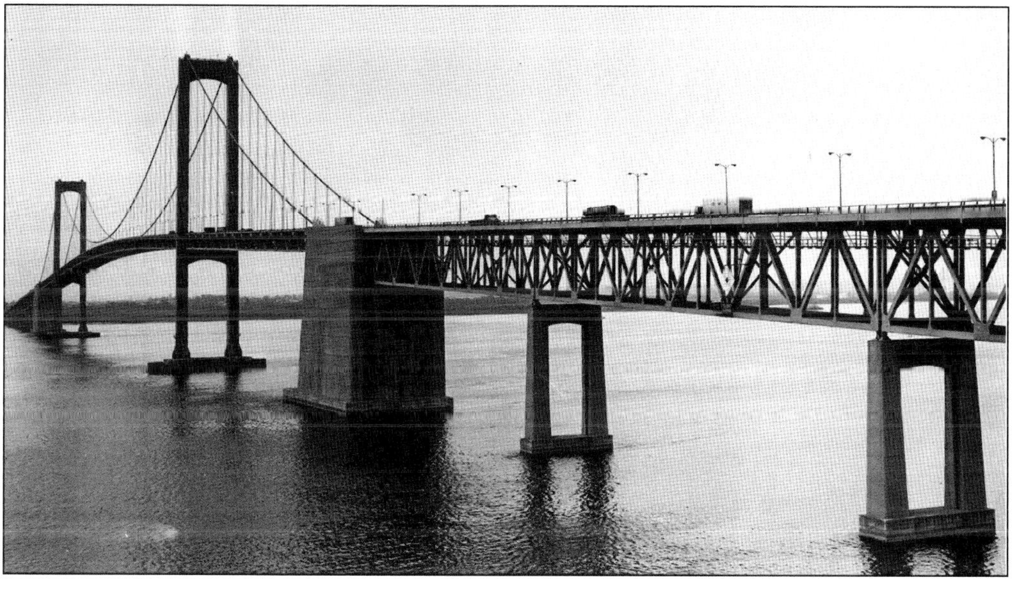

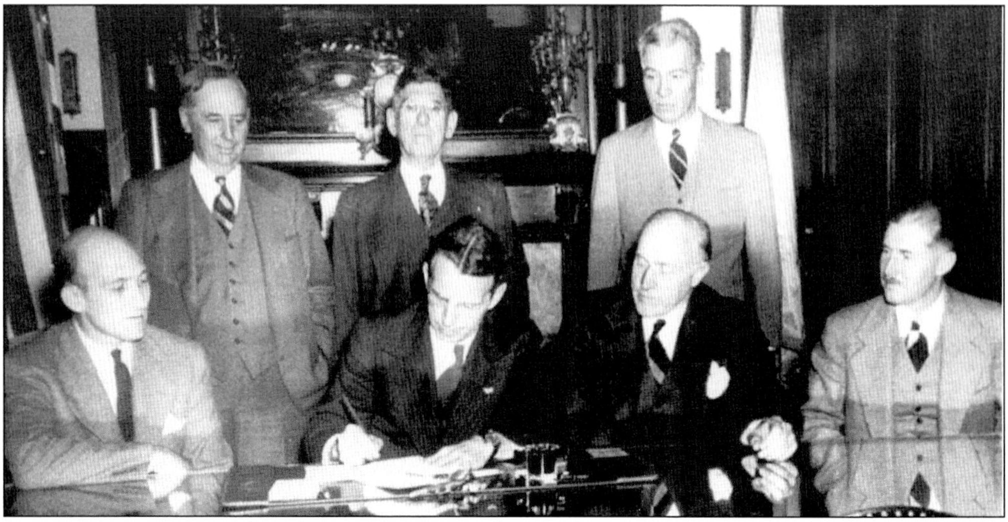

Gov. Alfred E. Driscoll signs the original bill to authorize construction of the New Jersey Turnpike. On October 27, 1948, the New Jersey Turnpike Authority Act (Chapter 454, Public Laws 1948) was approved "to facilitate vehicular traffic in the state of New Jersey by providing for the construction, maintenance, repair, and operation of Turnpike projects; creating the New Jersey Turnpike Authority and defining its powers and duties; providing for financing such projects by the issuance of Turnpike revenue bonds of the Authority, payable solely from tolls and other revenues; and providing for the collection of tolls and other revenues to pay the cost of construction, maintenance, repair, and operation of such projects and to pay such bonds and the interest thereon." Individuals shown, from left to right, are as follows: (first row) Herbert W. Voorhees (president, farm bureau), Governor Driscoll, Spencer Miller Jr. (state highway commissioner), and Charles M. Noble (state highway engineer); (second row) Edward W. Kilpatrick (assistant state highway engineer), Louis St. John (vice president, Atlantic City Planning and Improvement Association), and Kenneth B. Walton (member, Atlantic City Planning and Improvement Association).

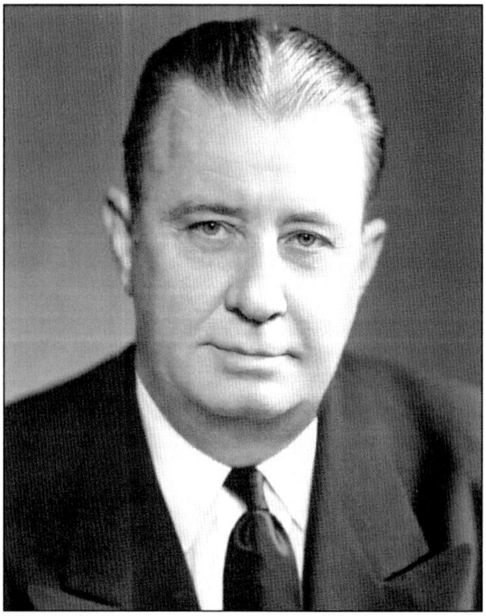

Paul L. Troast was appointed chairman of the New Jersey Turnpike Authority on March 31, 1949, by Gov. Alfred E. Driscoll to undertake the building of the 118-mile turnpike. Gen. W. W. Wanamaker, executive director of the Turnpike Authority, described Troast as "the chairman, the builder, a man of relentless drive, resourcefulness, energy, and vision, who gets to the heart of problems with astounding speed and directness, who gets things done without running roughshod over anyone." Troast served as chairman for more than eight years to the successful completion of "America's miracle road," without compensation, until the appointment of his successor in 1957.

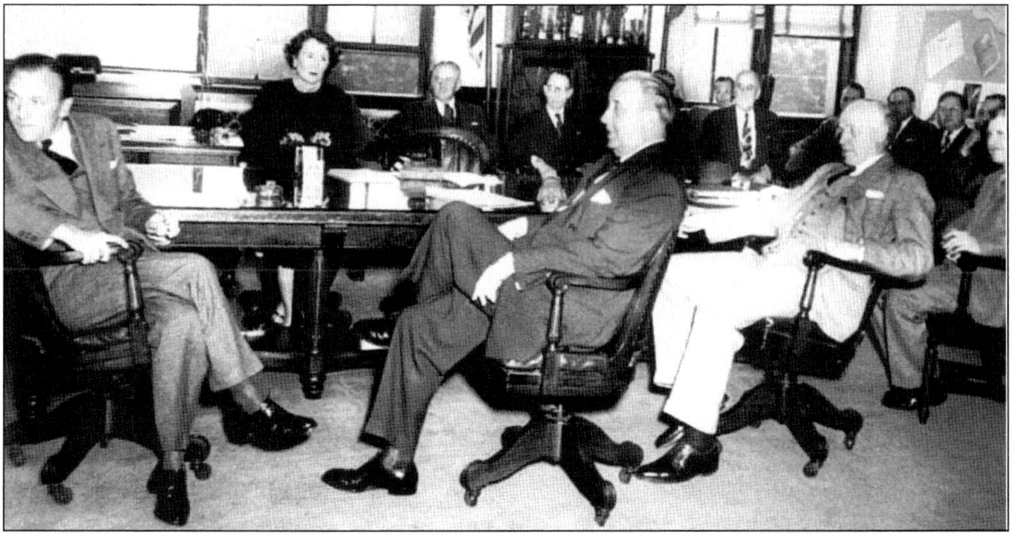

This meeting of the Authority was called into session by Chairman Paul Troast (center foreground) at the offices of the New Jersey Highway Department in Trenton at 2:30 p.m. on Tuesday, May 17, 1949. Present are Commissioner George F. Smith (far left) and Chief Engineer Charles M. Noble (far right); as well as Henry J. Woods Jr.; Commissioner Spencer Miller Jr. of the Highway Department; Mr. Ammann of Ammann and Whitney; Mr. Edwards of Edwards & Kelcey; Mr. Porter of O. J. Porter & Company Associated; General Robinson of Frederic R. Harris Inc.; Mr. Cather, Mr. Richards, Mr. McGonigee, and Mr. Brave of DeLeuw, Cather & Company; Colonel Needles of Howard, Needles, Tammen & Bergendoff; Mr. Warfield of Coverdale & Colpitts; Mr. Johansen, emeritus of the Highway Department; and members of the press. Seated across from the chairman is Lillian Schwartz, temporary secretary.

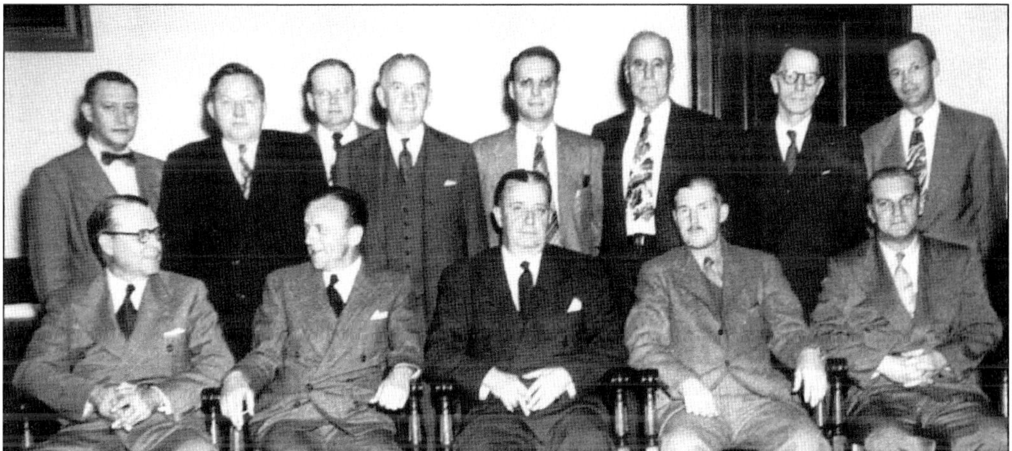

In this May 17, 1949 photograph of a meeting held only weeks after the Turnpike Authority was formed, Chairman Troast (seated center) convenes with Vice Chairman George F. Smith (seated second from left) and Chief Engineer Charles M. Noble (seated second from right), among others, at the statehouse in Trenton. Smith was president of Johnson & Johnson at the time he was appointed by Governor Driscoll and confirmed by the Senate as a member for the term ending March 31, 1954. On March 31, 1949, the same day Paul Troast was designated chairman by the governor, Smith was designated vice chairman. Smith served his full term of five years and several months until his successor, Joseph Morecraft Jr., was appointed by Gov. Robert B. Meyner.

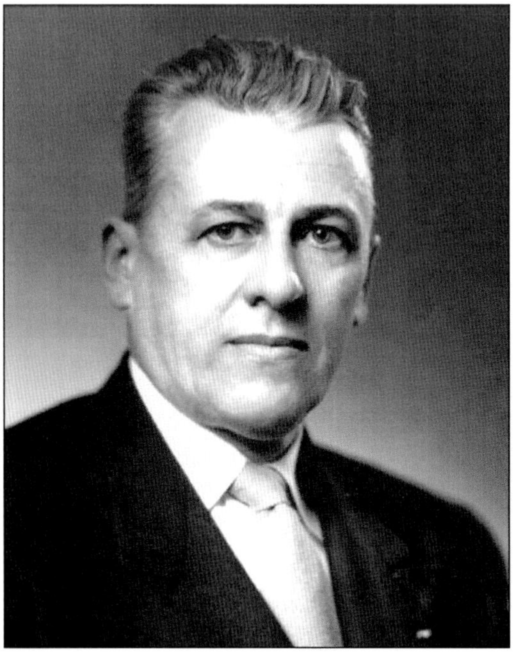

A veteran of 31 years' service in the U.S. Army Corps of Engineers and a graduate of West Point, Brig. Gen. W. W. Wanamaker was appointed executive director of the Authority on December 5, 1949. Upon completion of the turnpike, Wanamaker credited the outstanding work of the eight engineering firms and the two architectural firms who planned and supervised the construction of the turnpike. He felt that the successful completion of the project was due to the efforts of two groups—one group being Troast, Smith, and Lester. The second group was comprised of the more than 10,000 workers who actually built the turnpike. "The turnpike stands as a worthy tribute to the skill and resourcefulness of the construction industry, to American methods of private enterprise, and as a fitting memorial to the unfortunate few who lost their lives in its construction."

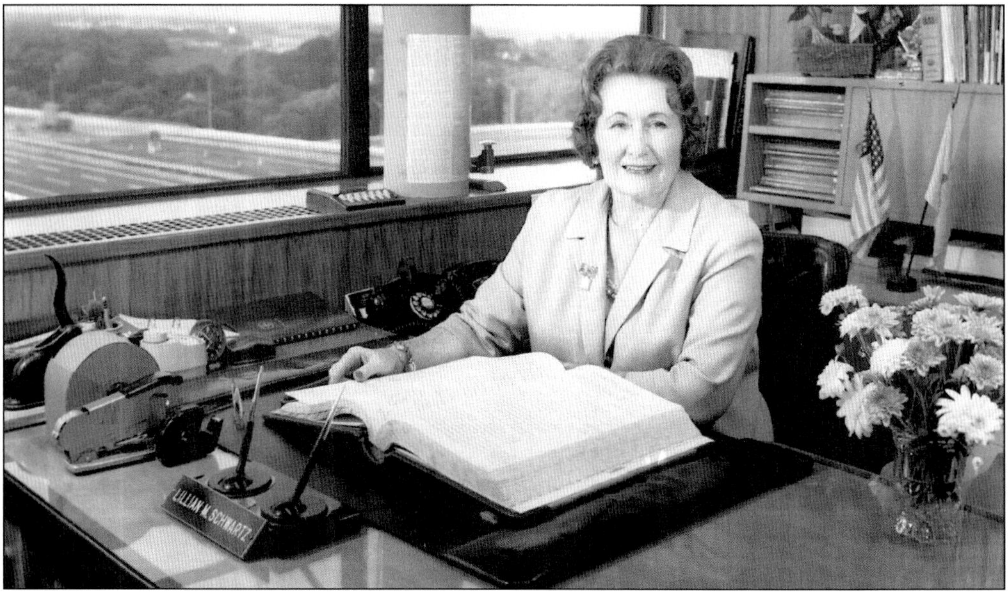

By the end of 1949, approximately 22 employees were hired, some on loan from the state Highway Department. They referred to themselves as the "Forty-Niners." Lillian M. Schwartz was the first person hired by the Turnpike Authority; she was hired as a temporary secretary on April 6, 1949, and was permanently appointed as recording secretary on November 6, 1949. At first she was told she would only work a day or two per week as secretary and assistant treasurer of the Turnpike Authority. However, during the early daily meetings of the Authority it was not uncommon for her to work well beyond a normal work day. Lillian preserved every piece of turnpike business as though future historians were standing at her back. She is remembered as the original Forty-Niner and "the First Lady of the Turnpike." Lillian retired from the Authority in 1982.

Aerial photographs, taken *c.* March 1950, show the proposed alignment of the New Jersey Turnpike. This photograph shows the proposed alignment through Hightstown, near Interchange 8 in the southern section of the state, where the turnpike traversed rolling land. Interchanges from New Brunswick to the south were planned to provide means for access to and from the rich agricultural areas of central and southern New Jersey, offering the growers in these areas direct and quick movement of their products into the metropolitan areas of New York and Philadelphia.

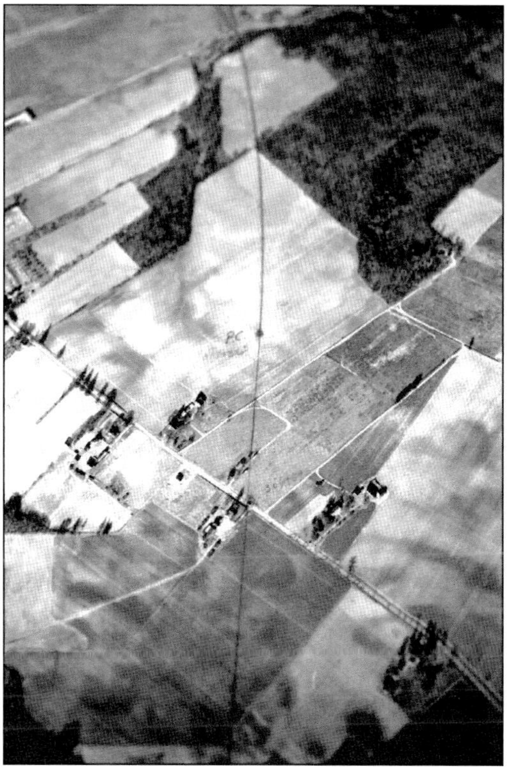

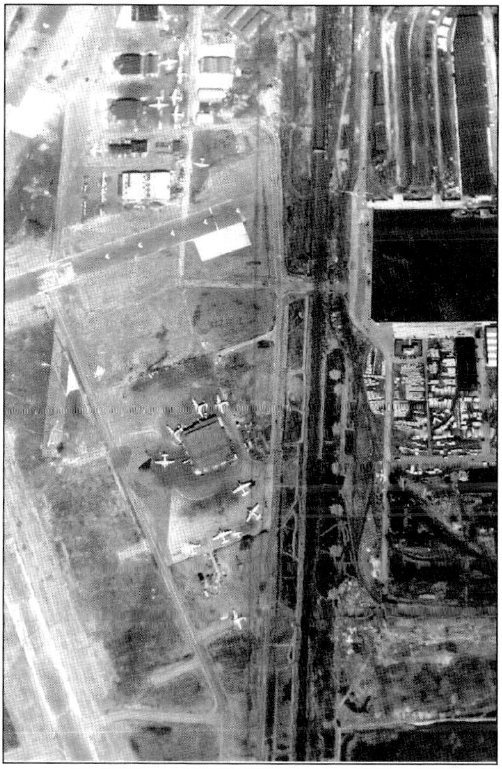

This aerial photograph shows a different view of the state, as the proposed alignment bisects Newark Airport and Port Newark in Newark, near Interchange 14. It was reported to the Authority in 1949 that Newark Airport was not being used by the international commercial airlines because the traffic congestion made it practically impossible to maintain flight schedules. The northern section of the turnpike passed through the intense industrial development of New Jersey, offering highly interesting vistas of the state not to be had by any other means of travel available in the 1950s.

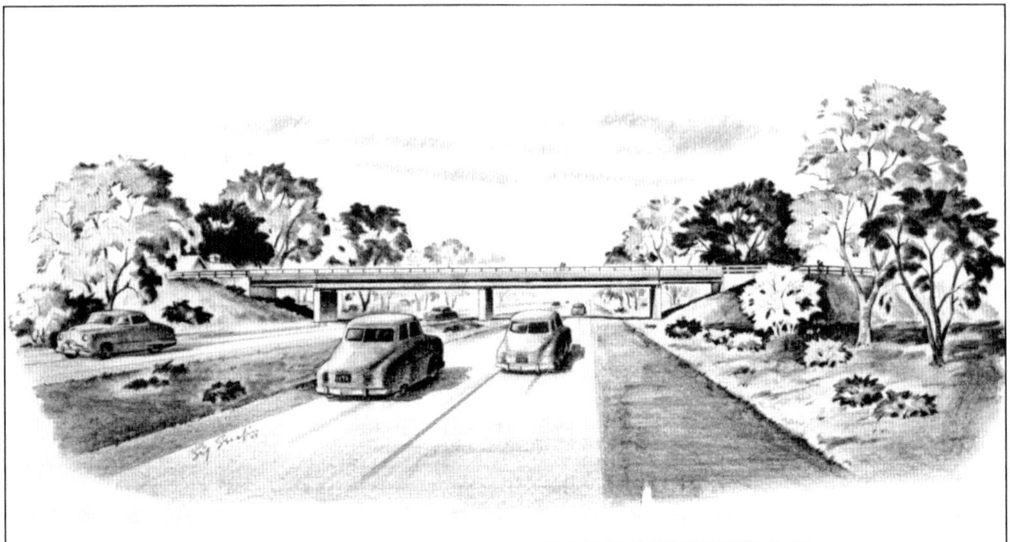

TYPICAL VIEW OF TURNPIKE NORTH OF NORTH CAMDEN INTERCHANGE SHOWING CROSSROAD BRIDGE

This artist's rendition of a typical view of the New Jersey Turnpike north of the North Camden Interchange shows a crossroad bridge. The illustration was part of the consolidated report of September 1949. The report stated: "Southward from New Brunswick, the New Jersey Turnpike will traverse rolling lands which are essentially agricultural. From these lands come the vegetables, grains, fruits, and dairy products, which typify 'the Garden State.'"

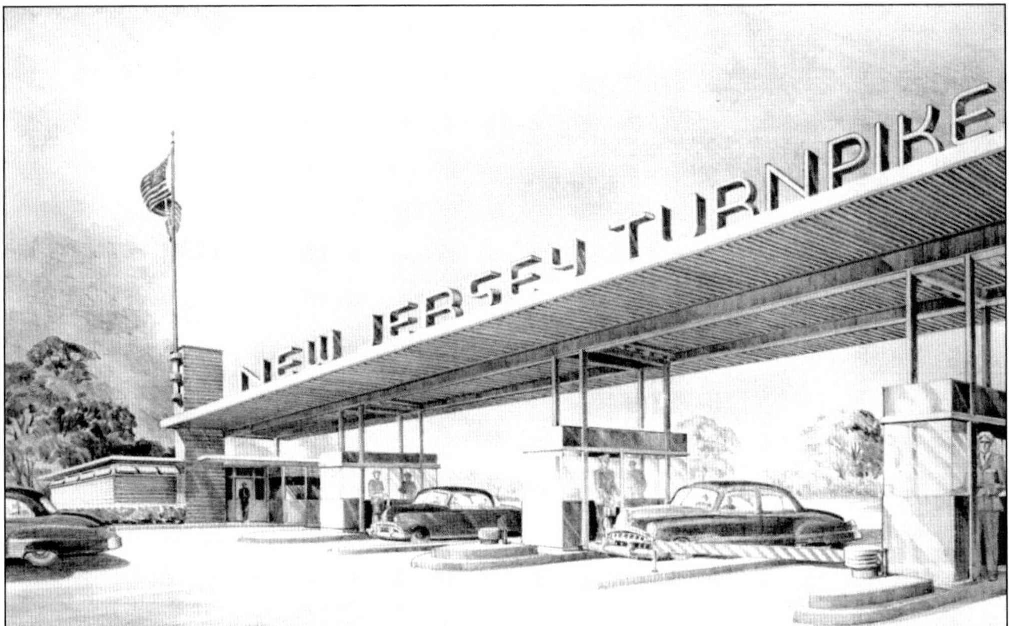

From an original press release, Chairman Troast stated: "In an express highway such as our Turnpike, it is imperative that the interchanges permit adequate and free-flowing traffic. Facilities which are improperly designed can seriously limit traffic volume on the Turnpike. Exit facilities which are incapable of easily accommodating vehicles under peak load conditions, such as highways to and from the shore resorts during vacation, can result in serious traffic congestion. Our interchanges will be so designed that these handicaps will not exist."

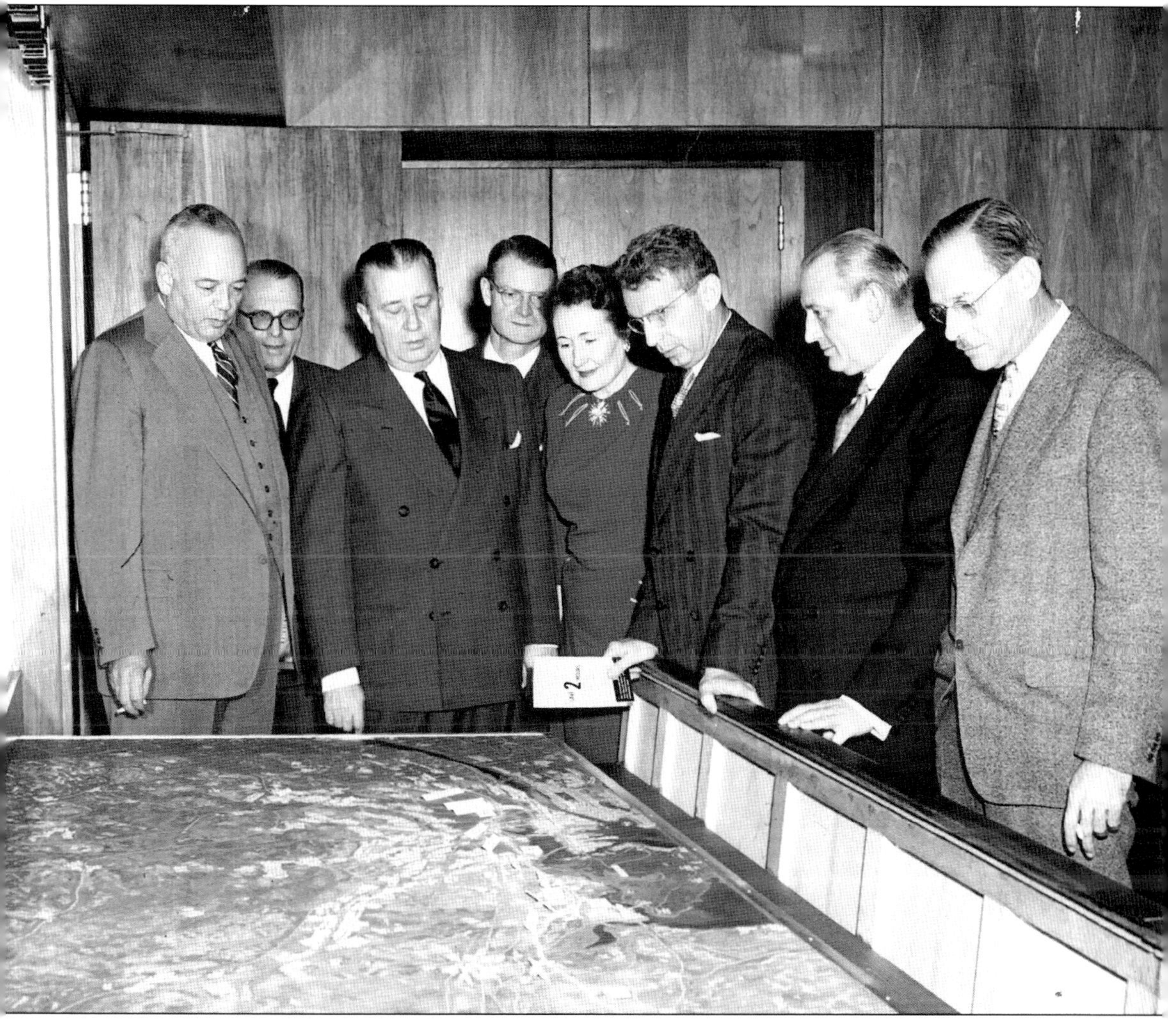

A 16-foot model of New Jersey's 118-mile turnpike was placed on display in the rotunda of the State Capitol. Built to scale of 1.3 inches to the mile, the model shows the route of this privately financed superhighway, its 17 traffic interchanges, and their connections leading to east–west public highways. The model was available for use at conventions and other public functions to acquaint motorists and truckers with the turnpike route and its connections to public highways. In his first inaugural address to the legislature on January 21, 1947, the governor of the state of New Jersey, the Honorable Alfred E. Driscoll, included these remarks: "In our industrial age it is hardly necessary to emphasize the importance of a properly planned highway system for the entire state. Without an even and steady flow of commerce, New Jersey, the great industrial workshop with its important agricultural and recreational areas, would wither and die. Our arteries of commerce and pleasure must be protected and improved." Reviewing the display with Governor Driscoll (third from right) are, from left to right, Maxwell Lester Jr. (commissioner), Paul Troast (chairman), Ward J. Herbert (counsel to the Authority), and Lillian Schwartz (secretary).

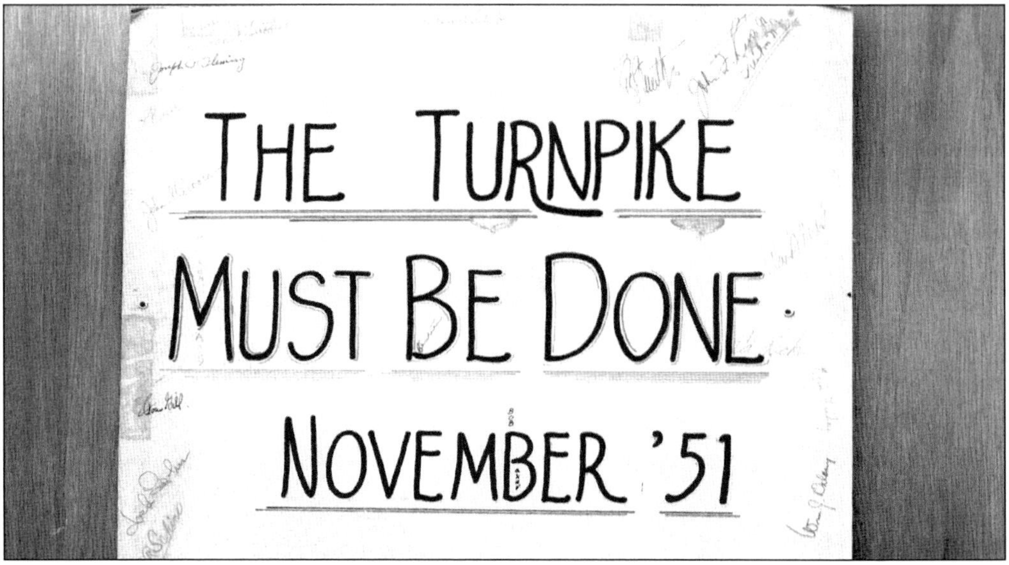

The Turnpike Authority occupied three rooms in the statehouse in Trenton, just around the corner from Governor Driscoll's office. These rooms served as the executive offices of the new authority. One of the first things Chairman Troast did was put the sign shown above on his office door. The notice was signed by a number of people involved in the turnpike project, including Turnpike Authority treasurer Maxwell Lester Jr. Additional office space was rented at 65 Prospect Street in Trenton.

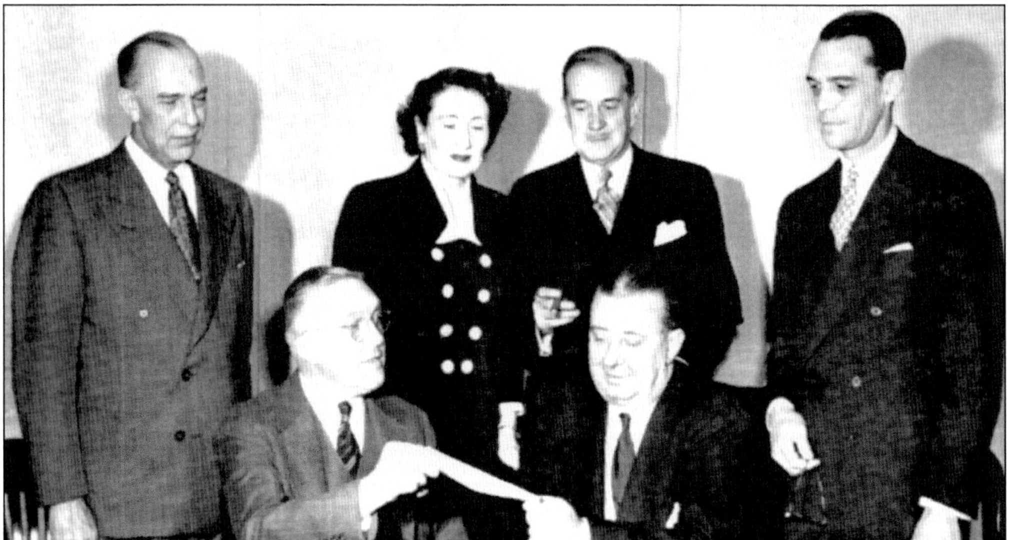

On February 17, 1950, New Jersey Turnpike Authority chairman Paul L. Troast (seated right) receives a check for $220 million from C. A. Buckley (seated left), vice president of Chase National Bank, to finance turnpike construction. The individuals standing are, from left to right, P. C. Beardsley (bank vice president); Lillian Schwartz (Authority secretary); L. Arnold Frey of Hawkins, Delafield, and Wood Bond Counsel; and Cheever Hardwick of Smith, Barney, and Company Fiscal Advisors. Fifty-three institutional investors, including forty-two insurance companies and five savings banks, agreed to make this loan to the Authority for the building of its trans-state toll expressway.

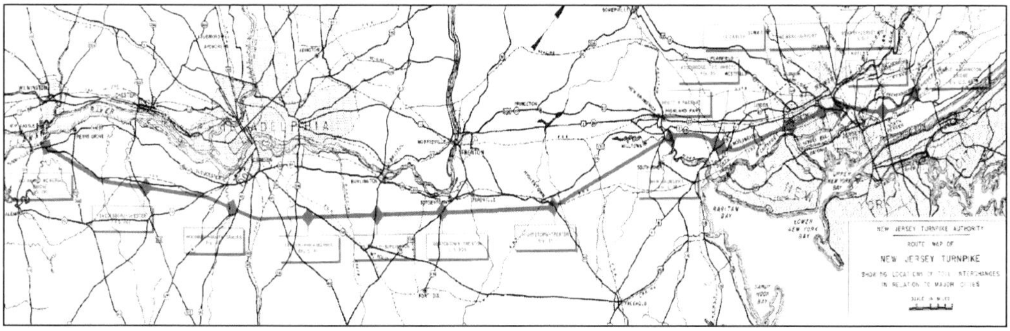

Spanning the state from north to south for 118 miles, the new turnpike, through interchanges, serves New Jersey's highly populous and industrial areas in the north and its rich agricultural lands in the south. It also connects with important public highways and thus serves motorists to and from the state's renowned shore resorts to the east and those traveling to and from the west, south, and north. The 118-mile turnpike was originally planned to have its northern terminus at Alpine. The terminus was soon changed to Route 6, which provided access to and from the George Washington Bridge over the Hudson River. The southern terminus at the Delaware Memorial Bridge, the first interchange, was near Swedesboro, where traffic to and from the Delaware Memorial Bridge across the Delaware River was served.

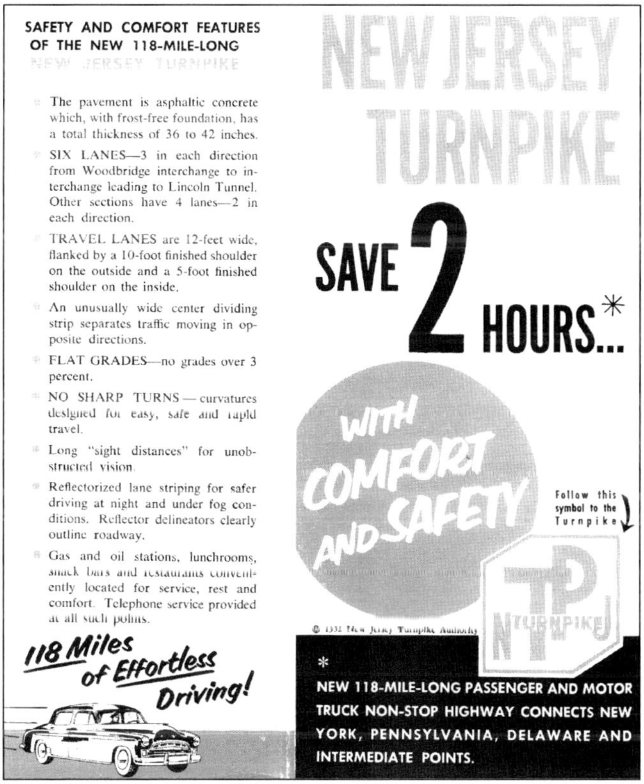

This New Jersey Turnpike advertisement boasts reduced travel time and safety on the world's most modern express highway. For the full 118 miles, motorists on the turnpike enjoyed uninterrupted travel since there were no crossroads, no left turns, and no red lights for its entire length. Only two stops were necessary: one at the point of entrance to pick up a ticket, and the other at the point of exit to pay the toll. Because of these factors and the safe, higher speeds permitted on the turnpike, the savings in travel time were substantial as compared to travel on other public highways.

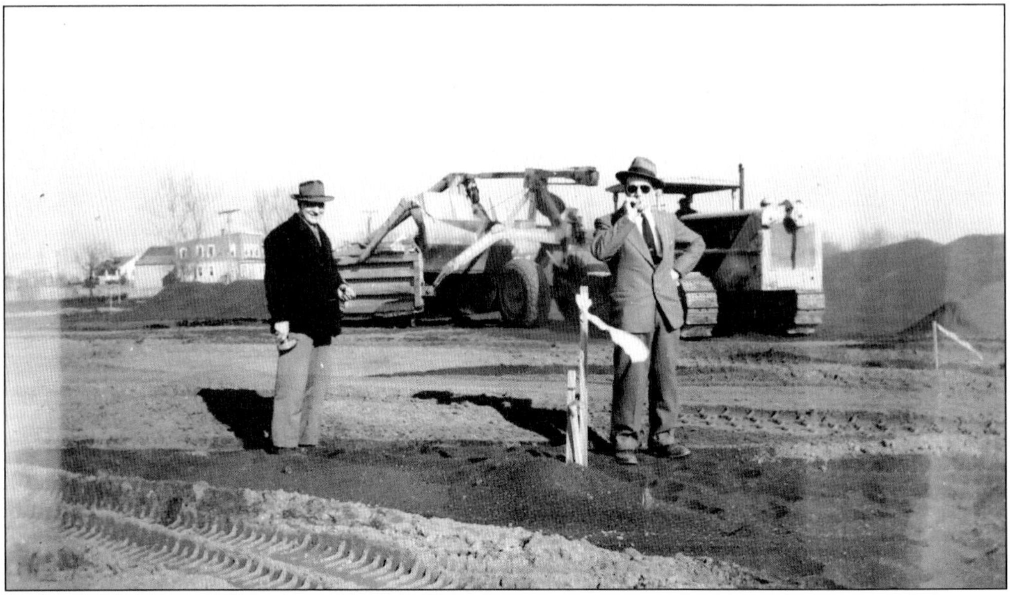

In January 1994, B. R. Rapacki forwarded a photograph album that belonged to his father, Bronislaw B. Rapacki (left). Rapacki, along with James O'Brien (right) worked for Frank Grad and Sons, associate architects for the Turnpike Authority. The top photograph shows Rapacki and O'Brien as they survey and stake construction site No. 10 in Woodbridge. Rapacki's own notes identify the photograph below as the "N. J. Turnpike, Looking south from Hartford Rd., Mt. Laurel Twnship., Burlington County, September 1950."

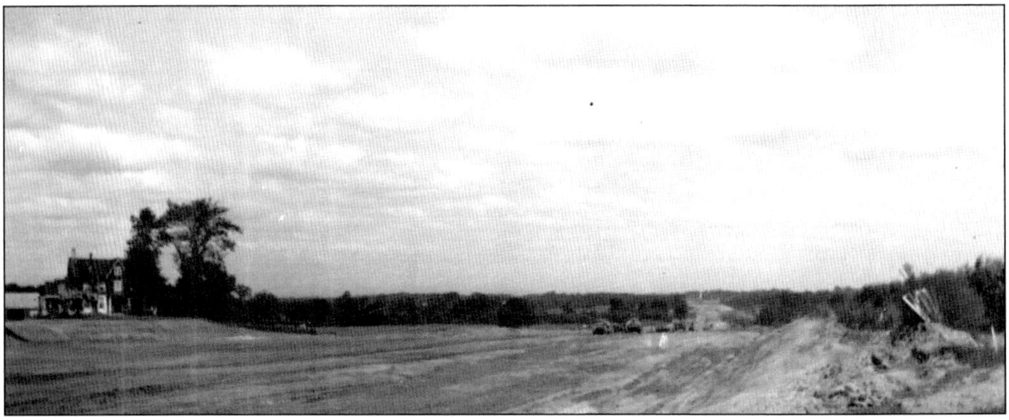

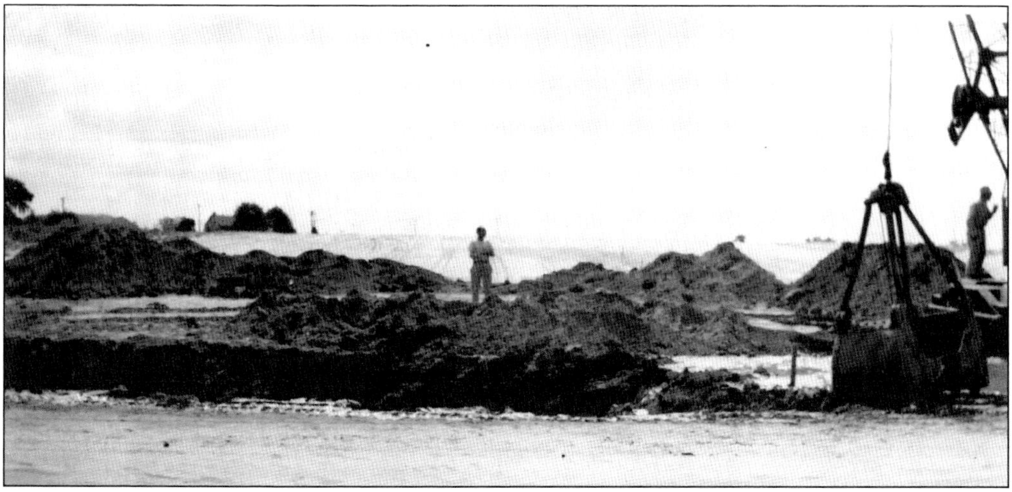

The top photograph is identified as: "N. J. Turnpike, Exc. For overpass foundations. Looking north from Hartford Rd. Mt. Laurel Township, Burlington, Co. 9/50." Upon receiving this photograph album, Robert Dale, director of operations, wrote to B. R. Rapacki: "The care which your late father took in compiling and documenting these photographs is remarkable evidence of the same care which thousands of men and women took in building this superhighway. Thank you for the insight into your family history, and thank you for helping us to remember ours."

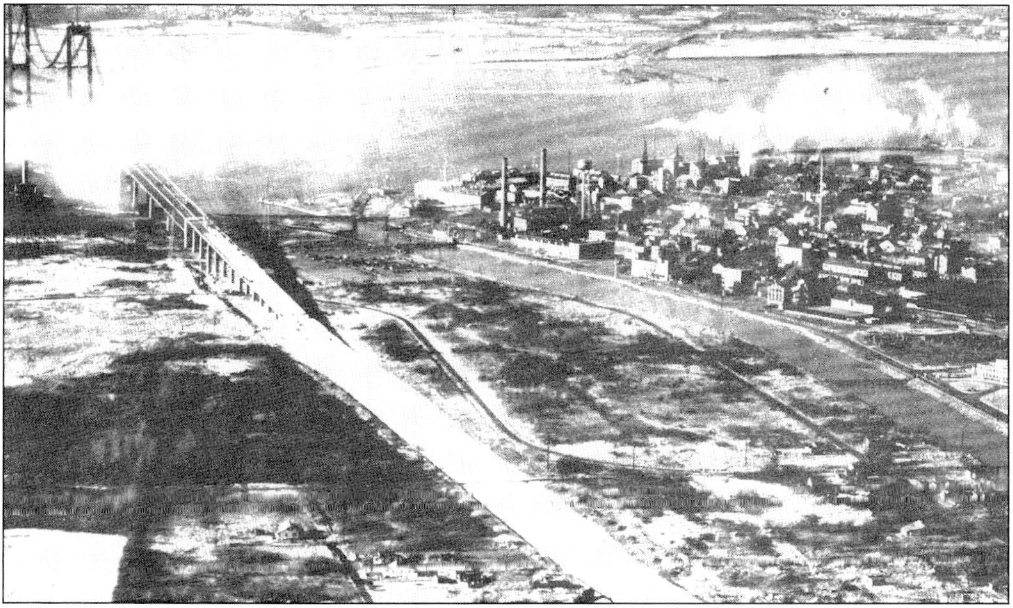

Interchange 1, near Swedesboro, provided direct access to and from the Delaware Memorial Bridge, which opened to traffic on August 16, 1951. Prior to the bridge's opening, the peak day numbers on the New Castle–Pennsville Ferry had been 17,000 vehicles. At that time, cars were lined up two abreast for seven miles, and the story of the congestion made the front page of New York newspapers. It appeared that the highways leading to the bridge could not reasonably handle many more cars. On the first Sunday after the bridge was opened, 36,000 vehicles passed over it, and the turnpike was not yet in use. The completed turnpike now connects directly with the Delaware Memorial Bridge, and both facilities supplement each other to the very great benefit of the motorist.

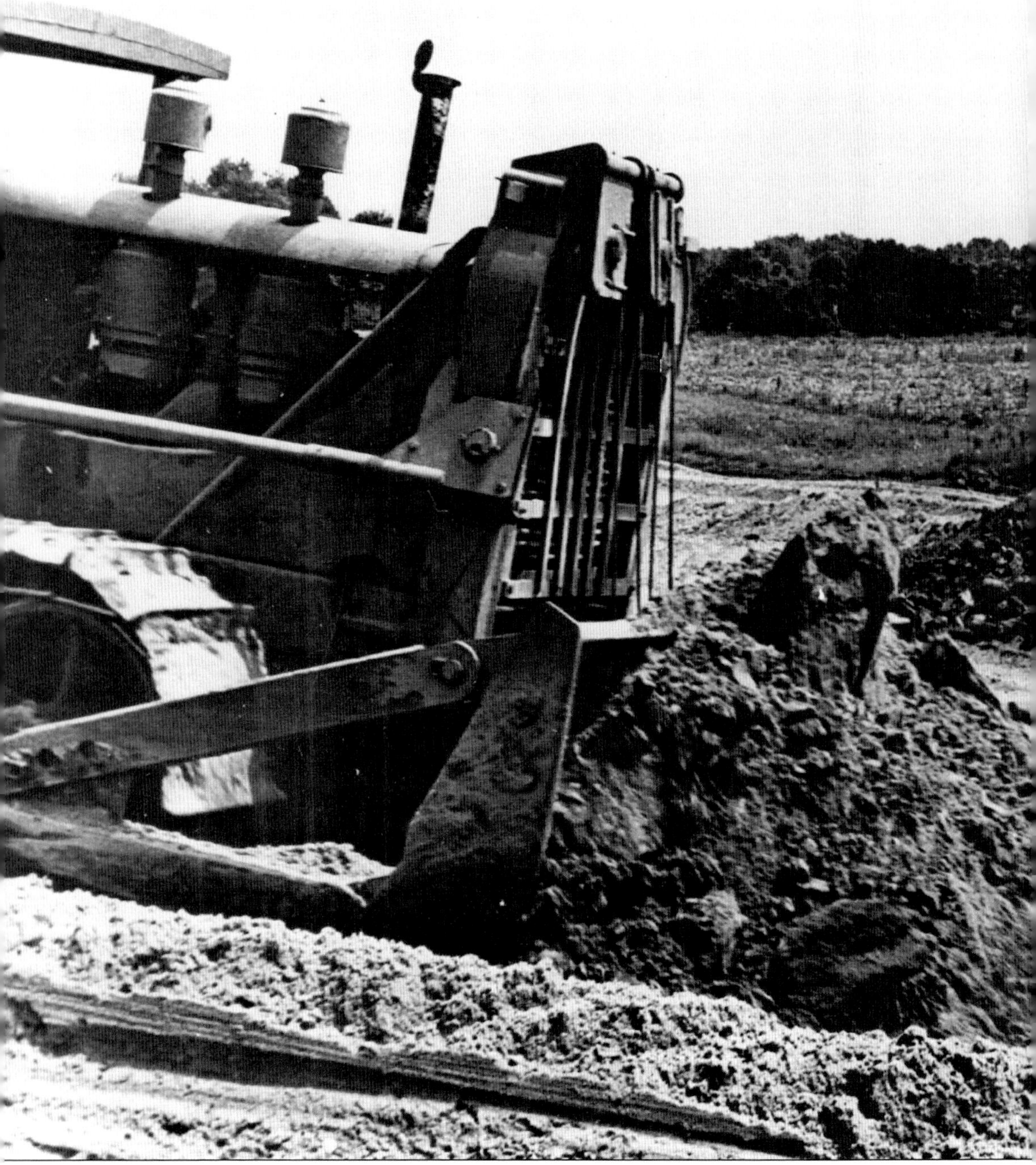

To expedite land negotiations for the 118-mile turnpike, the Authority's real estate division hired local experts familiar with the property holdings and values in each of the 10 counties through which the turnpike passes. Up north in Secaucus, the turnpike agents held their noses while they negotiated with some 30 pig farmers whose establishments blocked the right-of-way. Further south, in Gloucester County, the real estate staff told an

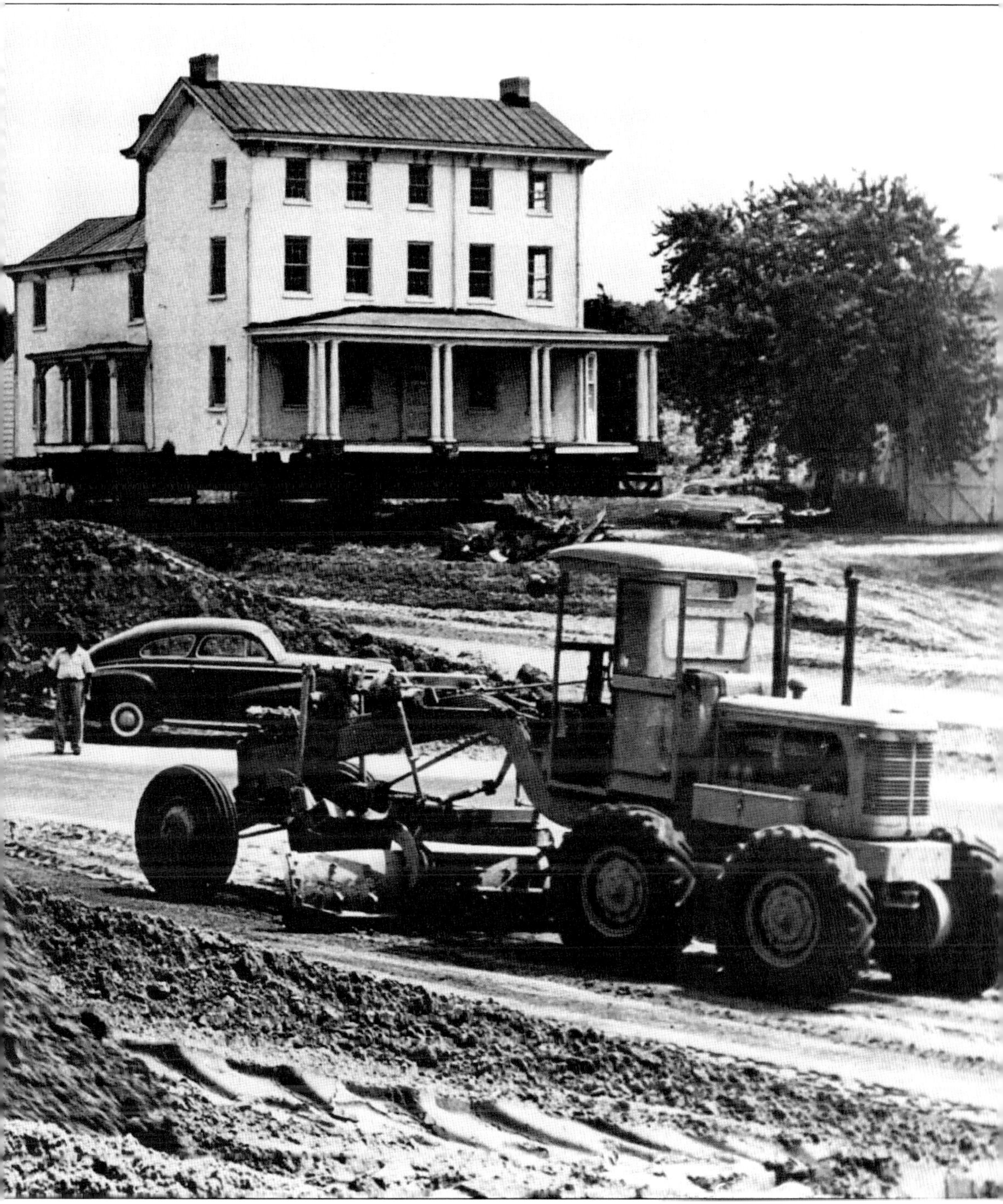

embarrassed property owner that he had been paying taxes on the wrong house for 16 years. In the photograph above, while road-building equipment churned away, the home of E. P. Sweeten of Woodbury Heights sat on rollers, waiting to be moved. The New Jersey Turnpike Authority paid about $17.5 million for the land it needed, according to the *Saturday Evening Post* in its December 8, 1951 issue.

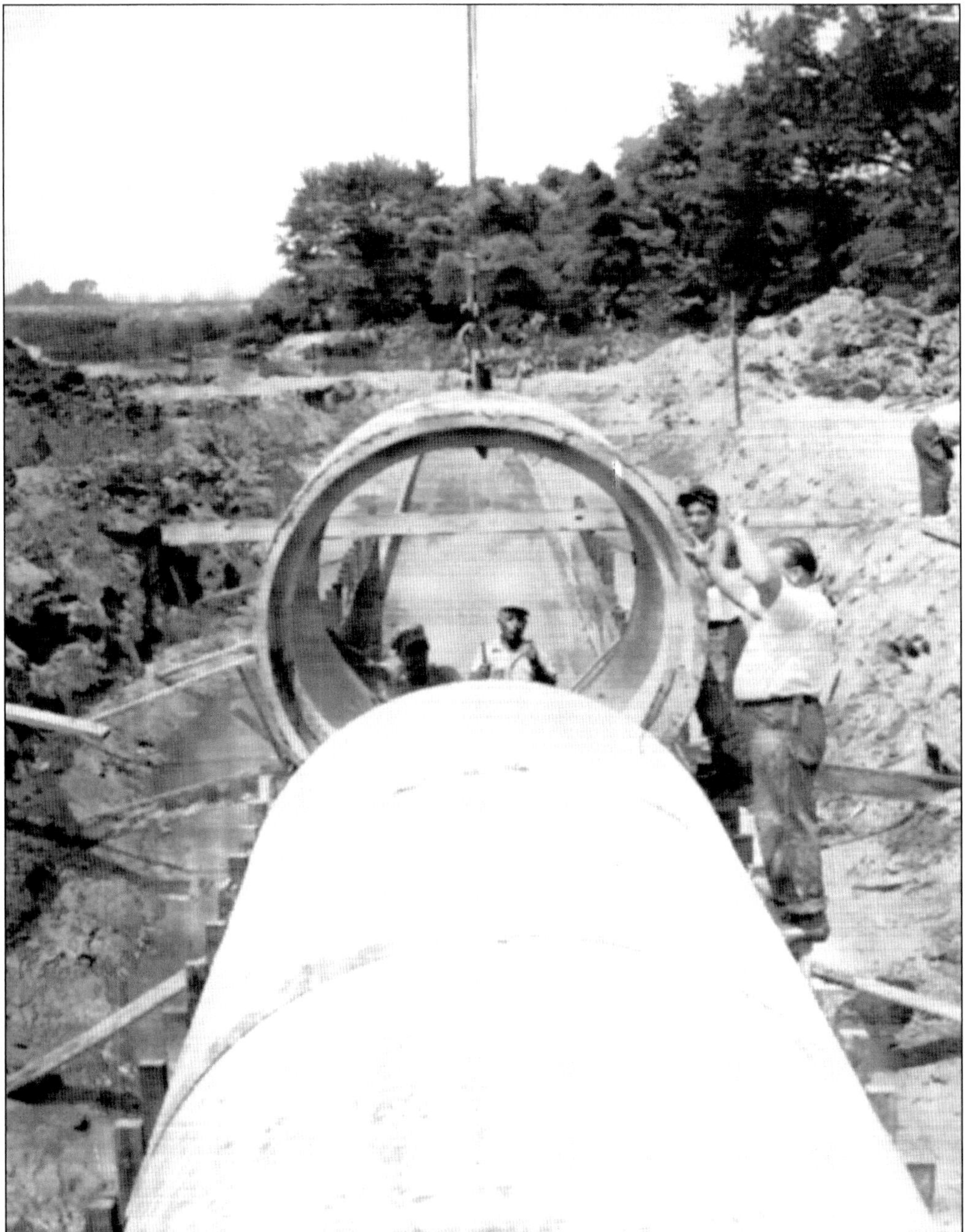

Almost the height of the average man (66 inches), this drain is being installed by the Savin Construction Company on the route of the New Jersey Turnpike. The drain crosses Beaver Creek, a branch of Big Timber Creek, and removes subsurface water from under the roadbed of the new superhighway.

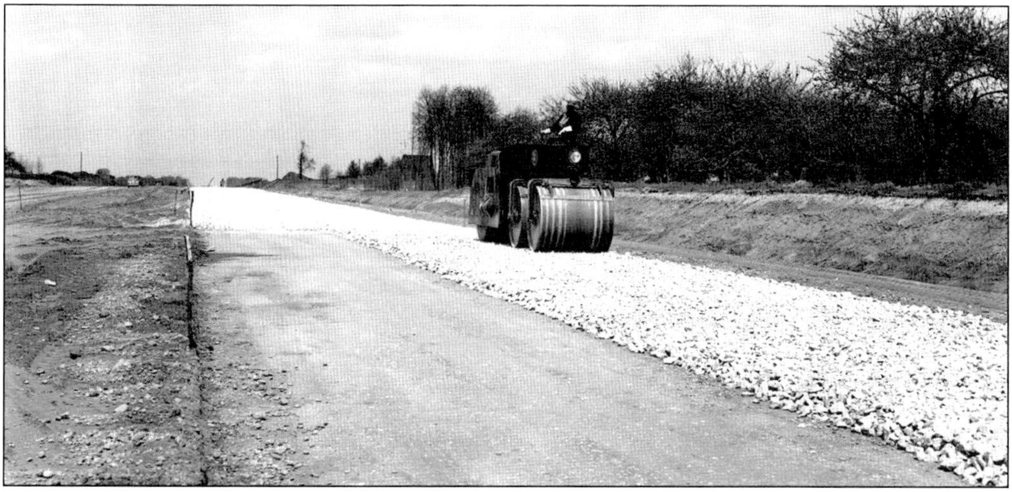

The pavement that was chosen had to stand up under extremely heavy truck loads, as well as provide good, economical service for the life of the Turnpike Authority bonds. Both concrete and asphalt had their advantages and disadvantages, but there were no clear-cut answers. Employees of the Savin Construction Company, contractors for Contract 60, Section 2, are shown rolling stone prior to applying asphalt on northbound lanes south of Route 40 (Marlton Pike) on April 25, 1951. The first course of macadam stone was placed on a compacted, frost-resistant subbase. The six-inch subbase was specified to consist of well-graded crushed rock, slag, or gravel of a durable and frost-free character. It was felt that such a choice encouraged the use of local materials and was economical.

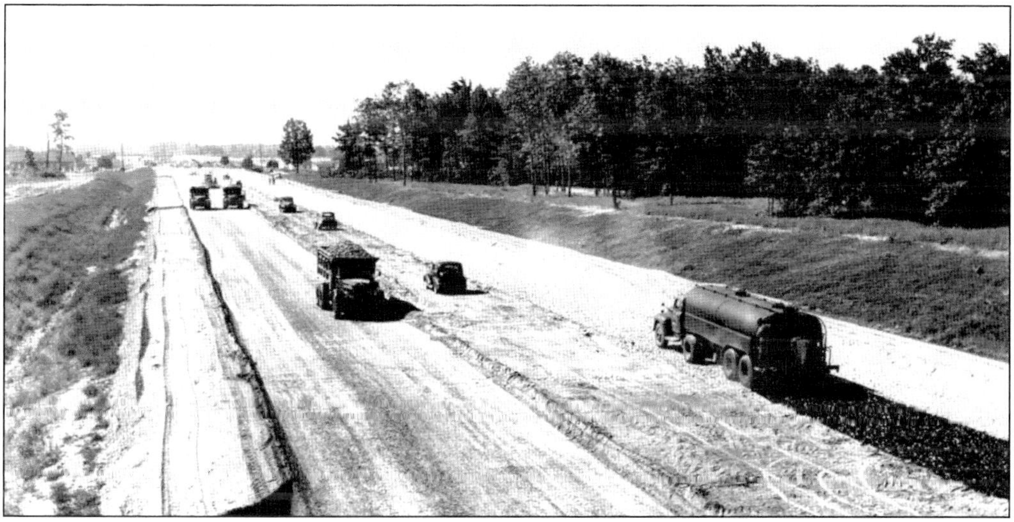

Ultimately, four options were presented to the Turnpike Authority: pave with concrete (rigid pavement); pave with asphalt (flexible pavement); pave with both; or take bids for both materials, and choose the least expensive bid. In the end, 12-inch-thick flexible asphalt was adopted at a bid price $5 million less than 10-inch-thick rigid concrete. Here, Geo. H. Brewster and Sons, contractor for Contract 62, Section 4, utilizes dump trucks to install the base stone on the northbound lane of the turnpike, while tank trucks apply penetrating asphalt on the southbound lanes. Trucks hauled asphalt directly from New Jersey and Pennsylvania refineries. This construction activity was photographed on September 6, 1951, looking south from Wykoff Road.

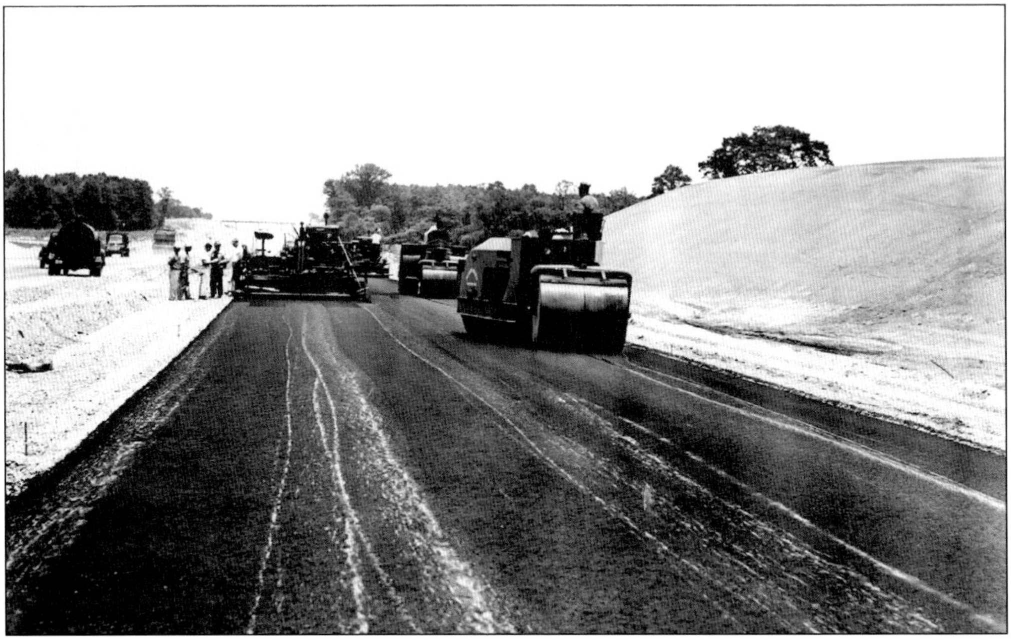

These photographs show the rolling operation of the first course of asphaltic concrete in Camden County. The asphaltic concrete was planned to be laid in a two-and-a-half-inch binder course and a two-inch surface course. From a May 10, 1951 press release, the Authority reported that these layers "must meet the Authority's severe specifications so that it will provide a smooth, even, non-skid surface for motorists and truckers for the full 118 miles."

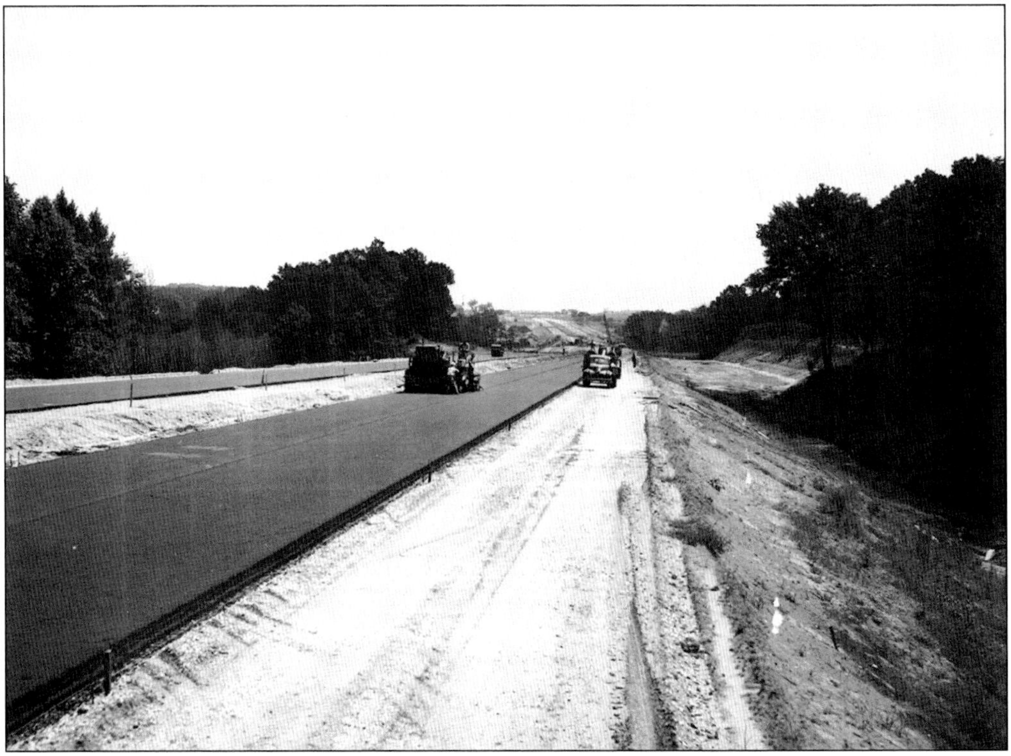

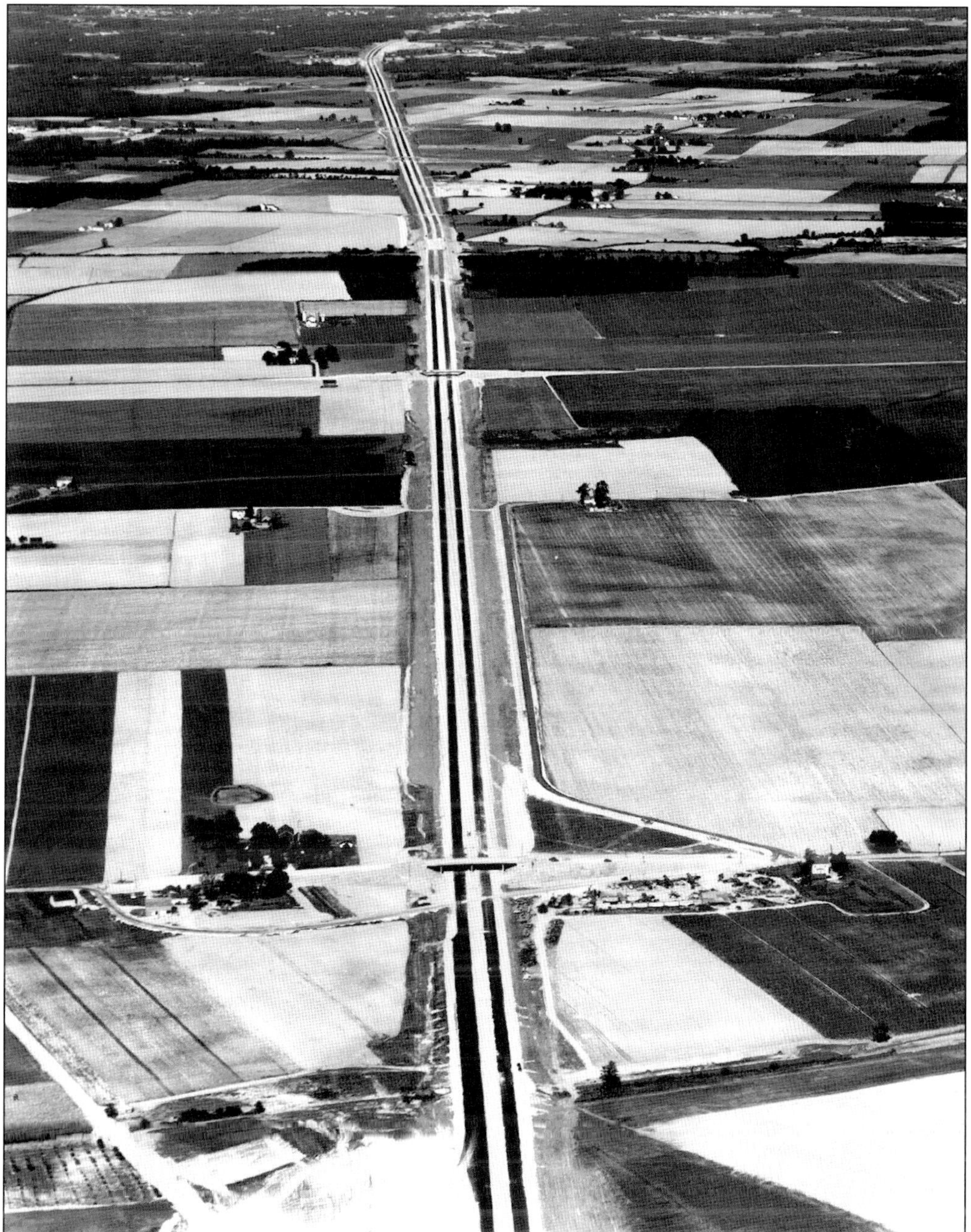

This is an aerial view of the nearly completed roadway through farmlands in Cranbury. Chairman Troast stated: "The pavement will provide turnpike users with an excellent surface, combining all the safety features available in any other highway and in all kinds of weather at high speeds. This turnpike will be as perfect a highway as can be built, and it will render outstanding service in the public interest."

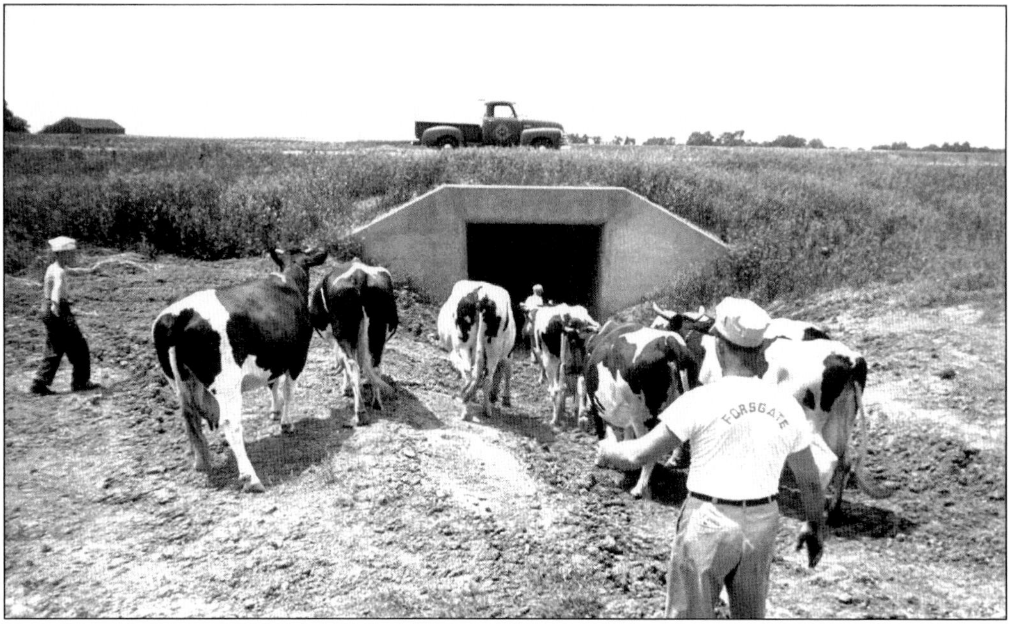

A hodgepodge of detail faced the planners of the turnpike. They had the problem of getting the cows of Forsgate Farms back to their barn at milking time. These dairy cattle had been cut off from their barn by the new road, so they are being driven through a special underpass that was built for them by the Turnpike Authority.

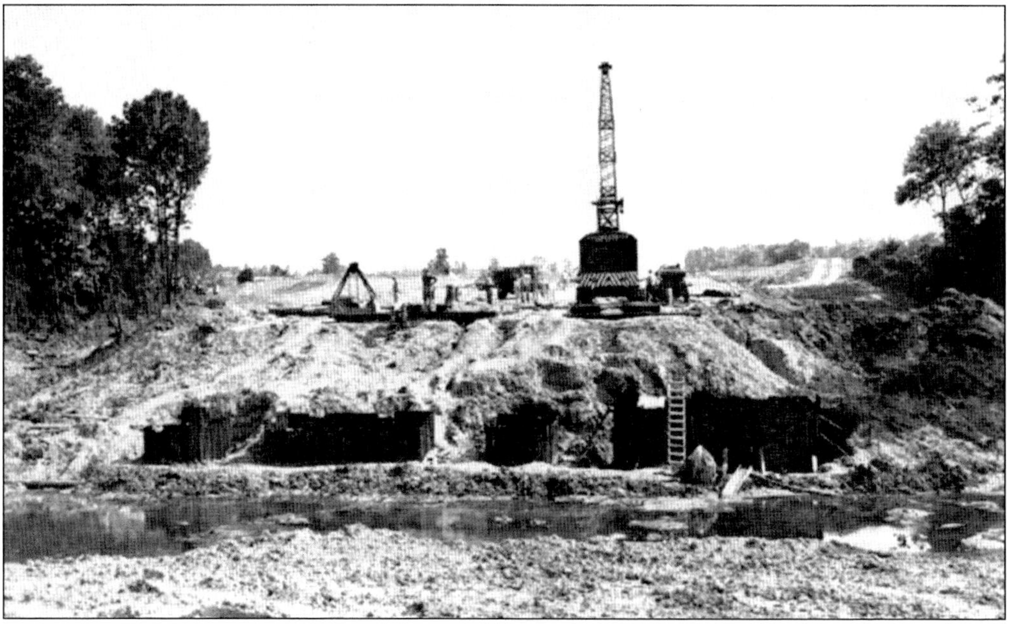

Here, looking south along the right-of-way of the New Jersey Turnpike, is one of the bridging problems encountered at the bend of the Millstone River, near Cranbury Station in Middlesex County. Sheeting piling had been driven into the ground to form a cofferdam, which when filled with concrete, supplied the pier support for a bridge to cross this river. In all, about 240 structures of various kinds, including the major bridges, became an integral part of the 118-mile turnpike.

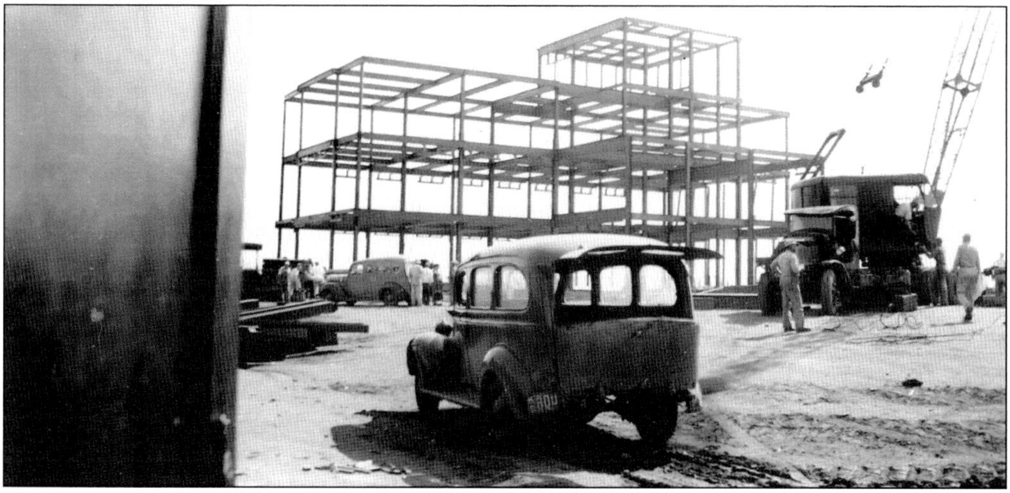

The Turnpike Authority's administration building is located in the center of a triangular plot of ground that is bounded on the west by Route S-28, on the north by School House Lane, and on the east by the turnpike itself. The original turnpike administration building, made of brick and limestone trim, is a three-story, penthouse-type of structure. When completed, the original structure supplied approximately 33,000 square feet of space. One of five of the Authority's microwave towers stands at the southern end of the administration building. A headline from the January 27, 1952 issue of the *Newark Sunday News* reads, "World's Most Modern Radio Network Spans New Jersey Turnpike." The $165,000 network interconnects state police cars on patrol, the turnpike's three police divisions at Newark, East Brunswick, and Moorestown, all 20 interchanges, the six turnpike maintenance stations, and repair trucks from service stations all along the highway.

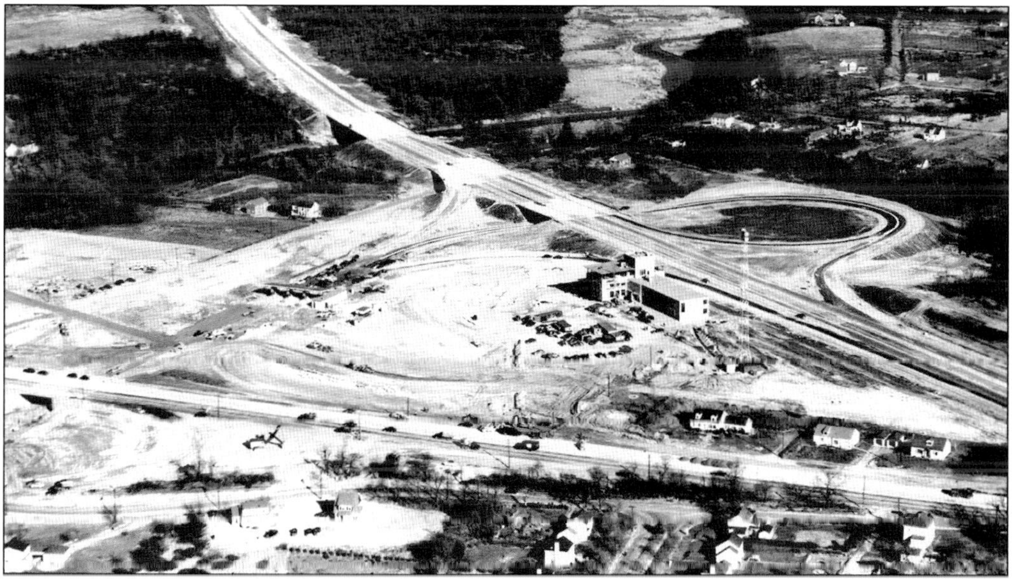

In an original press release dated October 2, 1950, George F. Smith, vice chairman of the Turnpike Authority stated: "The selection of East Brunswick for the headquarters of the Authority is predicated on several important factors. It marks a favorable location with respect to the center of gravity of traffic on the Turnpike, and it is desirable geographically with respect to Trenton and the New York metropolitan area."

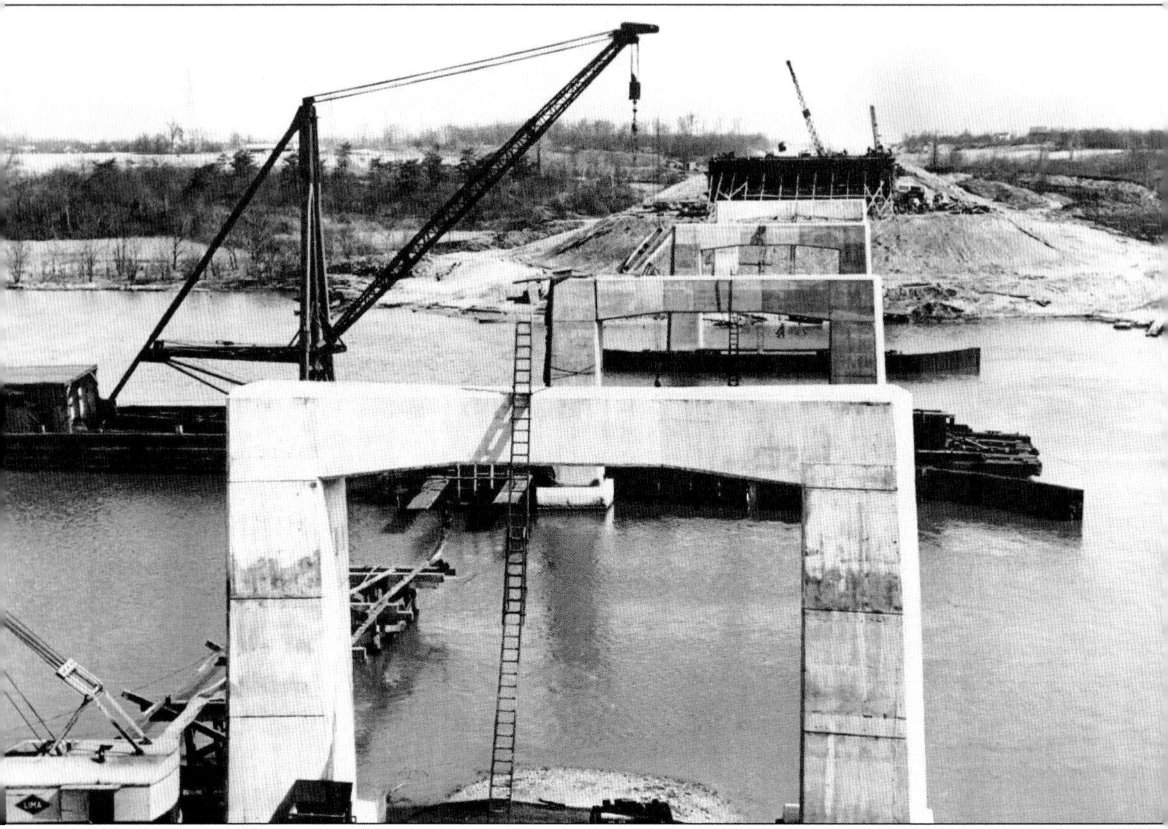

There are a total of 148 structures required for the 87-mile section of road between Deepwater and Bonhamtown along the New Jersey Turnpike. The Raritan River Bridge is the largest in the southern section of the turnpike, crossing the Raritan River downstream from the present College Bridge (U.S. Route 1). The bridge spans the Raritan River between New Brunswick and the town of Raritan, and it is an integral part of the 118-mile superhighway constructed by the Authority. The bridge's overall length is 805 feet. The center span directly over the channel is 213 feet in length, one of the longest for bridges of this plate-girder type built in the United States during the time of its construction. "More than 2,100 tons of steel and about 1,300 cubic yards of concrete will be used in the superstructure of this bridge," stated George F. Smith. "Like all other major bridges of the turnpike, this crossing over the Raritan will be of the fixed span, deck type, permitting motorists a clear view in all directions at all times. There will be no steel superstructure to interfere with vision." Originally built for six lanes, today four three-lane roadways with shoulders now span this river.

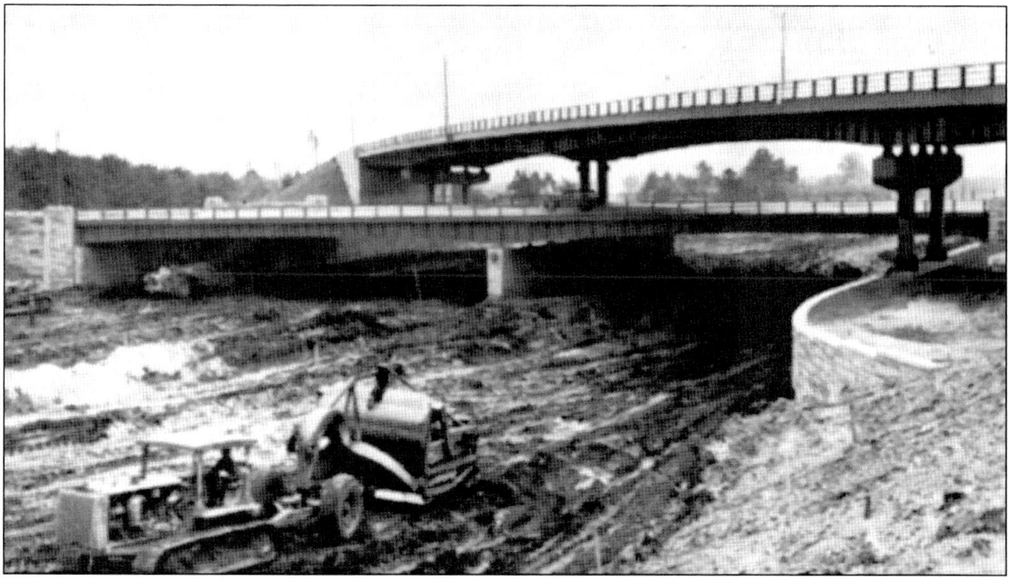

Many unusual engineering problems presented themselves during the construction of the New Jersey Turnpike. One of the most unusual is that of boring under two existing roadways in Middlesex County. Located directly on the alignment of the turnpike were the Route 4 Parkway (the lower road), and Woodbridge Avenue (the upper road) in Woodbridge Township. Seen underneath are turnapulls engaged in removing dirt to provide safe and rapid transportation for passenger cars and commercial vehicles on the turnpike.

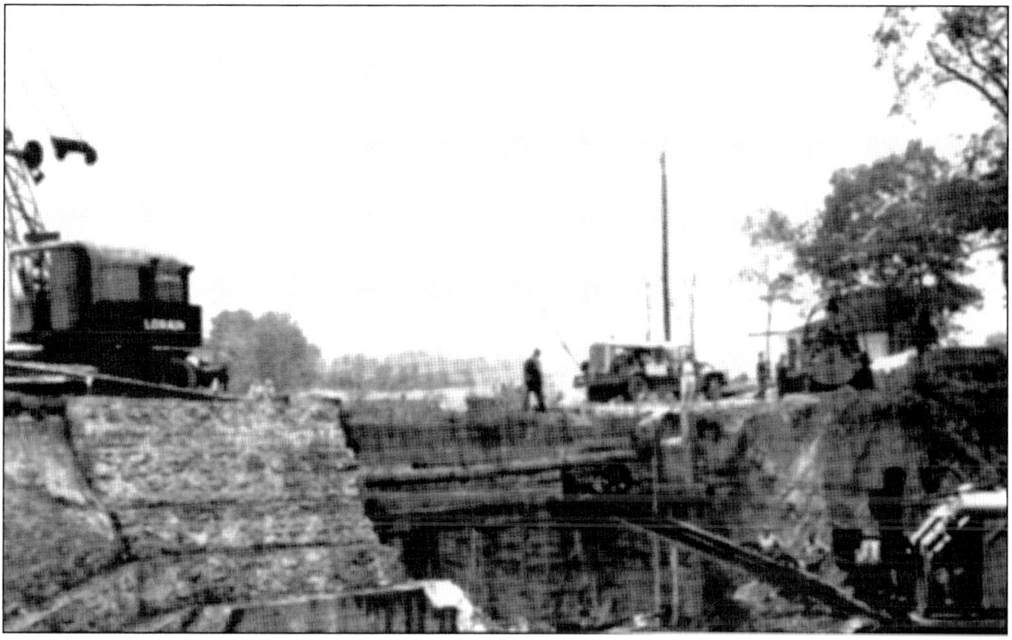

Contractors engaged in construction of the New Jersey Turnpike uncovered an old brick culvert over Mill Brook, underneath the Old York Road (Woodbridge Avenue), the historical main highway between New York and Philadelphia near Woodbridge in Middlesex County. The photograph shows demolition of the brickwork and concrete of the old culvert, and the construction of the new box culvert to carry Mill Brook underneath the new roadway.

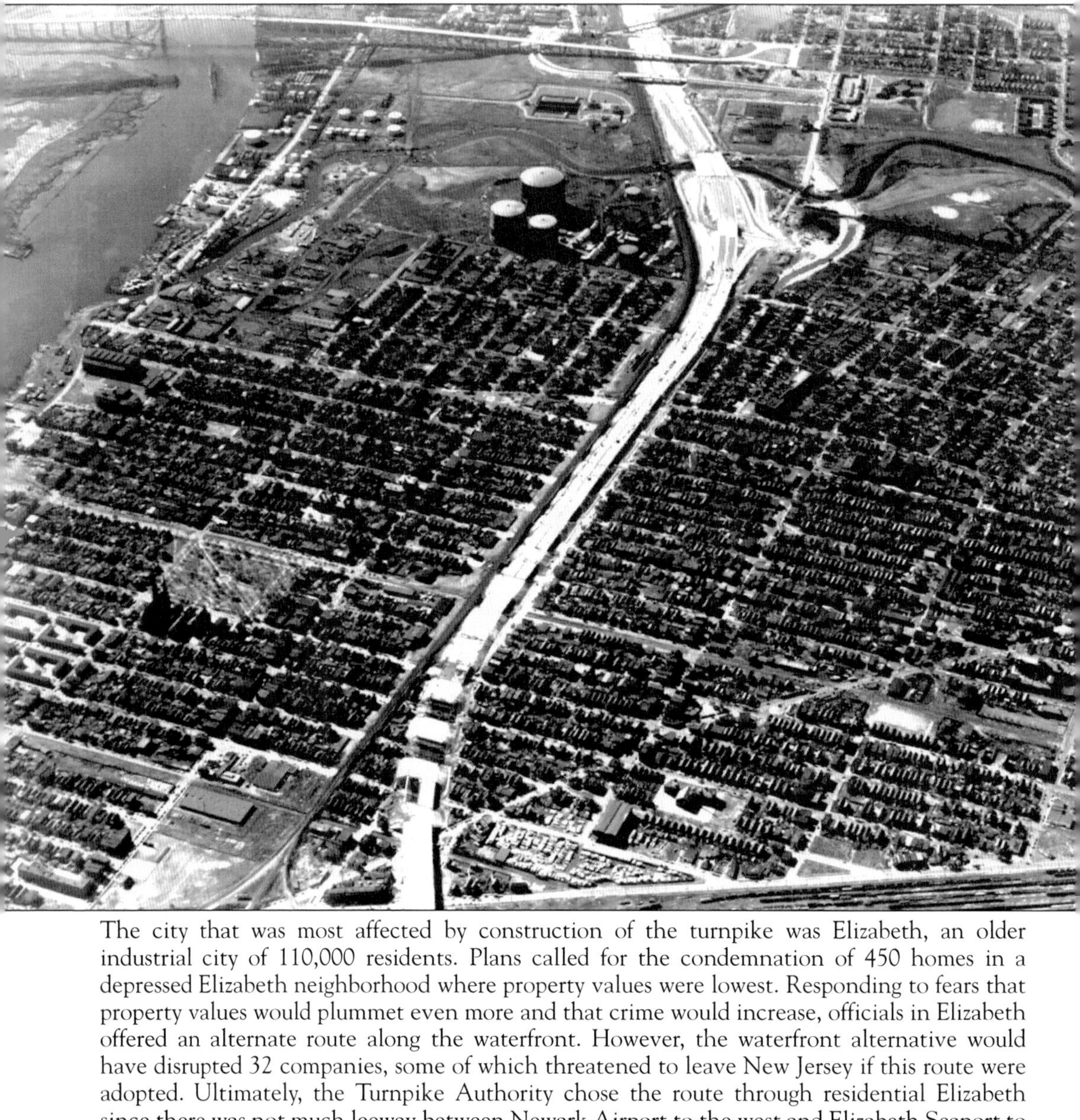

The city that was most affected by construction of the turnpike was Elizabeth, an older industrial city of 110,000 residents. Plans called for the condemnation of 450 homes in a depressed Elizabeth neighborhood where property values were lowest. Responding to fears that property values would plummet even more and that crime would increase, officials in Elizabeth offered an alternate route along the waterfront. However, the waterfront alternative would have disrupted 32 companies, some of which threatened to leave New Jersey if this route were adopted. Ultimately, the Turnpike Authority chose the route through residential Elizabeth since there was not much leeway between Newark Airport to the west and Elizabeth Seaport to the east. Once in the city, the Turnpike Authority had to construct overpasses and underpasses for local streets, railroad tracks, pipelines, and other utilities, an undertaking that significantly added to construction costs.

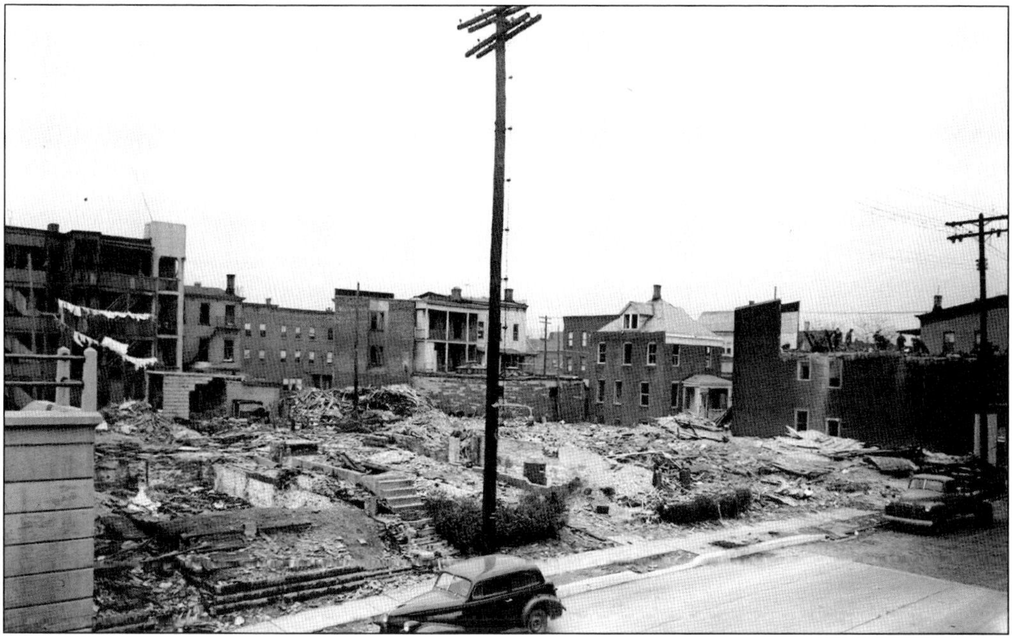

An original photograph dated December 7, 1950, shows a general view of the site of Livingston Street Bridge, looking south. Rubble and debris are the only remnants of this Elizabeth neighborhood that was cleared to make way for the superhighway. To the right, workers on the second level of a corner home continue the demolition.

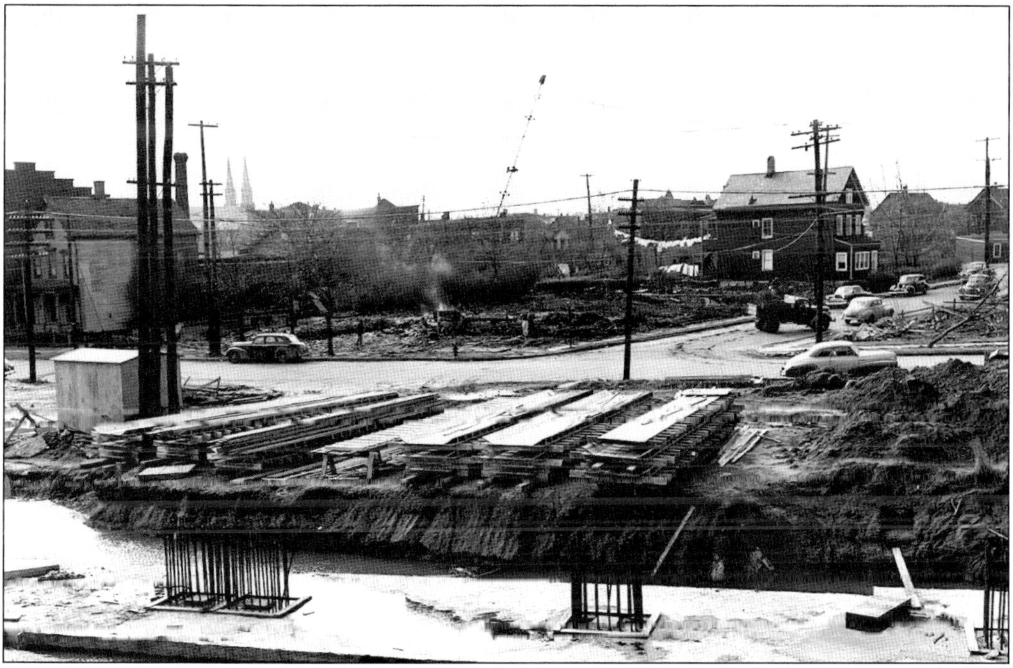

This photograph is a view of the site of bridge piers Nos. 3, 4, 5, and 6, and the Trumbull Street Viaduct, looking south from the Central Railroad embankment in Elizabeth. Schiller Street crosses the Trumbull Street Viaduct near the center of the photograph, and the spires of St. Patrick's Church are visible to the left.

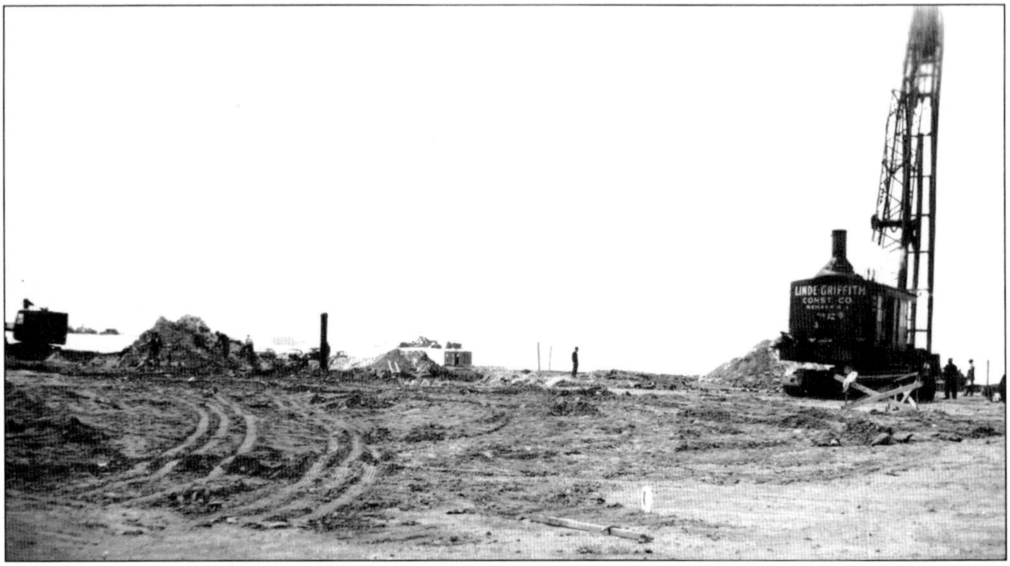

Above, in an original photograph dated May 4, 1951, workers are seen driving test piles at a construction site in Elizabeth. The bottom photograph shows Julius DiRenzo (with back to camera) and Ed Wood (right of center) checking the elevation of the south foundation wall of Maintenance Building District 5 in Elizabeth on May 1, 1951.

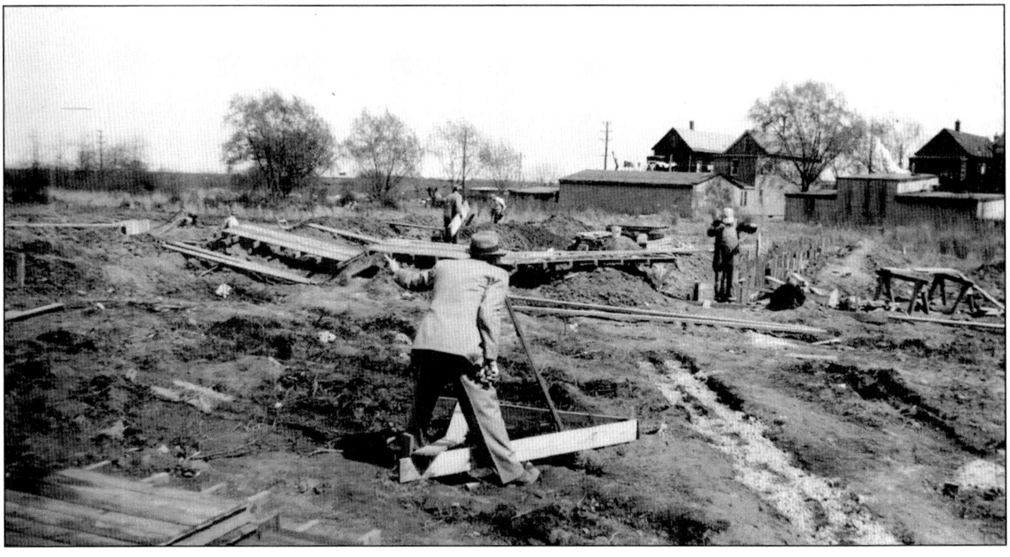

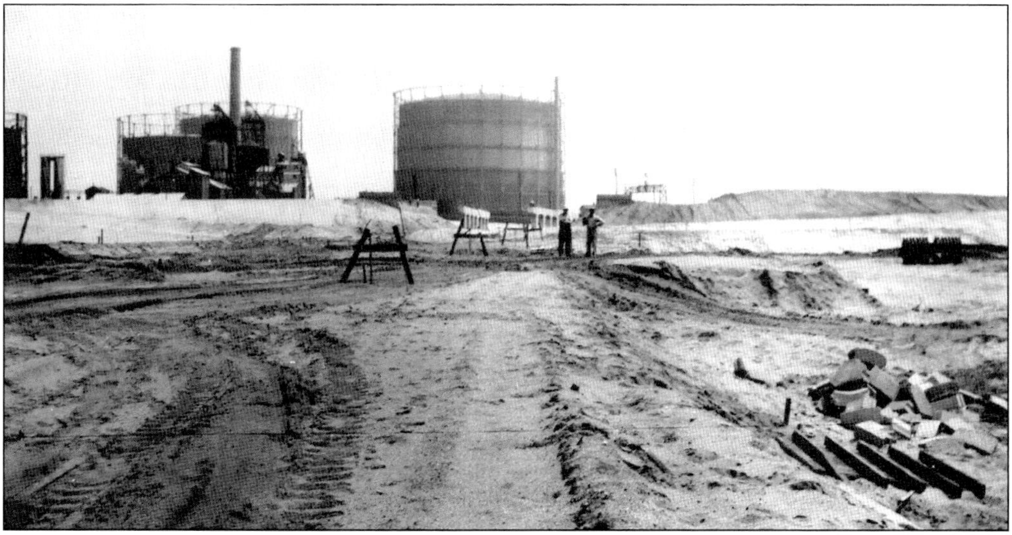

This photograph shows the site of Interchange 12. Contractors are preparing the land for construction of this plaza in the northern section of the New Jersey Turnpike. Refinery storage tanks and stacks can be seen in the background.

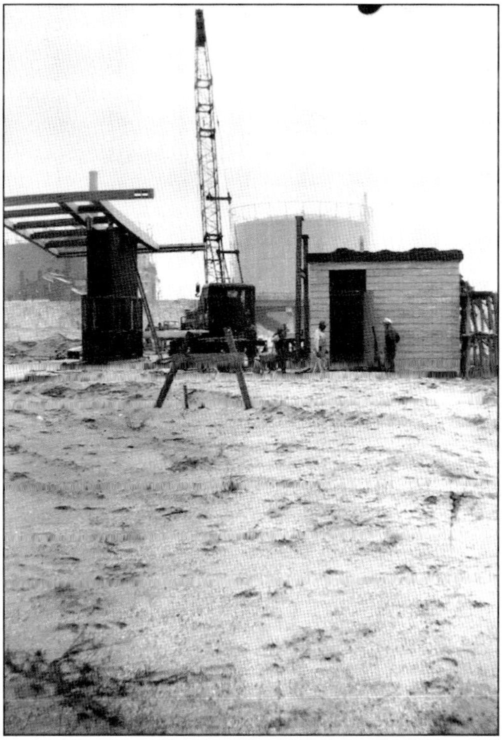

Contractors employed by the Turnpike Authority are in the process of erecting a canopy over the toll plaza at Interchange 12. Prefabricated, welded steel-plate construction was chosen for toll booths. Each booth serves two traffic lanes.

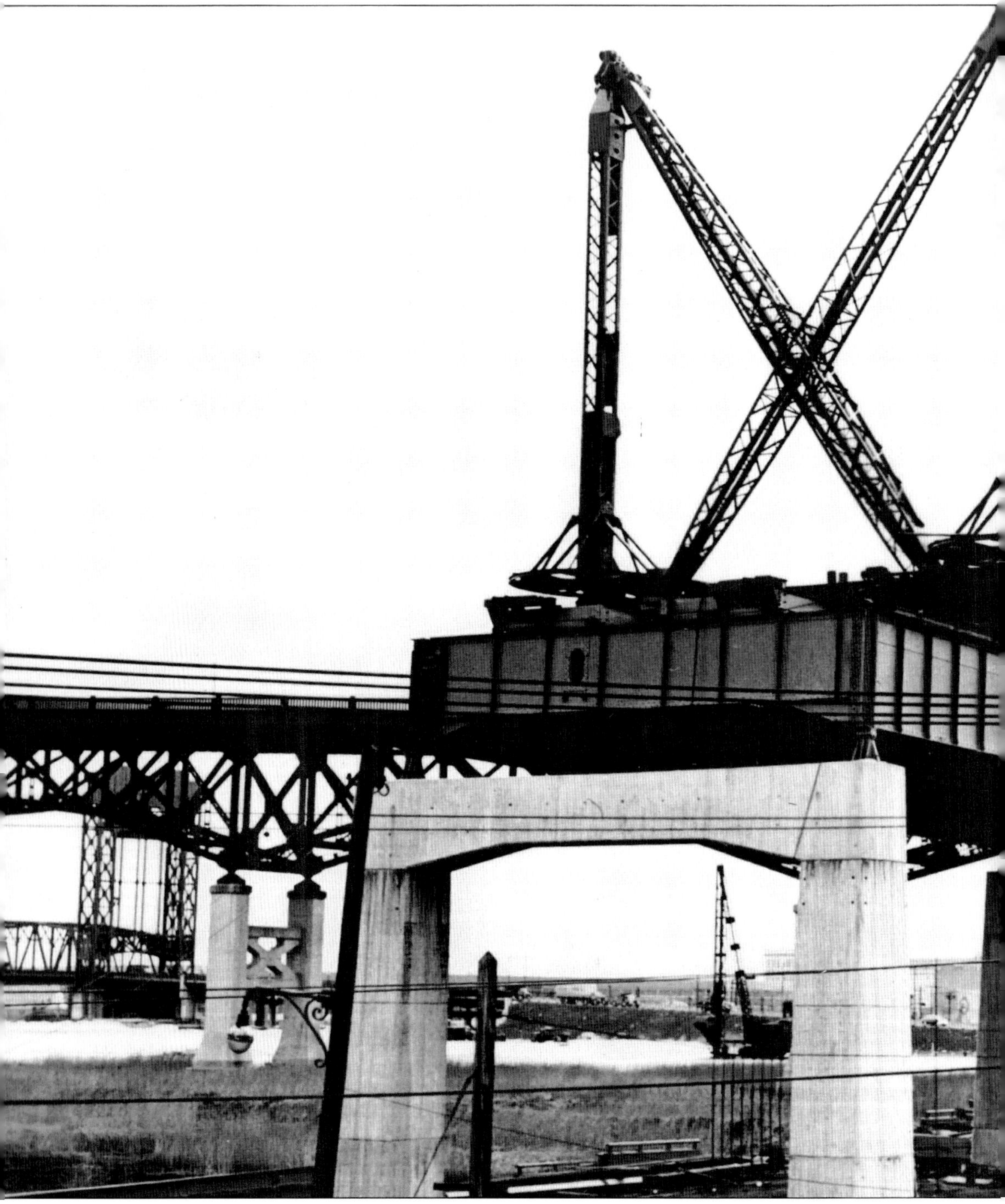

A unique double-boom stiff-leg derrick from Bethlehem Steel Company speeds the erection of steelwork for the Authority's largest original structure. Friendly competition with U.S. Steel, which was erecting the nearby Hackensack River Bridge, helped the Authority meet its opening-date deadline. Crossing the Pulaski Skyway posed one of the many problems for engineers of the Turnpike Authority—whether to pass over or under it. At its intersection with

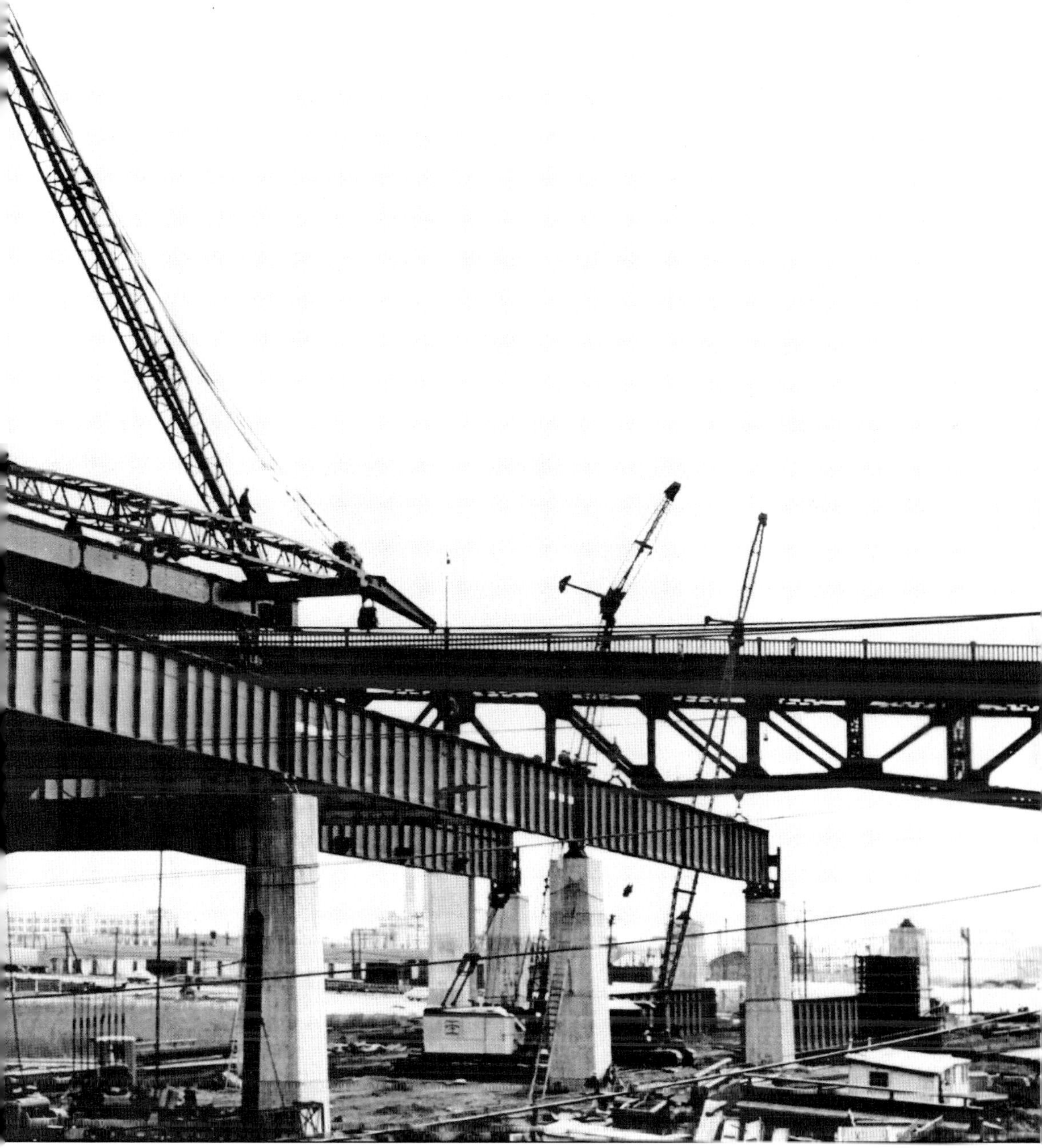

the turnpike, the Pulaski Skyway is 90 feet high. If engineers went over the skyway, they would have to elevate the turnpike high above the ground, which would have been an expensive undertaking. When it was found that the clearance of the underpass was still greater than that provided by many existing structures, and at a considerable cost savings, the decision was made to proceed with design and construction accordingly.

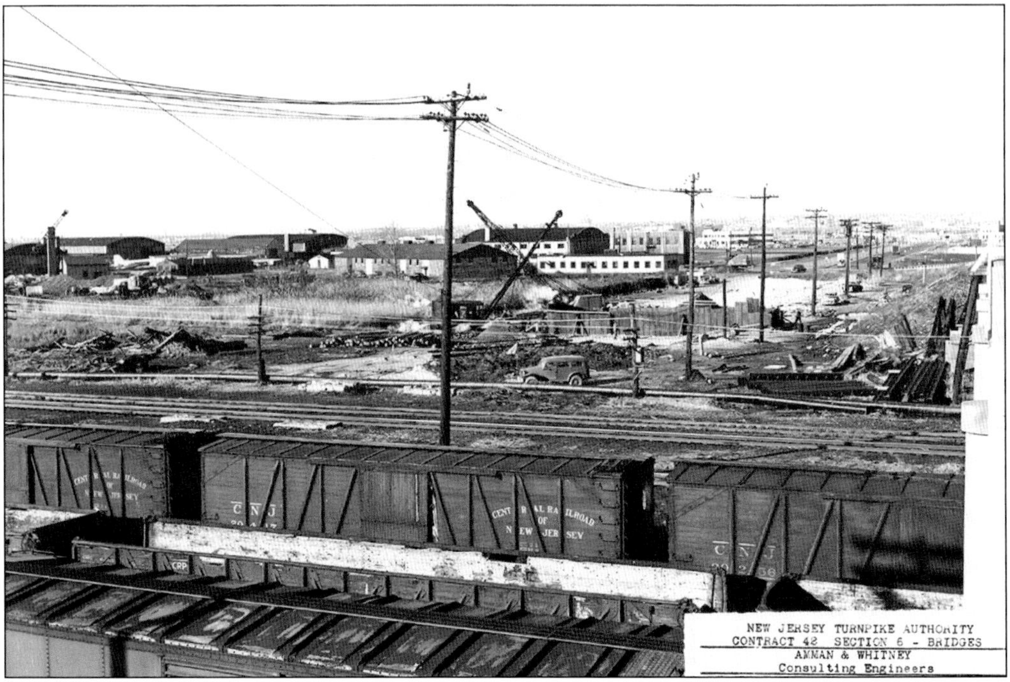

Looking west from the existing ramp in Newark, this general view of the site of the Port Street Viaduct is from an original photograph dated December 5, 1950. Central Railroad of New Jersey train cars are seen in foreground.

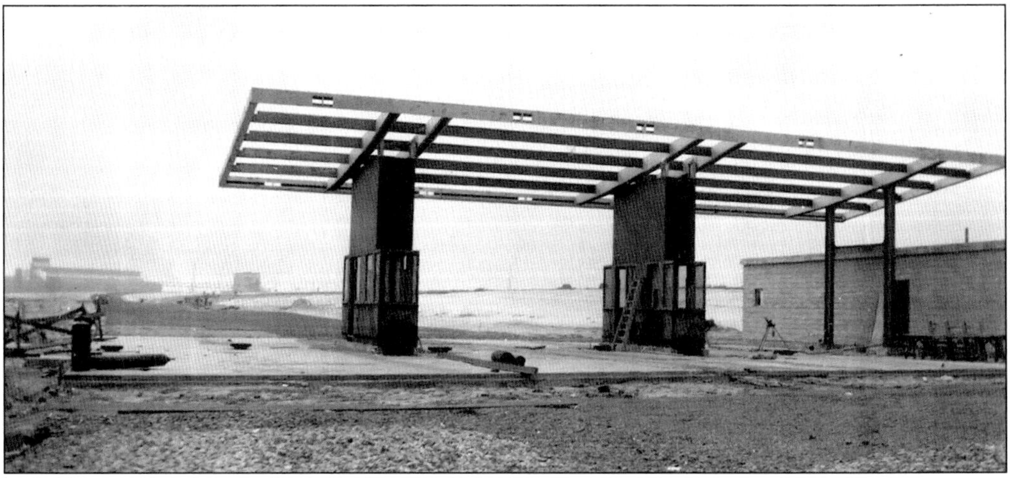

This image from an original photograph dated November 10, 1951, shows Toll Plaza 14 in a view to the south. The booths appear to be complete; however, the canopy has only been framed out at this stage. The original Interchange 14 gave patrons access to the nearby communities of Newark and Jersey City.

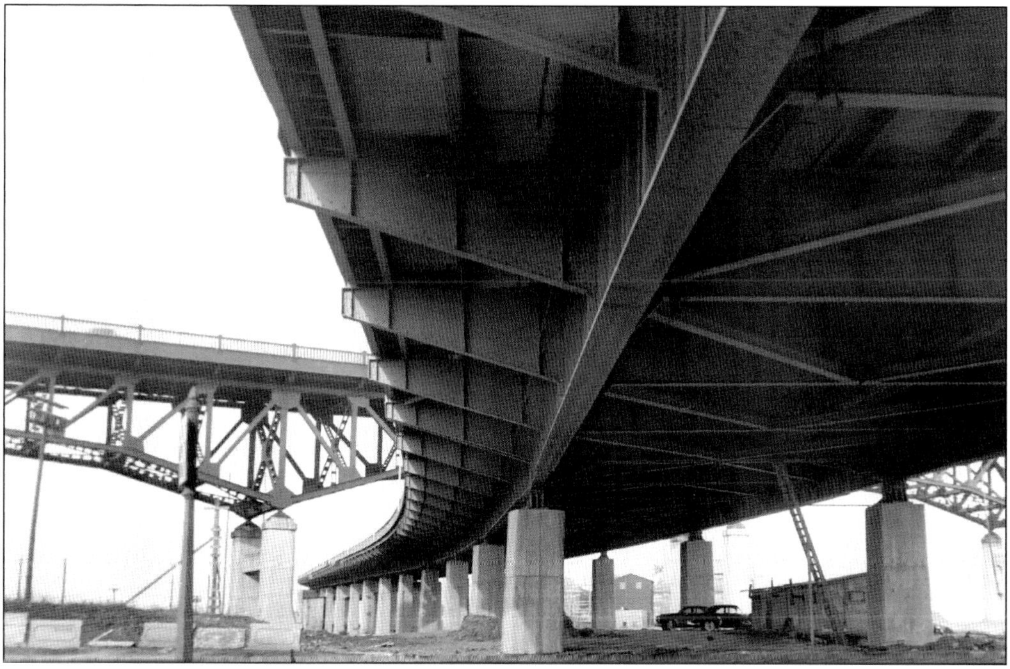

This view from below the turnpike shows girders and the underside of the roadway near Interchange 15. More than 15 feet of clearance was provided on New Jersey's Passaic River Bridge where it passes under the Pulaski Skyway in Newark. This clearance is more than adequate to provide for the passage of the highest trucks and loads on the public highways, with a margin of two and a half feet above those loads.

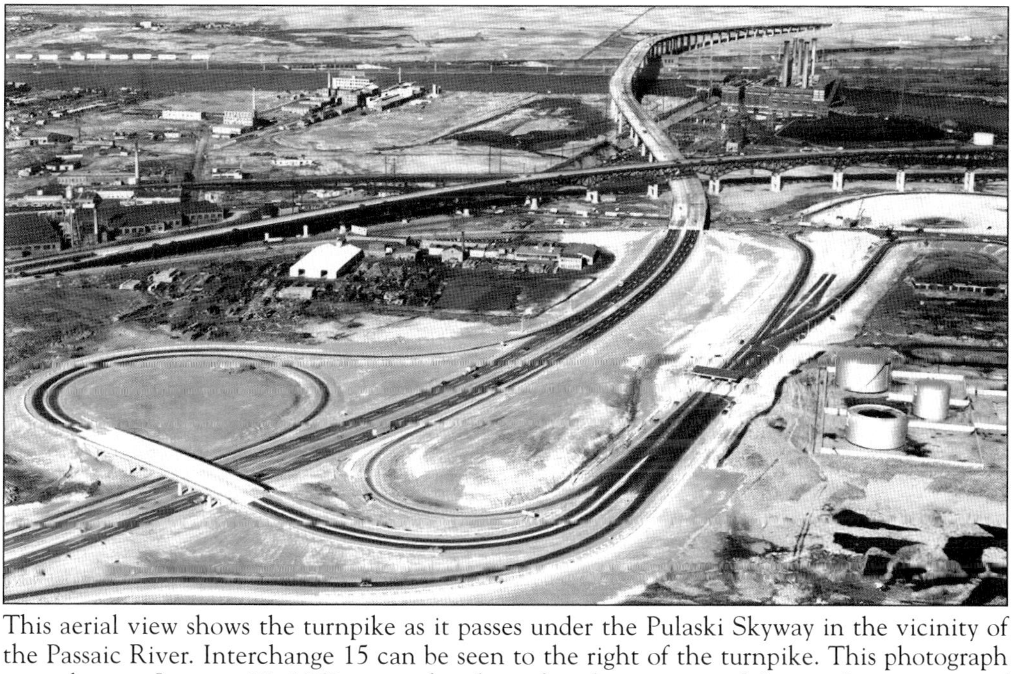

This aerial view shows the turnpike as it passes under the Pulaski Skyway in the vicinity of the Passaic River. Interchange 15 can be seen to the right of the turnpike. This photograph was taken on January 18, 1952, just a few days after the opening of the northern section of the roadway.

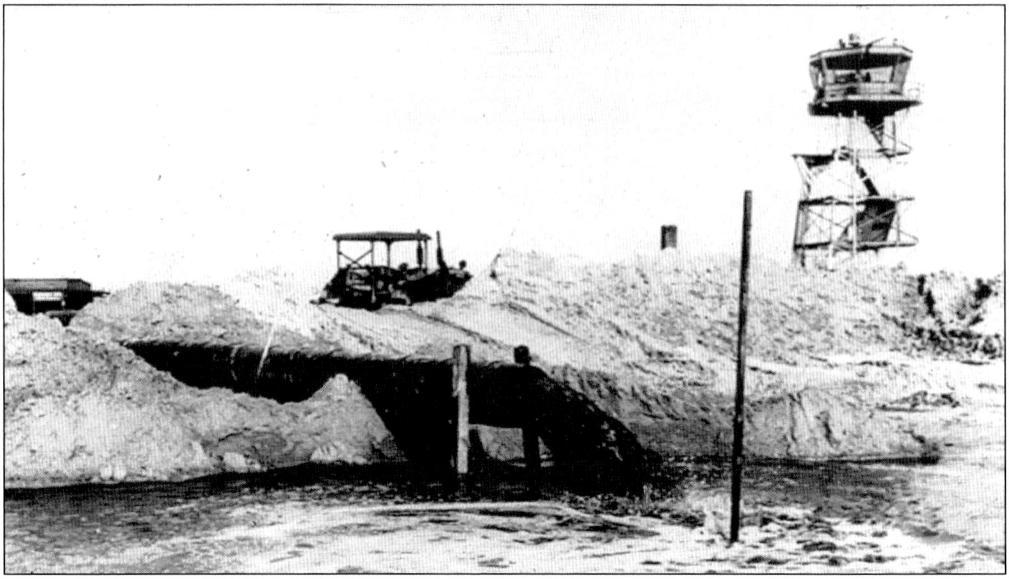

To provide a stable base, more than six million cubic yards of ocean sand is literally being poured on the meadows in Newark and Elizabeth. Called Operation Sand by the engineers working on the project, the sand is first dredged out of the Jamaica Bay and also the New York Bay near Coney Island by two large hopper dredges and dipper dredges operating on a round-the-clock basis. The hopper dredges, each more than 270 feet long and 47 feet wide, then transport the sand to the dock at Pork Newark. Here, mixed with water, it is pumped thousands of feet through a 20-inch pipe to its destination on the meadows. A maze of machinery with massive pumps, the hopper dredges operating from the dock at Port Newark to the sand banks carry crews of more than 40 men who work four-hour shifts. Arriving at the dredging scene, the dredger drops a 30-foot pipe with a bell-shaped nozzle to the bay floor, and the pumps start bringing up sand and pouring it into the large hoppers inside the boat. Once filled, the dredge turns about and heads for Port Newark, where it connects to the 20-inch pipeline running to the roadbed. Again the giant pumps start functioning, and the sand mixed with water is forced through 9,000 feet of pipe at the end. The heavy sand drops by gravity to the marshy ground, and the water is carried off through a drainable ditch at the end of the 324-foot right-of-way. Along its course, the pipeline passes through an electric booster station with a 1,200-horsepower capacity. (Courtesy of the Newark Library.)

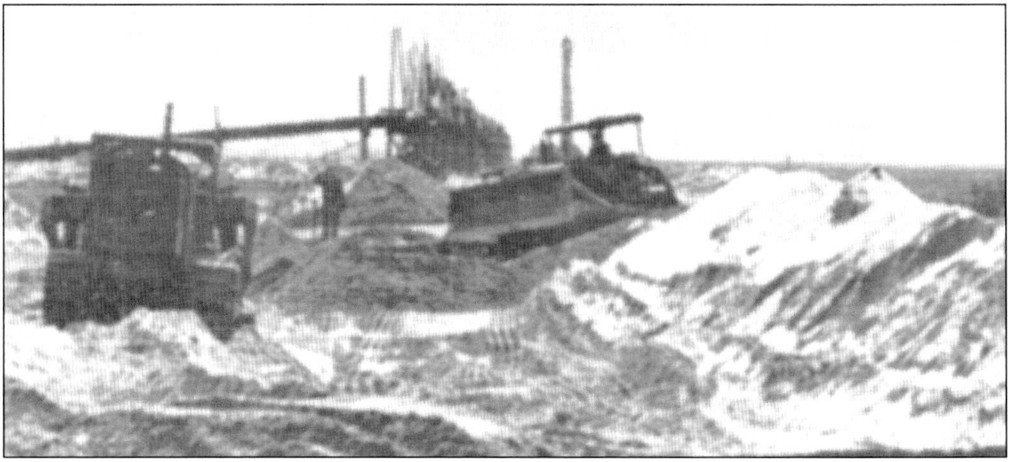

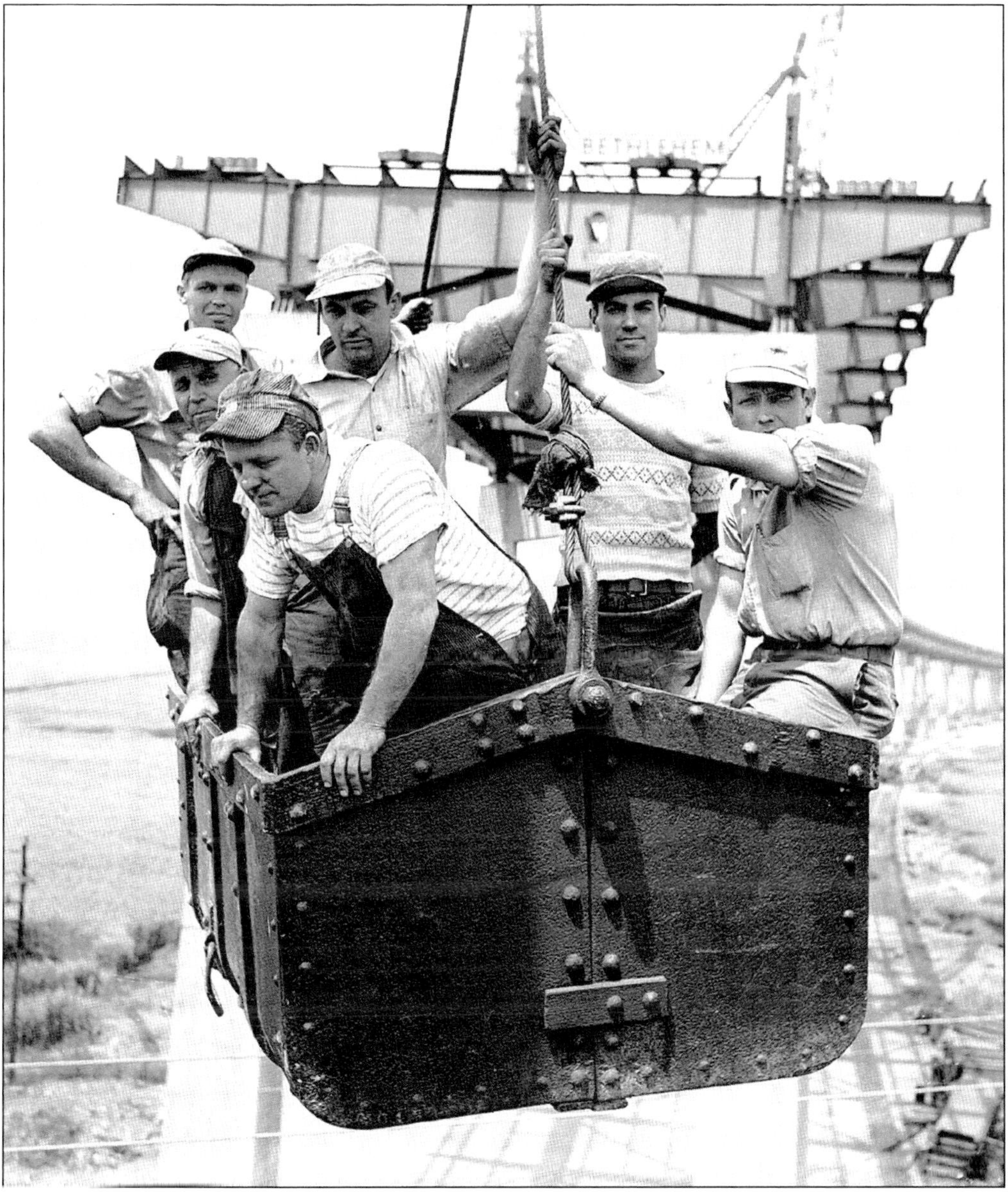

Workers ride a lift during the construction of the New Jersey Turnpike, June 1951. The Bethlehem Steel logo sits atop the girders of the unfinished Passaic River Bridge in the background. (Courtesy of Getty Images.)

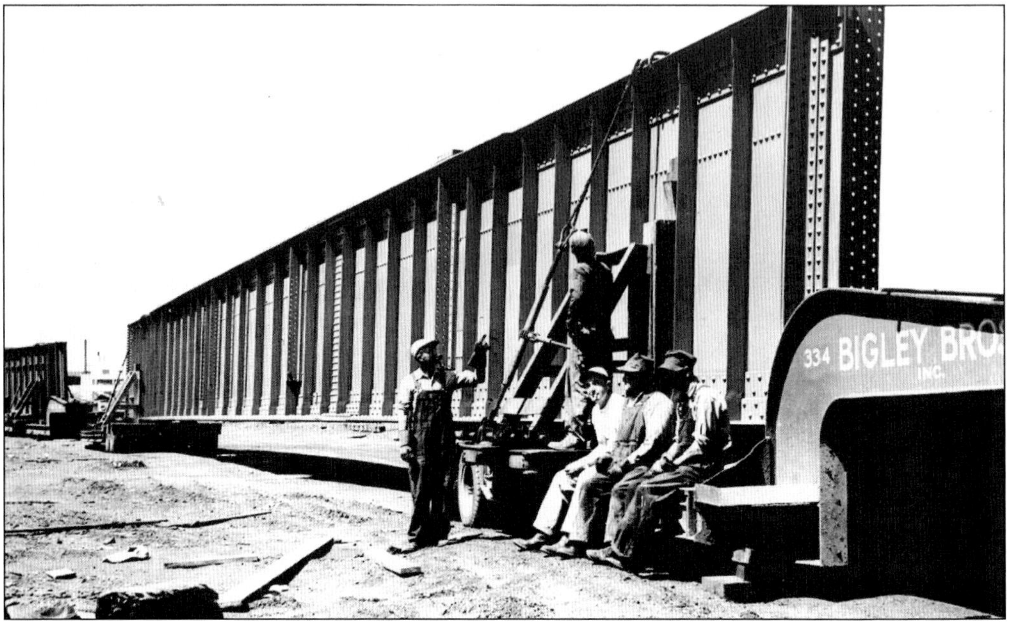

Taking a break, construction workers sit on huge steel girders for the Passaic River Bridge. The girders are lined up and are on wheels to be transported to their final destination near the construction site.

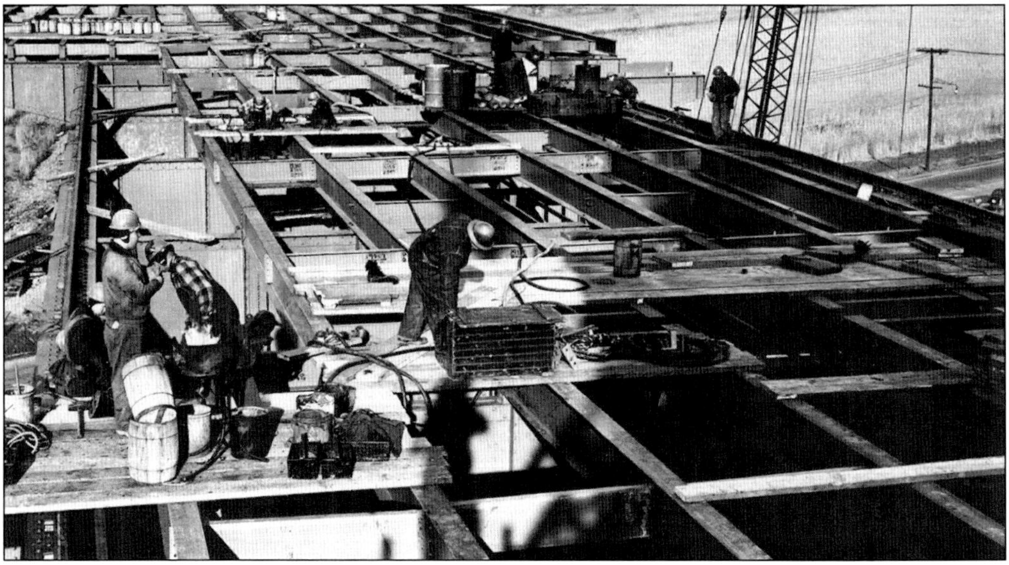

Iron workers are seen completing the secondary steelwork to support the roadway deck of the Authority's original alignment bridge over the Passaic River. When it appeared that the timely completion of the structure could be jeopardized because of a delay by the Bethlehem Steel Company, Governor Driscoll contacted the company president, Arthur B. Homer, to strongly voice his dissatisfaction. In a frank phone conversation with Homer, Driscoll explained that if the turnpike was not opened on schedule, it would be necessary for the Authority to advise the bondholders and the general public that the fault lay with the Bethlehem Steel Company. While the conversation was friendly and frank, it was clearly stated that Governor Driscoll was "mad as hell."

A twin-boom stiff-leg derrick is ready to lift a massive riveted plate girder over the Pennsylvania Railroad mainline, which is now Amtrak's Northeast Corridor. Adding shoulders to this bridge in 1973 cost four times what it cost for the original construction. "The river span over the Passaic River will be approximately 375 feet, the longest on record in the United States for this plate-girder type of bridge," said Paul L. Troast, chairman of the New Jersey Turnpike Authority. The full length of the structure will be almost 7,000 feet. It will start at a point near Raymond Boulevard, Newark, in Essex County, pass under the Pulaski Skyway, and end in Kearny in Hudson County.

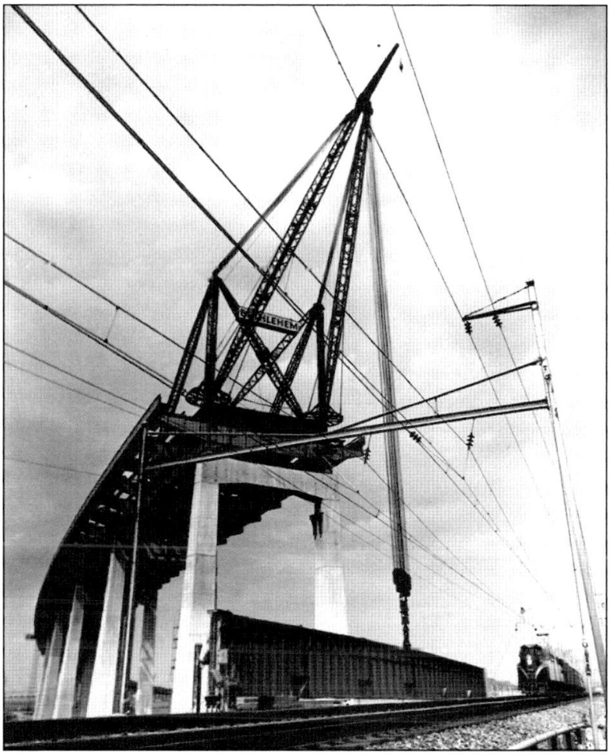

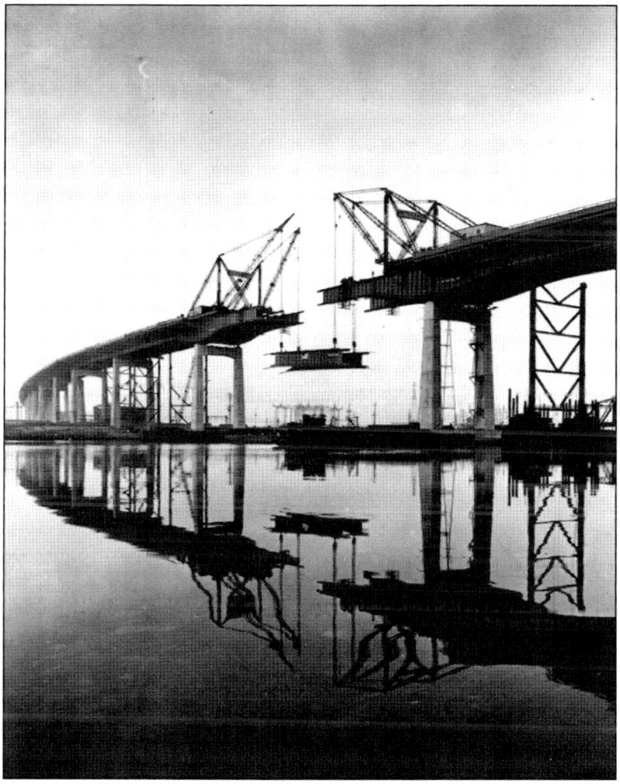

This photograph shows the closure of the main span, as twin-boom stiff-leg derricks lift both main girders together. These girders weigh approximately 175 tons each. The Passaic River Bridge is the largest structure on the 118-mile New Jersey Turnpike. It passes over five railroads and four major streets, besides the river itself.

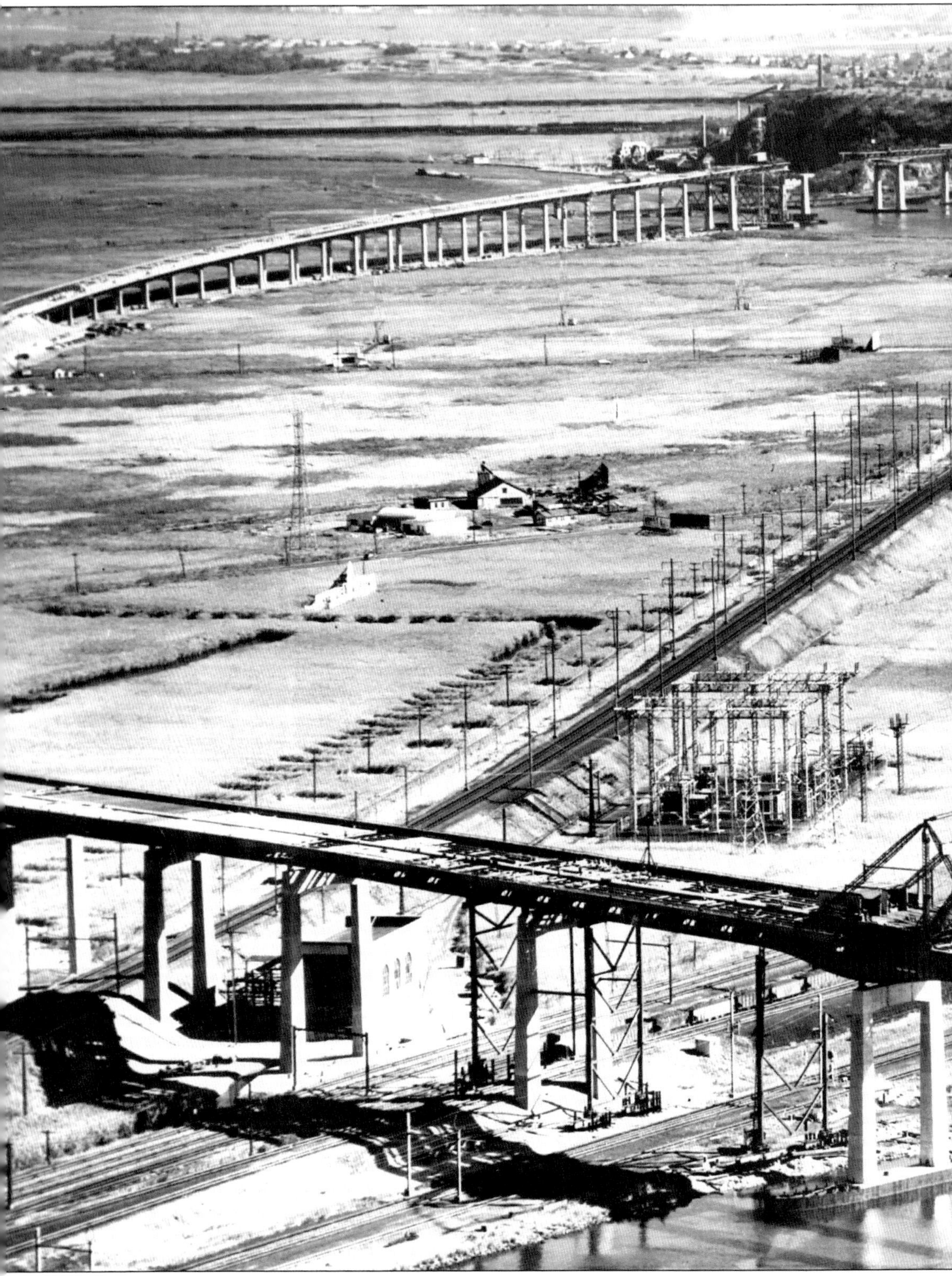

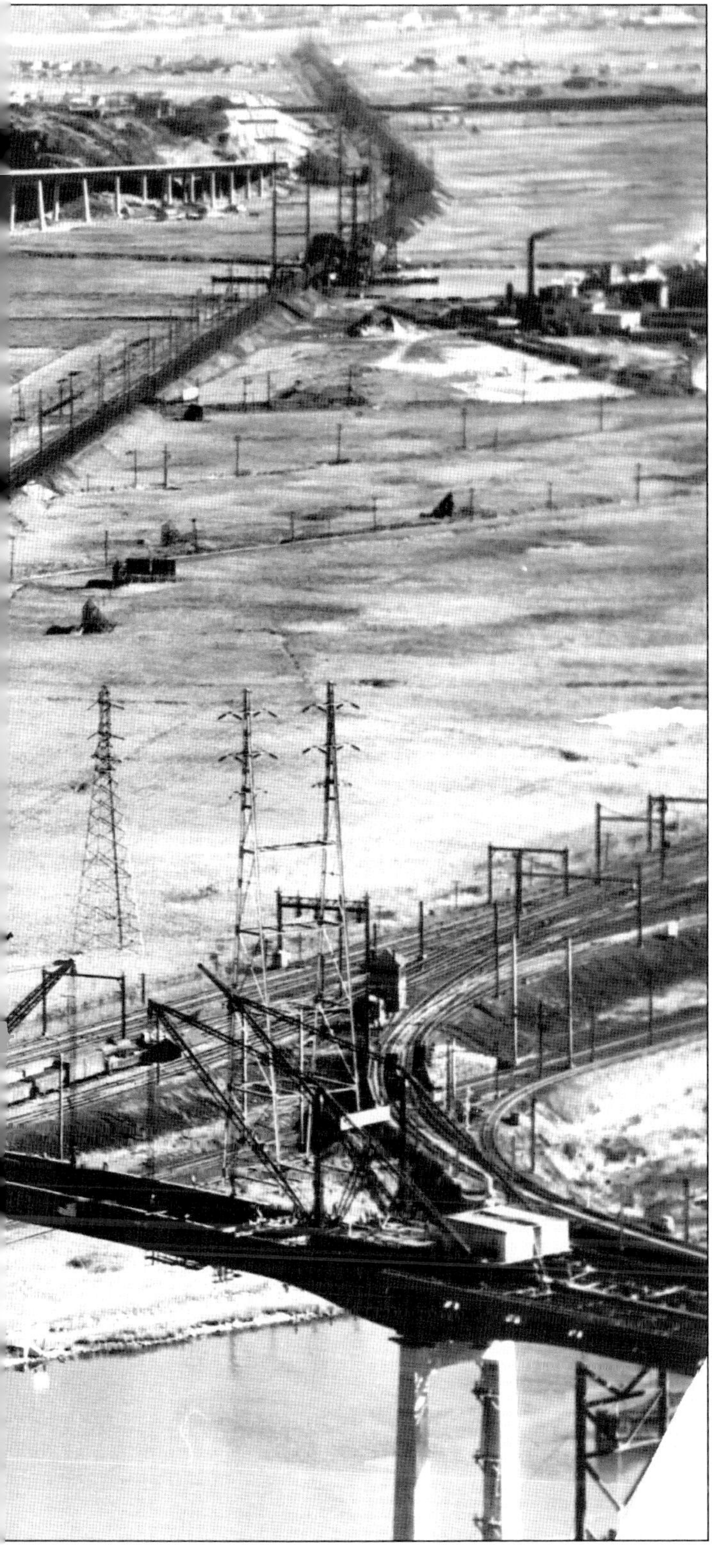

In the foreground, twin girders have been lifted into place on the Passaic River Bridge. Troast had the following to say about the Passaic: "A fixed, high-level structure, this bridge will provide an under clearance of 110 feet from mean high water, thus permitting clearance of all navigation, and assuring uninterrupted operation of vehicles traveling on the turnpike. It will be of deck construction, which will enable clear vision for drivers in all directions with no overhead steelwork." The 6,955-foot-long Passaic River Bridge cost $13.7 million to construct. In the background, construction on the Hackensack River Bridge progresses simultaneously.

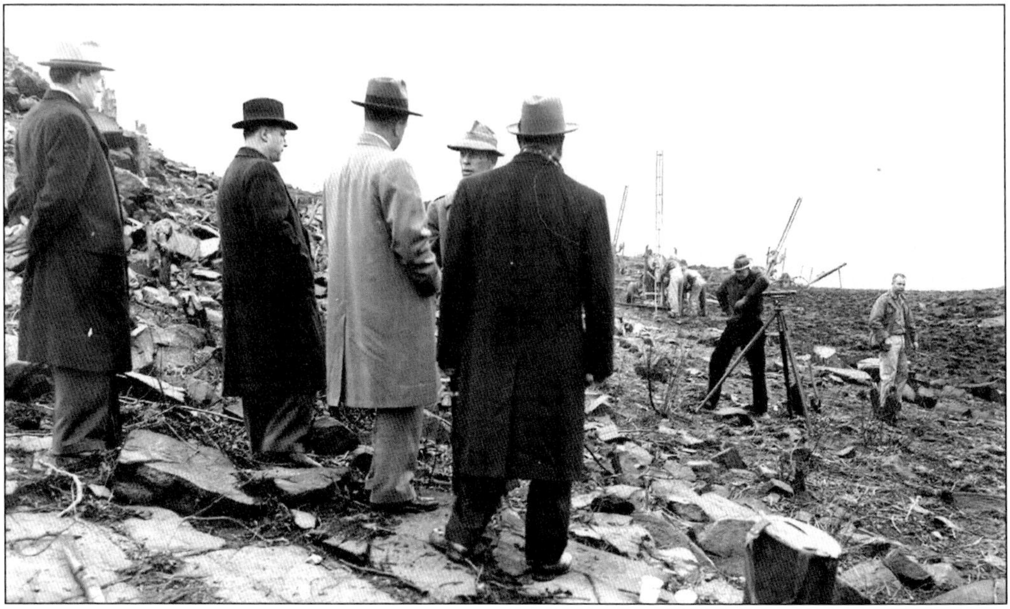

A flurry of activity takes place on Laurel Hill in Secaucus as contractors survey and prepare for the first cut through this rock formation on March 22, 1950.

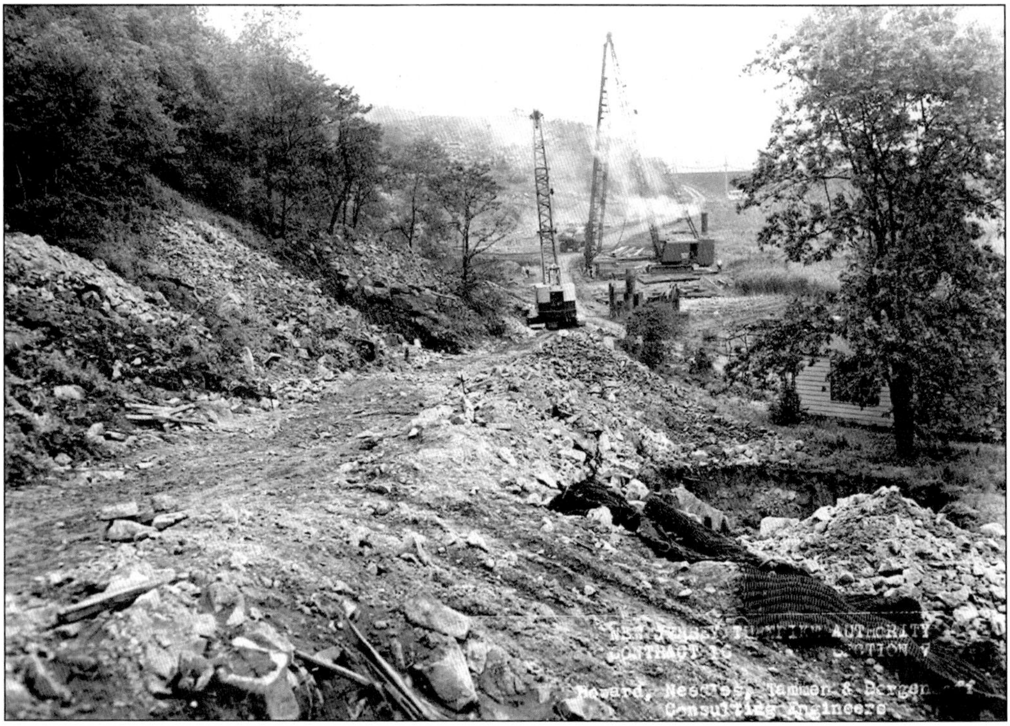

From an original photograph dated June 15, 1950, this view looking northeast from Pier N-8, shows progress on Piers N-9, N-10, N-11, and N-12 on the Hackensack River Bridge. This bridge is the second largest on the turnpike, with an overall length of 5,613 feet from the center bearings of the two abutments on either side of the river. Approximately 16,000 tons of steel are being used in the construction of the superstructure of the Hackensack River Bridge.

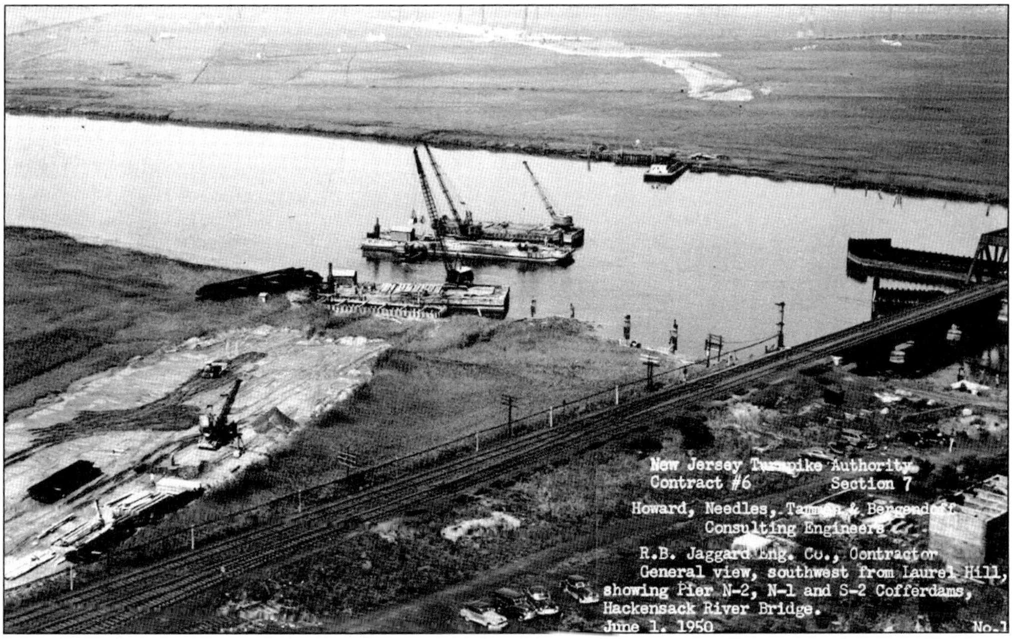

This general view, looking southwest from Laurel Hill, shows Pier N-2, N-1, and S-2 cofferdams on the Hackensack River Bridge on June 1, 1950. This is a six-lane structure, with three lanes in each direction. Travel lanes are 12 feet in width, with a separation between north and southbound lanes. The outside curbs are flanked by three-foot safety walks.

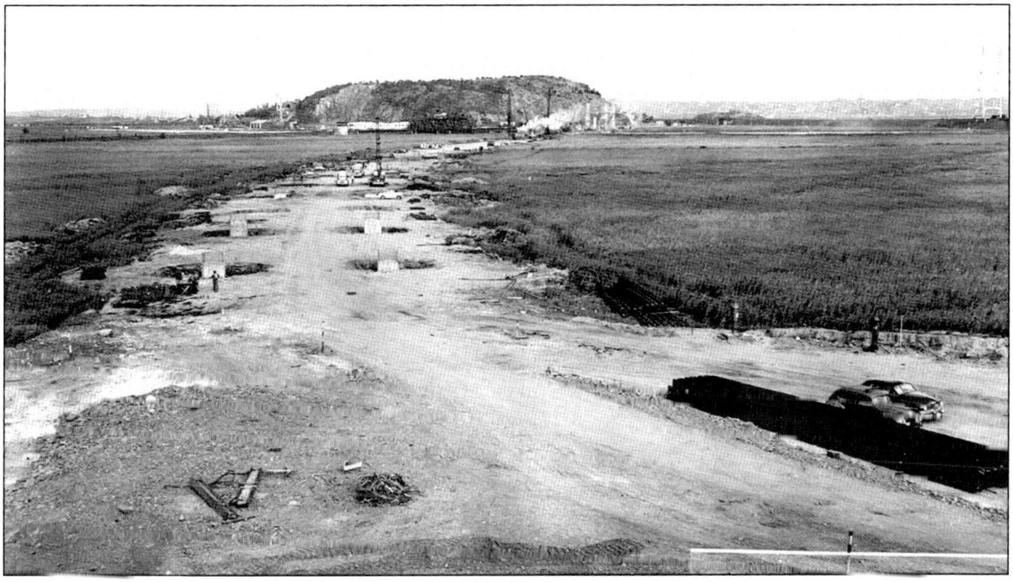

This view looking northeast from the south abutment shows progress on Piers S-22 to S-12 on the Hackensack River Bridge, on October 4, 1950. A very extensive study was made of the comparative economy of using wood piles, steel H-piles, and cast-in-place piles. Because of the great depth to rock in some areas, especially along most of the Hackensack River Bridge, it would have been necessary to obtain a large part of the wood piles from the West Coast. The steel H-piles, with their greater carrying capacity, permitted the use of smaller footings with a minimum of reinforcing steel, and indicated appreciable economy over the other types studied.

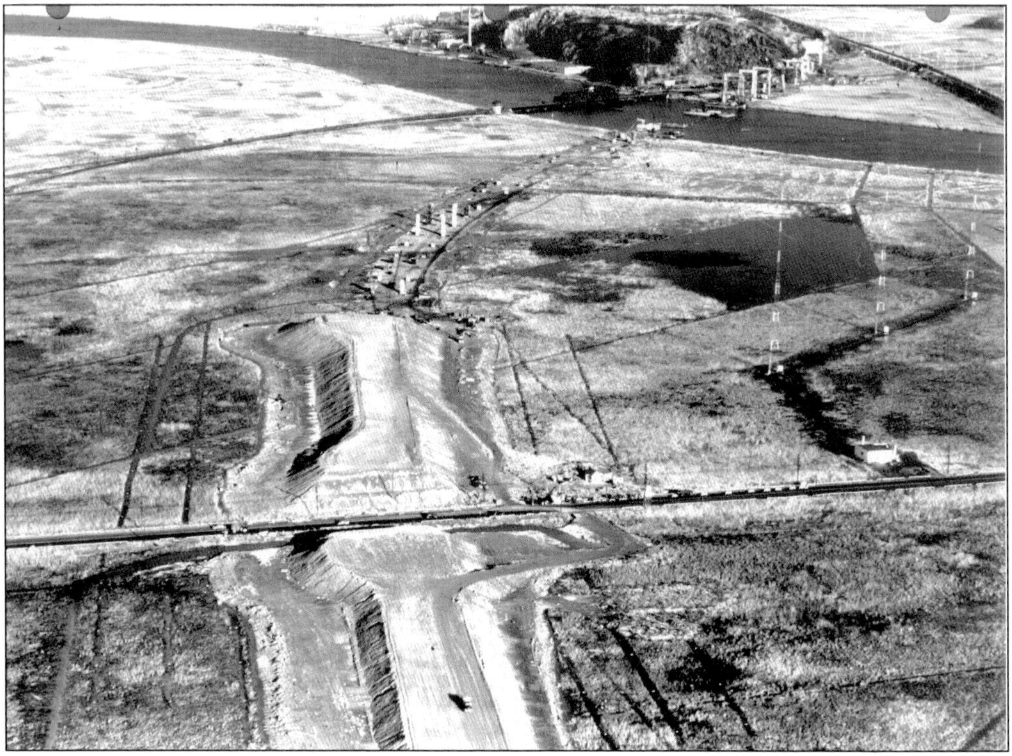

This original photograph dated February 6, 1951, shows an aerial view looking north toward the Hackensack River and Laurel Hill. Material in the foreground has been placed to build the approaches to the soon-to-be constructed Bellville Pike. The small building on the right housed one of the area's local radio stations.

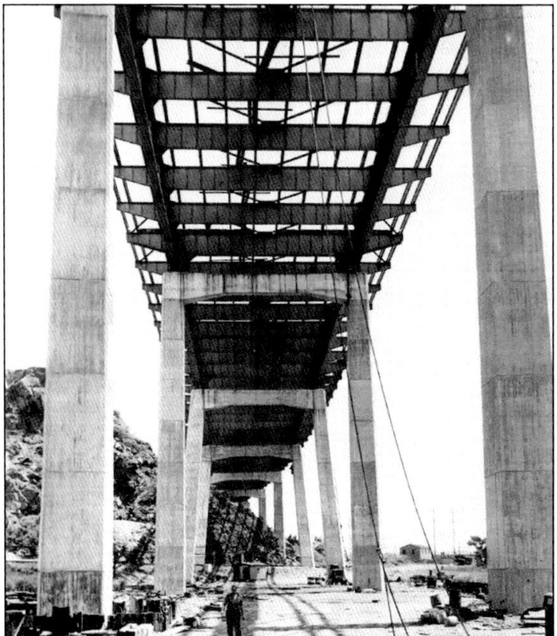

This photograph shows the underside of the Hackensack River Bridge, with primary steel in place. Deck construction is about to commence. Cement pilings are seen supporting 175-ton girders.

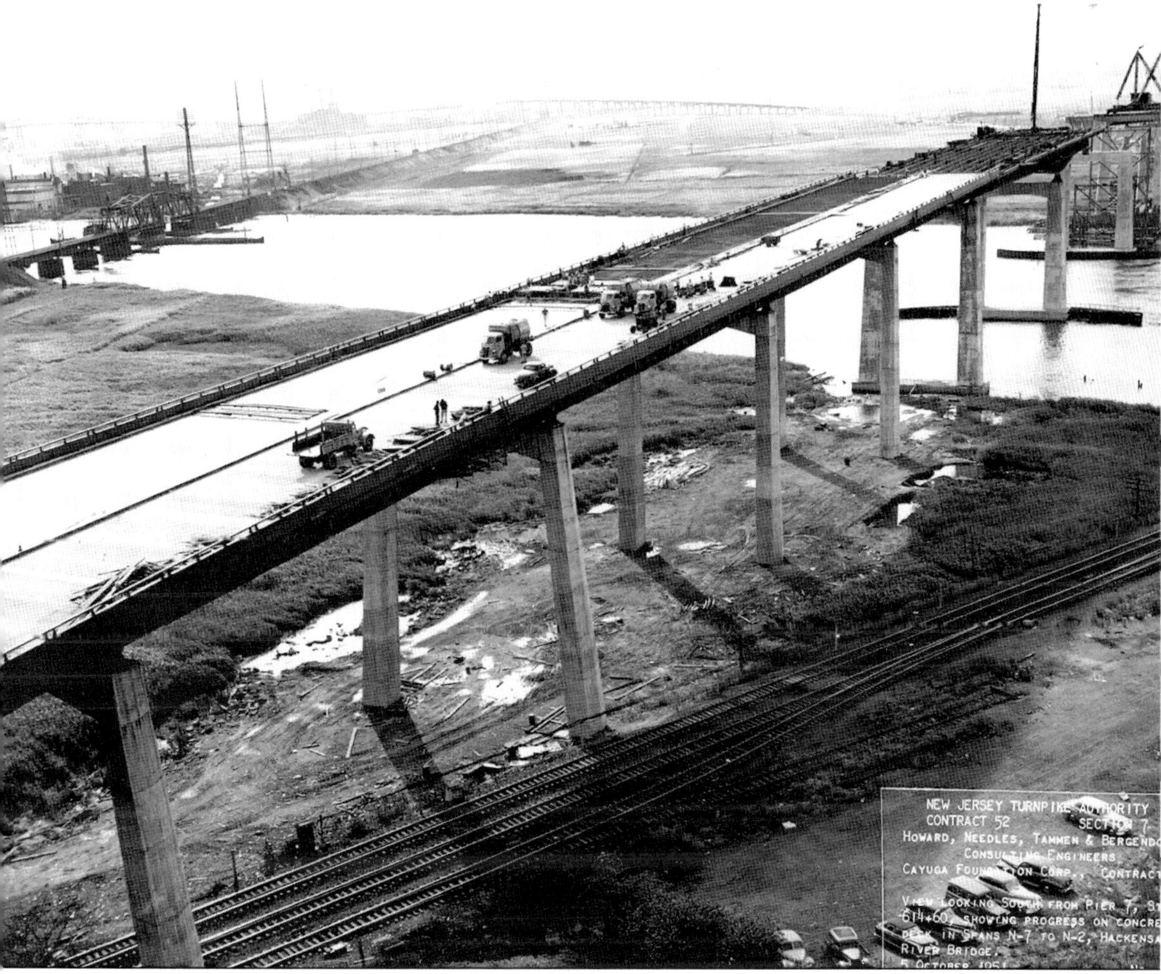

This original photograph dated October 5, 1951, shows a view looking south from Pier 7, Station 614+60, showing progress on construction of concrete deck in spans N-7 to N-2 on the Hackensack River Bridge. By October 1951, all piers were completed, and a traveler crane was erecting the final spans of the south approach. The Passaic River Bridge is seen in the background.

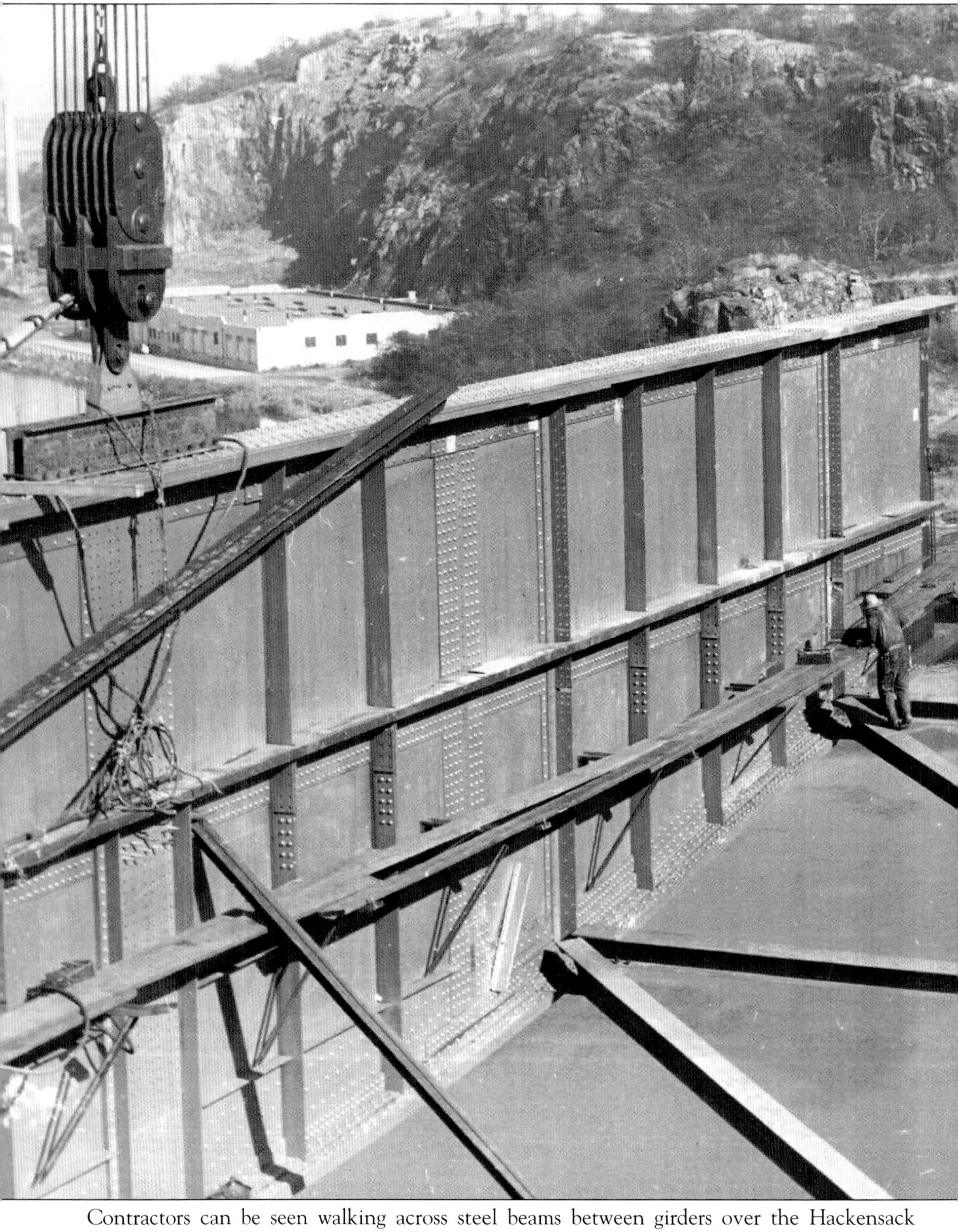

Contractors can be seen walking across steel beams between girders over the Hackensack River during bridge construction. The center span of the structure has not yet been put in place. Mount Laurel is visible in the background. On the Hackensack River Bridge, all

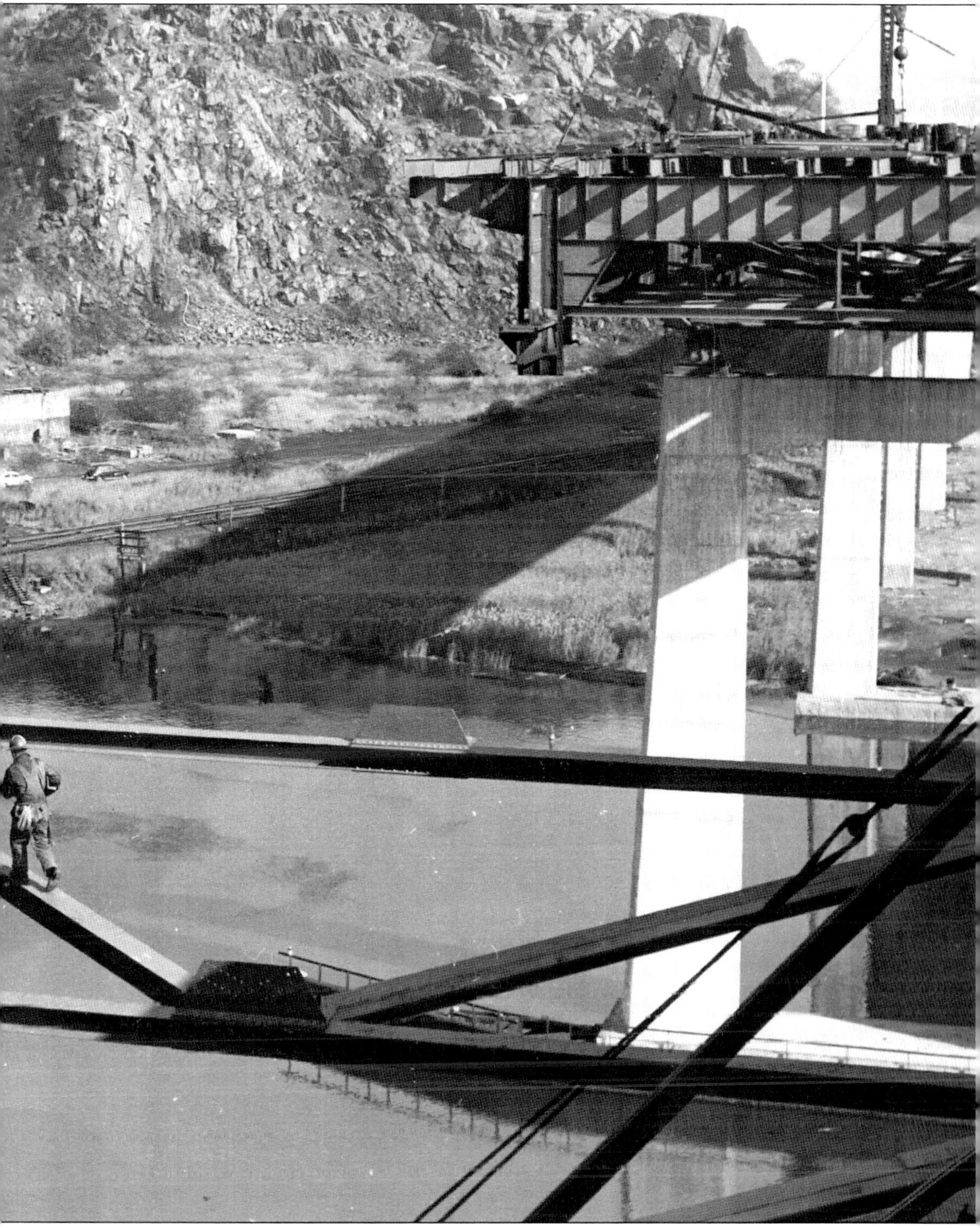

end- and center-span girder sections, shipped in upper and lower halves, were assembled prior to placement and raised as single units. In the case of the sections over the central piers, the lower and upper halves, averaging slightly over 90 tons each, were erected separately.

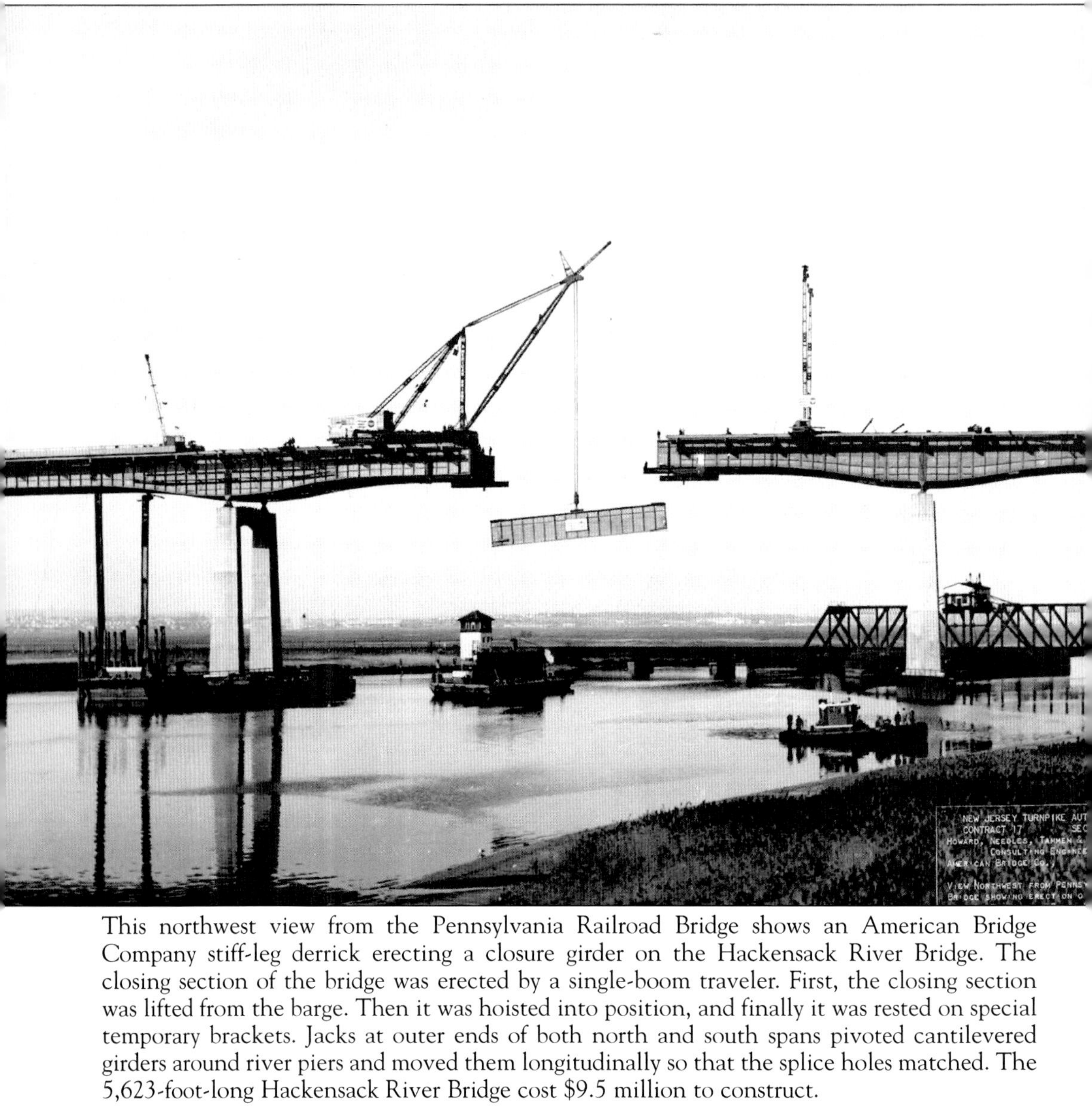

This northwest view from the Pennsylvania Railroad Bridge shows an American Bridge Company stiff-leg derrick erecting a closure girder on the Hackensack River Bridge. The closing section of the bridge was erected by a single-boom traveler. First, the closing section was lifted from the barge. Then it was hoisted into position, and finally it was rested on special temporary brackets. Jacks at outer ends of both north and south spans pivoted cantilevered girders around river piers and moved them longitudinally so that the splice holes matched. The 5,623-foot-long Hackensack River Bridge cost $9.5 million to construct.

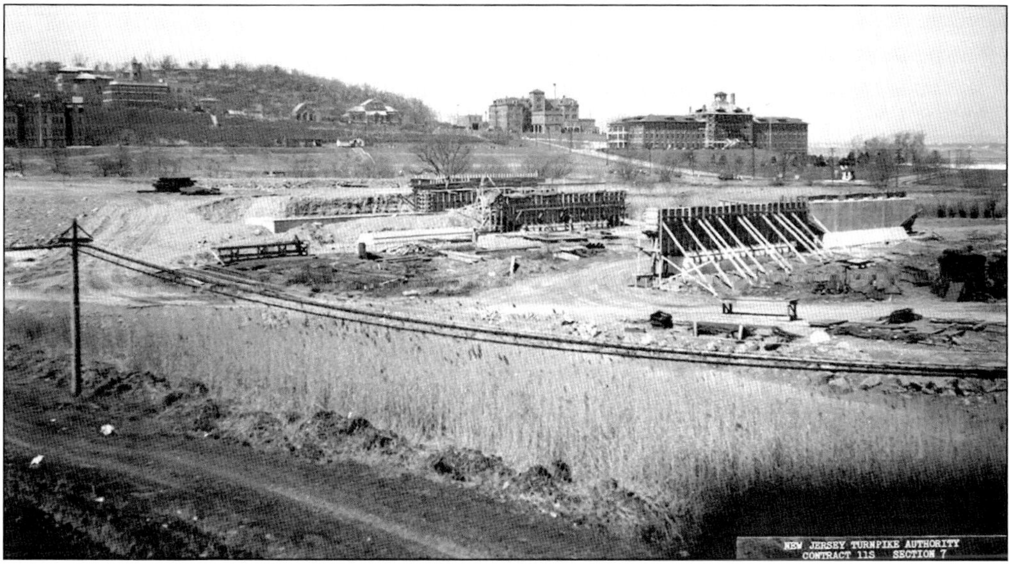

An original photograph dated April 2, 1951, shows a view looking southwest from the top of the Pennsylvania Railroad embankment opposite Station 647+50. Items shown, from right to left, are as follows: compressors; center pier, with left side stripped; south pier; and south abutment with forms in place for left side. "We have no intention of disturbing the graves which are in that [Snake Hill] cemetery," Troast said in a 1950 press release. "The cost of such moving, aside from the problems involved, is almost unpredictable and might easily be greater than the cost of the structure. For this reason we have decided to build this structure which will add considerably to the cost of the Turnpike in that area." Some 50 years later, in 2002, a widening project in Secaucus prompted the Authority to follow through with the disinterment of Potter's Field. This bridge is being removed and replaced with an embankment under the configuration of the new Secaucus Interchange, which is scheduled to be completed by the end of 2005.

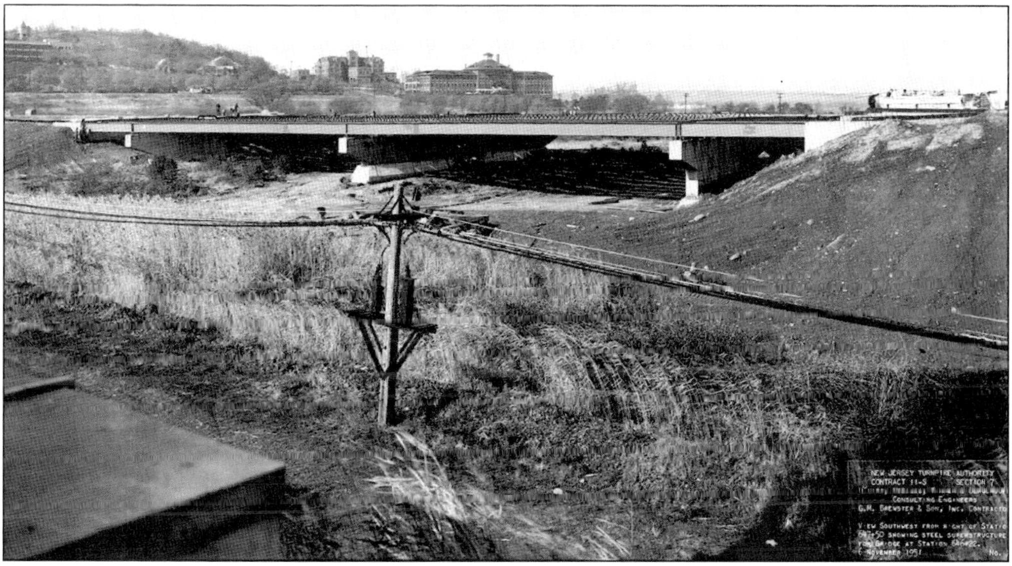

This southwest view from the right of Station 647+50 shows the steel superstructure for the bridge over Potter's Field at Station 646+22 on November 6, 1951. The Potter's Field burial site can be found directly under the bridge, between pilings supporting steel girders.

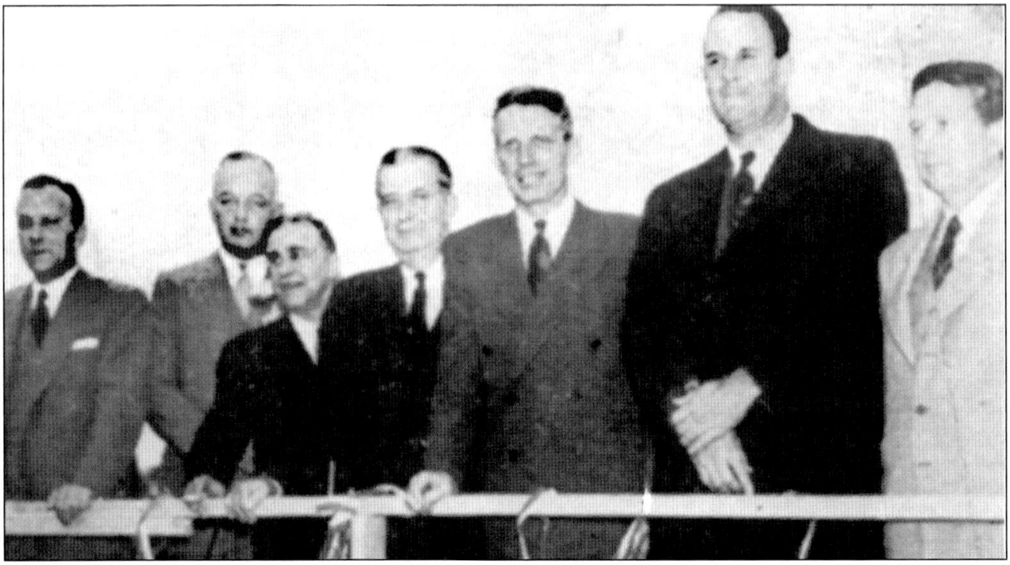

Opening ceremonies in Gloucester County took place at the Swedesboro Interchange with Sen. Harold W. Hannold as principal speaker. The attendees pictured are, from left to right, Vice Chairman Smith, Treasurer Lester, Mayor Charles Peterson of Woodbury, Chairman Troast, Governors Driscoll and Carvel, and Senator Hannold. (Courtesy of *New Jersey County Government* magazine.)

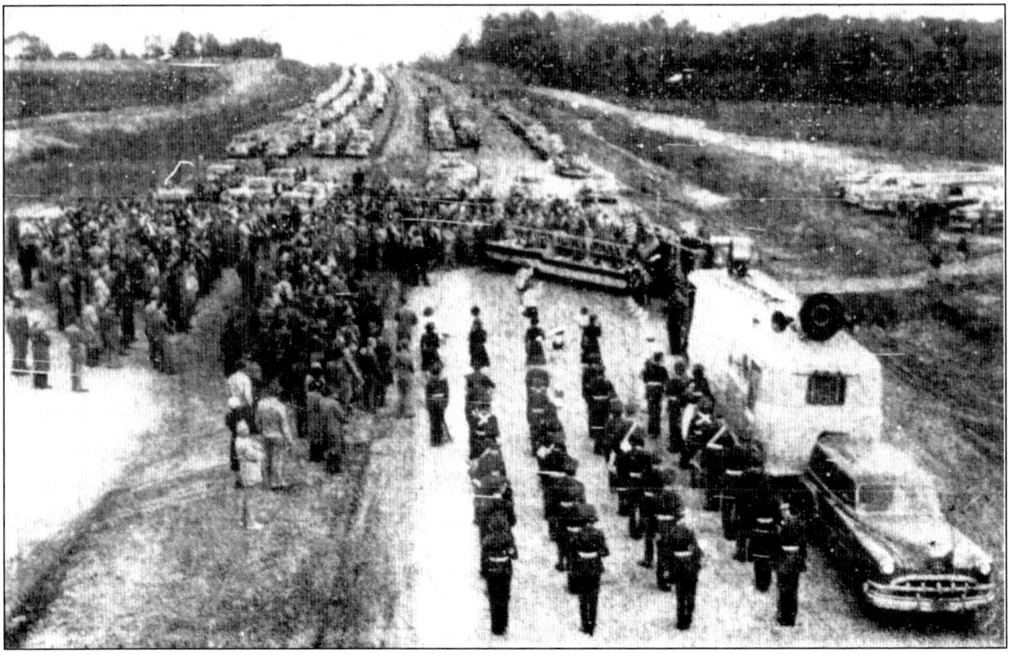

This dedication ceremony took place on the New Jersey Turnpike near Bordentown, with a long line of cars ready to make the first historic trip north to Woodbridge on October 31, 1951. Huge crowds gathered at every stop to witness the outdoor ceremonies, where high school bands took part by playing the national anthem. The ceremony was remembered as providing the Garden State's first grand tour through the finest farmlands, forests, cities, and industry sites in America. (Courtesy of the *Sunday Home News.*)

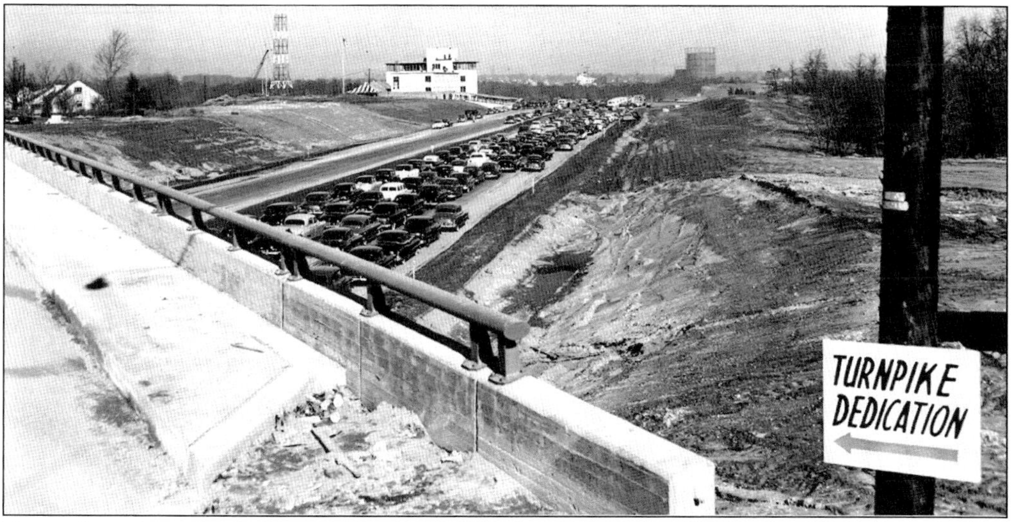

November 13, 1951, one week after the first cars took to the road in the southern part of the state, the New Jersey Turnpike Authority celebrated the beginning of the turnpike era with a series of ceremonies along the roadway in the central and northern parts of the state. Gov. Alfred E. Driscoll, Chairman Paul L. Troast, Commissioners Maxwell Lester and George F. Smith, and Executive Director W. W. Wanamaker, along with a host of dignitaries, marked the occasion in each of the four counties traversed by the turnpike at the time, followed by a celebratory procession along the length of the roadway.

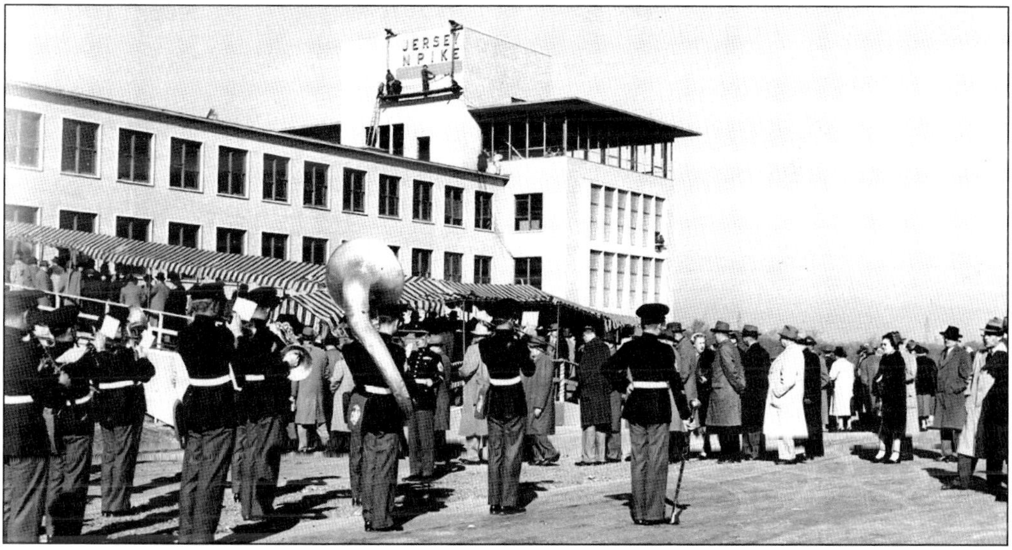

Workers atop the Turnpike Authority administration building are busy with the finishing touches as construction progresses on the third floor of the penthouse-style structure. A marching band plays a festive tune while guests attending the dedication visit with one another. The bittersweet ceremonies were marked with thanks and accolades for the more than 10,000 workers whose efforts made the completion of the turnpike possible in a remarkably short period of time. Officials also used the occasion to offer remembrances and sympathy for the six men who perished during the construction. Thanks to the efforts of thousands of workers and the vision of statewide leaders, the engineering marvel called the New Jersey Turnpike was ready to serve the state and, indeed, the nation.

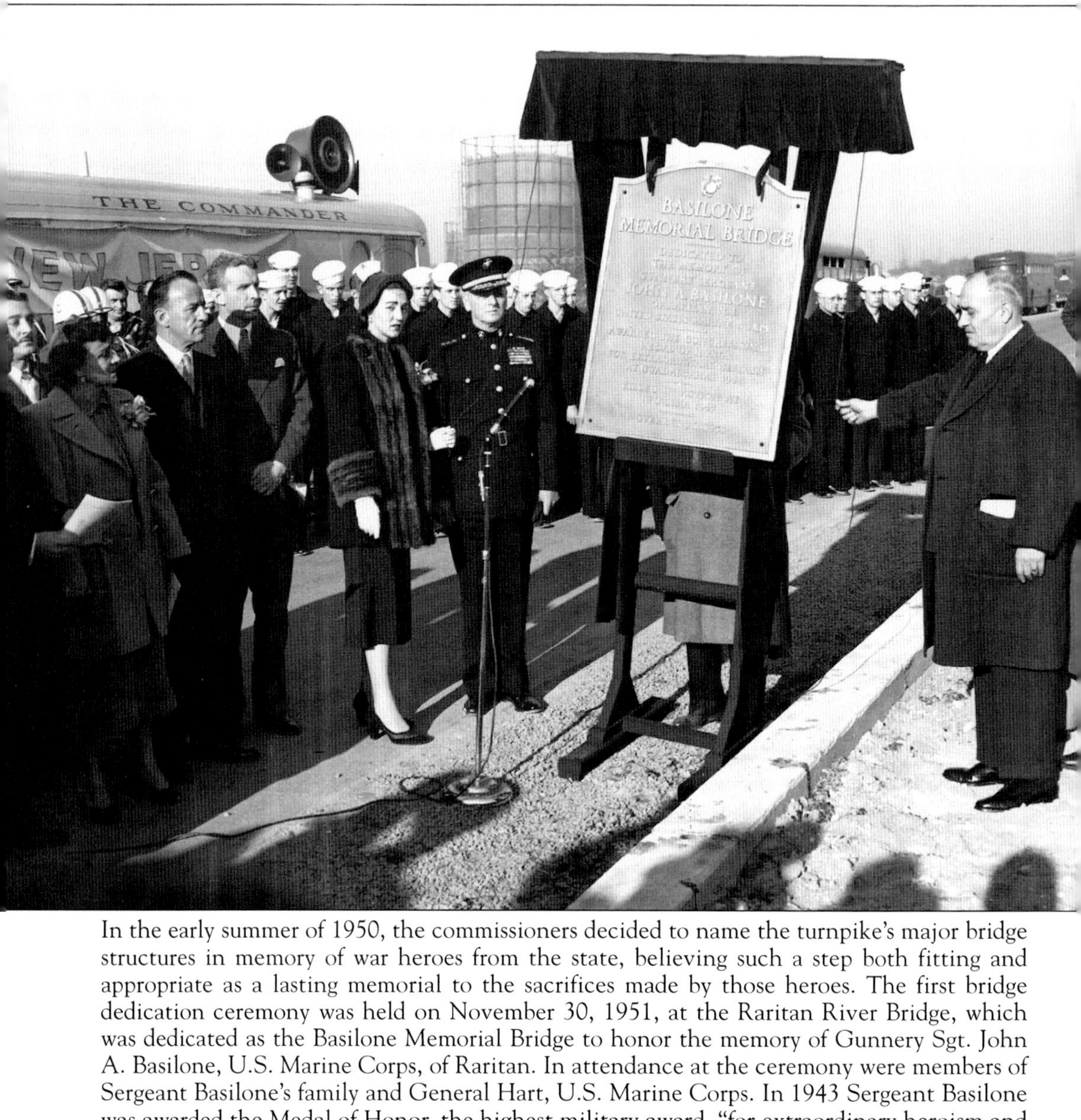

In the early summer of 1950, the commissioners decided to name the turnpike's major bridge structures in memory of war heroes from the state, believing such a step both fitting and appropriate as a lasting memorial to the sacrifices made by those heroes. The first bridge dedication ceremony was held on November 30, 1951, at the Raritan River Bridge, which was dedicated as the Basilone Memorial Bridge to honor the memory of Gunnery Sgt. John A. Basilone, U.S. Marine Corps, of Raritan. In attendance at the ceremony were members of Sergeant Basilone's family and General Hart, U.S. Marine Corps. In 1943 Sergeant Basilone was awarded the Medal of Honor, the highest military award, "for extraordinary heroism and conspicuous gallantry in action against enemy Japanese forces above and beyond the call of duty" in Guadalcanal on October 24 and 25, 1942. On those days, Sergeant Basilone "led soldiers in repelling a Japanese attack on crucial Henderson Field. Sergeant Basilone was killed in action at Iwo Jima on March 22, 1945, after he turned down a stateside commission and re-enlisted," according to Jeanette Rundquist of the *Star Ledger*.

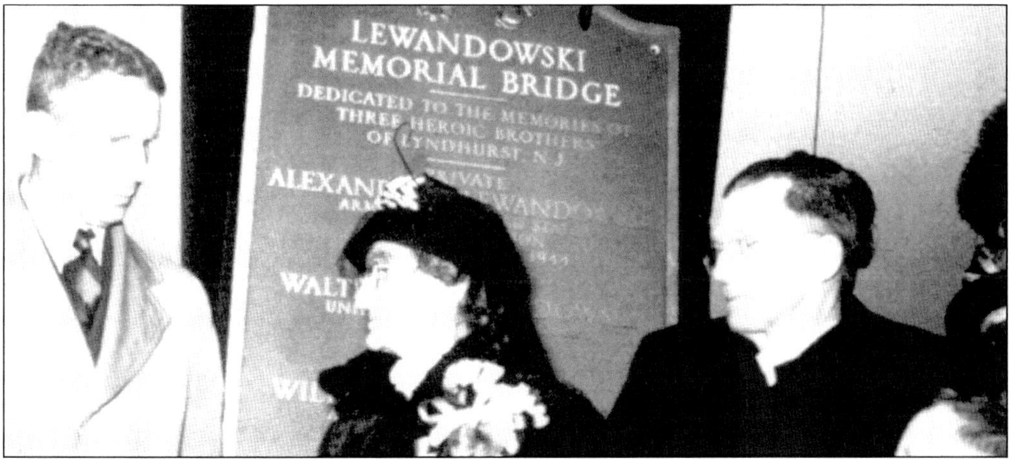

The Hackensack River Bridge was named in honor of the three Lewandowski brothers, who were killed in action during War World II within 18 months of each other. In attendance at the dedication ceremony were Governor Driscoll, members of the Lewandowski family, and clergy. At the age of 24, Walter M. Lewandowski, U.S. Marine Corps, was killed on July 21, 1944, the first day of the U.S. invasion of Guam. Nineteen-year-old Alexander F. Lewandowski, U.S. Army, was killed as his company fought near the Roer River in Apweiler, Germany. The third Lewandowski brother was killed on March 14, 1945; at the age of 27, William J. Lewandowski, a second lieutenant with the U.S. Air Force, was shot down as he was flying in his B-17 as part of a bomber mission in Germany. On October 31, 1998, Ted Lewandowski, the only surviving brother, spoke to the *Record* and said, with regard to his three fallen brothers: "They served their country. They did their job. I can thank God for that."

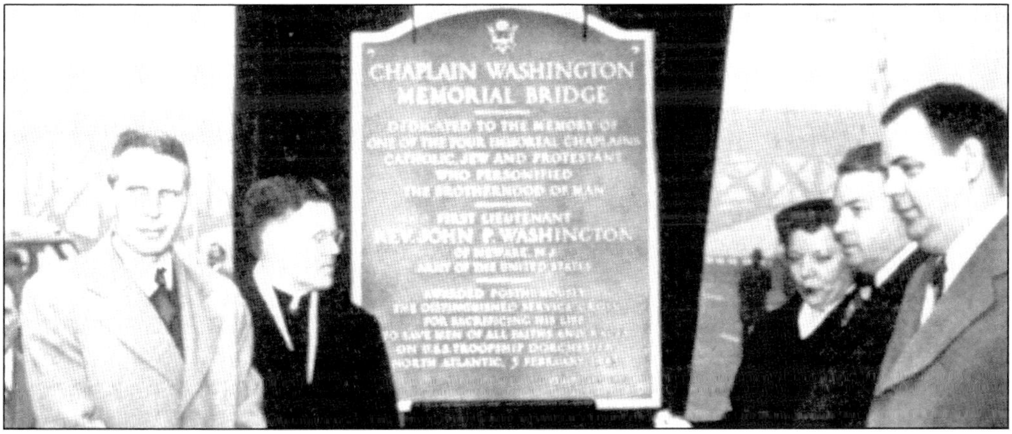

The Passaic River Bridge was named the Chaplain Washington Memorial Bridge after 1st Lt. Rev. John P. Washington, Army of the United States, who was one of the four chaplains who gave their lives to save their comrades during the sinking of the troopship *Dorchester* on February 23, 1943, in the North Atlantic. In attendance at the dedication ceremony were Governor Driscoll, along with Washington's relatives and pastor. According to accounts in the January 29, 1993 edition of the *Star Ledger*, "It took less than a half-hour for the *Dorchester* to slide beneath the ocean's surface after it was torpedoed by a German U-boat while en route to an American military base in Greenland." Chaplain Washington's death marked the first loss of a priest to the war, and he and his fellow chaplains were awarded both the Distinguished Service Cross and the Purple Heart. Posthumously, the four chaplains were awarded a special medal for heroism, which was created especially for them and was the only one ever given. There was also a 3¢ stamp issued in their honor.

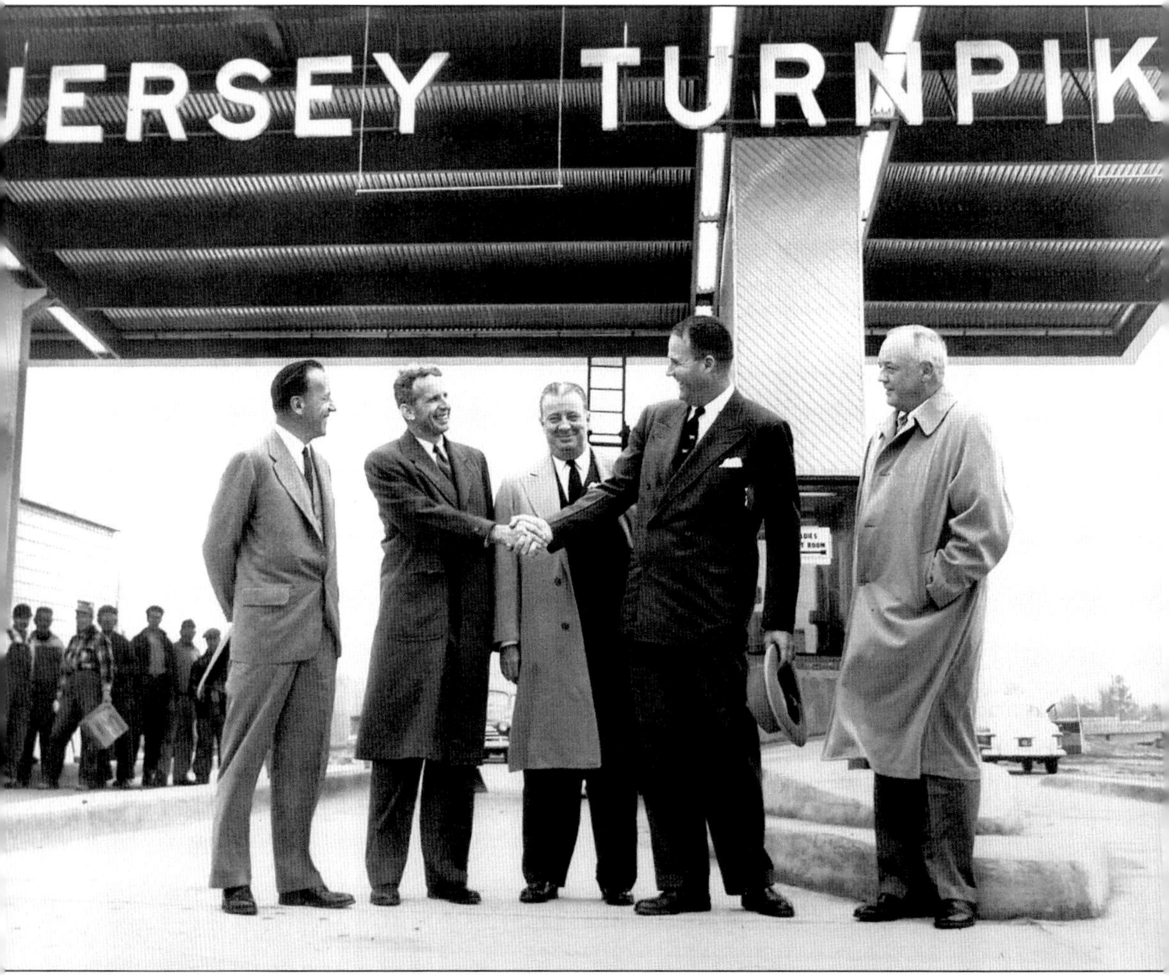

Governor Driscoll shakes hands with Delaware's Governor Carvel during the turnpike tour. Guests were brought to an official preview of the southern portion of the New Jersey Turnpike, and a tight schedule of sightseeing went awry. Some 800 persons received formal invitations from Governor Driscoll to accompany him on a tour of the 53 miles of superhighway from Bordentown to Deepwater. It was to be opened to the public at 8:00 in the morning on Monday. The 1,700 opening day guests whizzed along the black-topped road during the morning in their own cars and in buses provided by the Turnpike Authority. They stopped to hear speeches by Clarence Price, director of the Burlington County Board of Freeholders, and by Rep. Charles A. Wolverton (R-N.J.) before arriving at the Woodbury Armory. Pictured from left to right are George F. Smith, Governor Driscoll, Paul Troast, Governor Carvel, and Maxwell Lester.

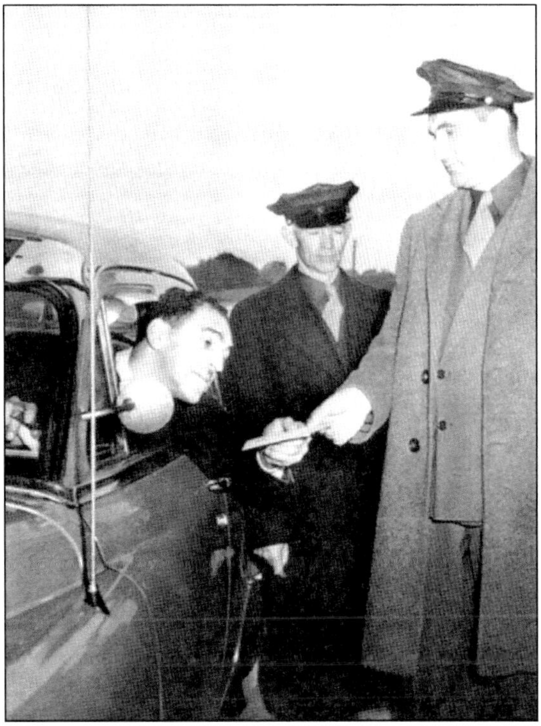

"Mr. First"—37-year-old Omero C. Catan of Woodside, Long Island—seen behind the wheel of his 1951 blue DeSoto sedan, paid the first toll of 15¢ to Toll Collector Sam Kostick for his 12-mile trip from Interchange 1 in Deepwater to Interchange 2 in Swedesboro. Toll Supervisor Archie Murphy looks on in the background. Catan was followed on that first day alone by an additional 4,225 vehicles, bringing the first day's toll collection total to approximately $1,996.

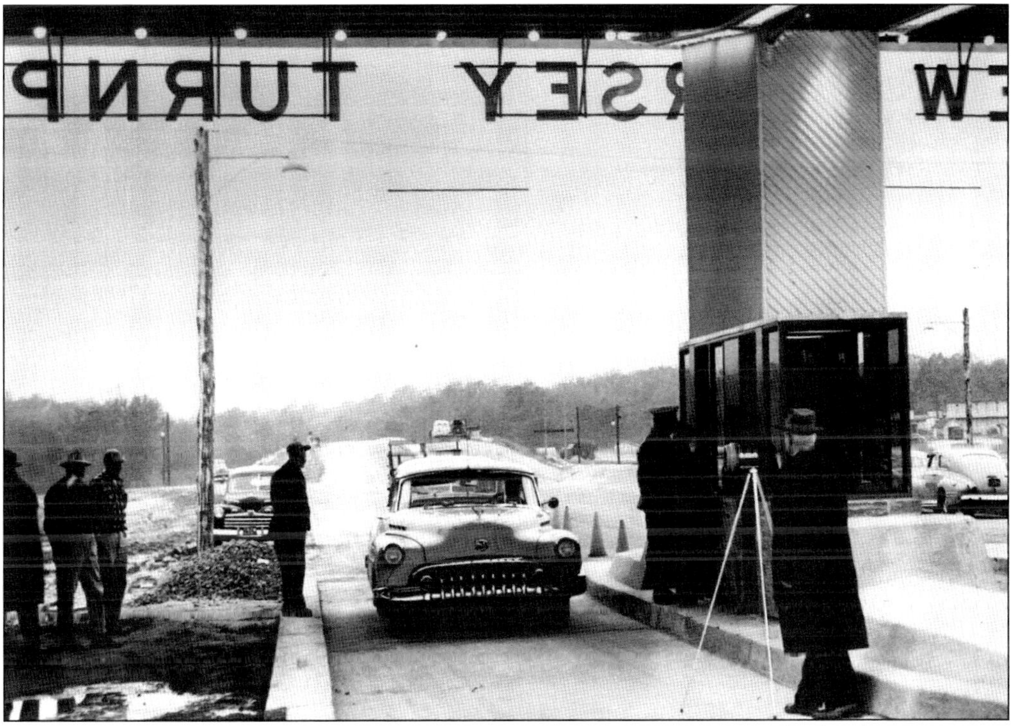

An original photograph taken November 5, 1951, shows the first vehicle about to enter Interchange 3. This interchange in Woodbury was one of seven plazas in a 53-mile stretch to open on the turnpike's first day of operation.

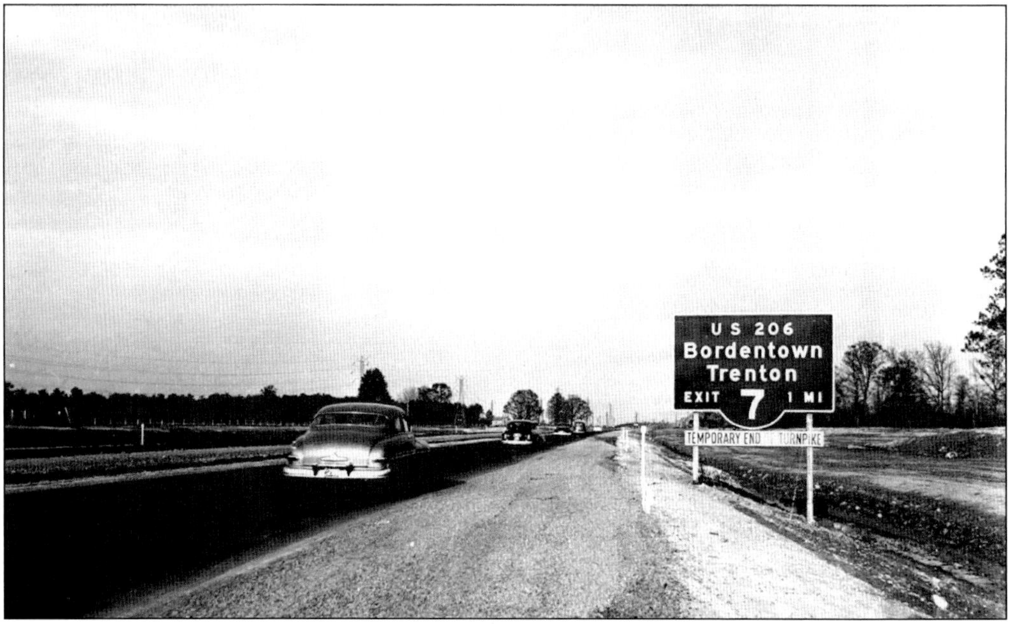

On November 5, 1951, a new era of transportation begins, as the New Jersey Turnpike Authority opens operations to serve the motoring public on the turnpike's first 53-mile stretch of roadway, extending from Interchange 1 in Deepwater to Interchange 7 in Bordentown. Following a grand-opening ceremony of a catered breakfast at the War Memorial Building in Trenton, 1,700 guests anxiously awaited their chance to be pioneering motorists and drive "the road of tomorrow."

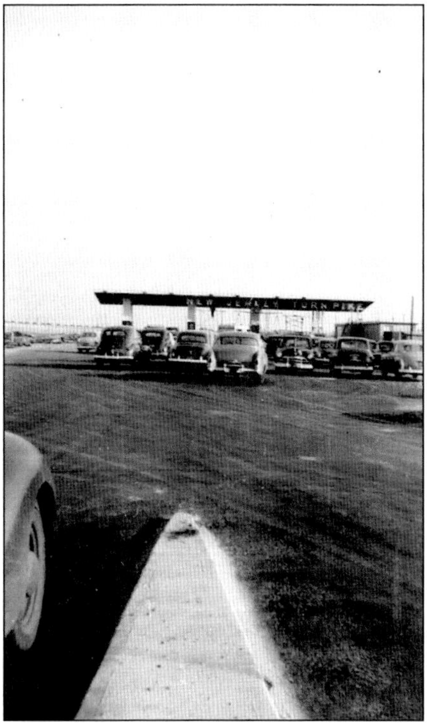

Cars await opening at the original Newark Airport Interchange 14 in January 1952. The Newark Airport Interchange serves as a most important collection and distribution point for traffic to and from Newark Airport, and it was a major factor in the heavy movement of passenger vehicles to and from the Pulaski Skyway and the Holland Tunnel. The interchange provides access to and from the Newark business and industrial districts and the Jersey City/Bayonne area.

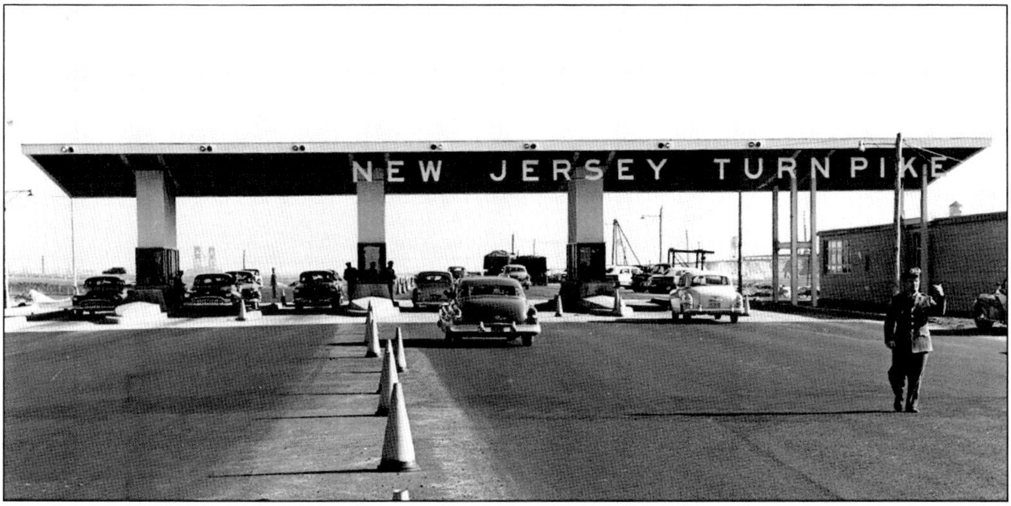

Toll collectors direct traffic into Newark Airport Interchange 14 on opening day, January 15, 1952. The completion of the New Jersey Turnpike provided another piece of what was called the "eastern turnpike complex." The first piece of the complex was completed in 1940 with the opening of the Pennsylvania Turnpike, followed in 1947 by the opening of the Maine Turnpike. This was followed by the completion of controlled-access toll expressways in a number of states: New Hampshire in 1950, Ohio in 1955, New York and Indiana in 1956, Massachusetts in 1957, Connecticut and Illinois in 1958, and Delaware and Maryland in 1963. By 1963, motorists could travel southward from Maine to Virginia, or westward from Maine to Illinois, without stopping at a traffic light. Much of the eastern turnpike complex was absorbed into the Interstate Highway System. (Courtesy of nycroads.com.)

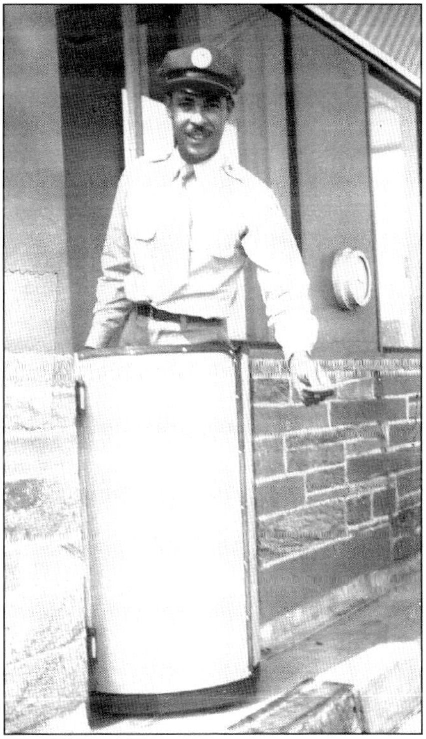

According to an article in the August 1952 edition of the *Afro American*, the New Jersey Turnpike Authority employed 175 toll collectors at 17 interchanges along the 118-mile superhighway, 13 of whom were African American. The article features accounts from toll collectors of color who commend the Authority for pleasant conditions on the turnpike and considerate supervisors. John L. Costly of East Orange stated: "There is no discrimination. Employees are advanced according to their ability and seniority." Wilbur Marshall (pictured) was one of the original African American collectors. In February 1953, Marshall was promoted to the office of administrative supervisor. He was the first African American to hold an executive post of this kind with the Authority. Marshall's daughter, Teresa Hale, is following in her father's footsteps. Teresa, a compliance manager, Equal Employment Opportunity, was hired by the Turnpike Authority in 2002 and is currently working at the turnpike administration building in East Brunswick.

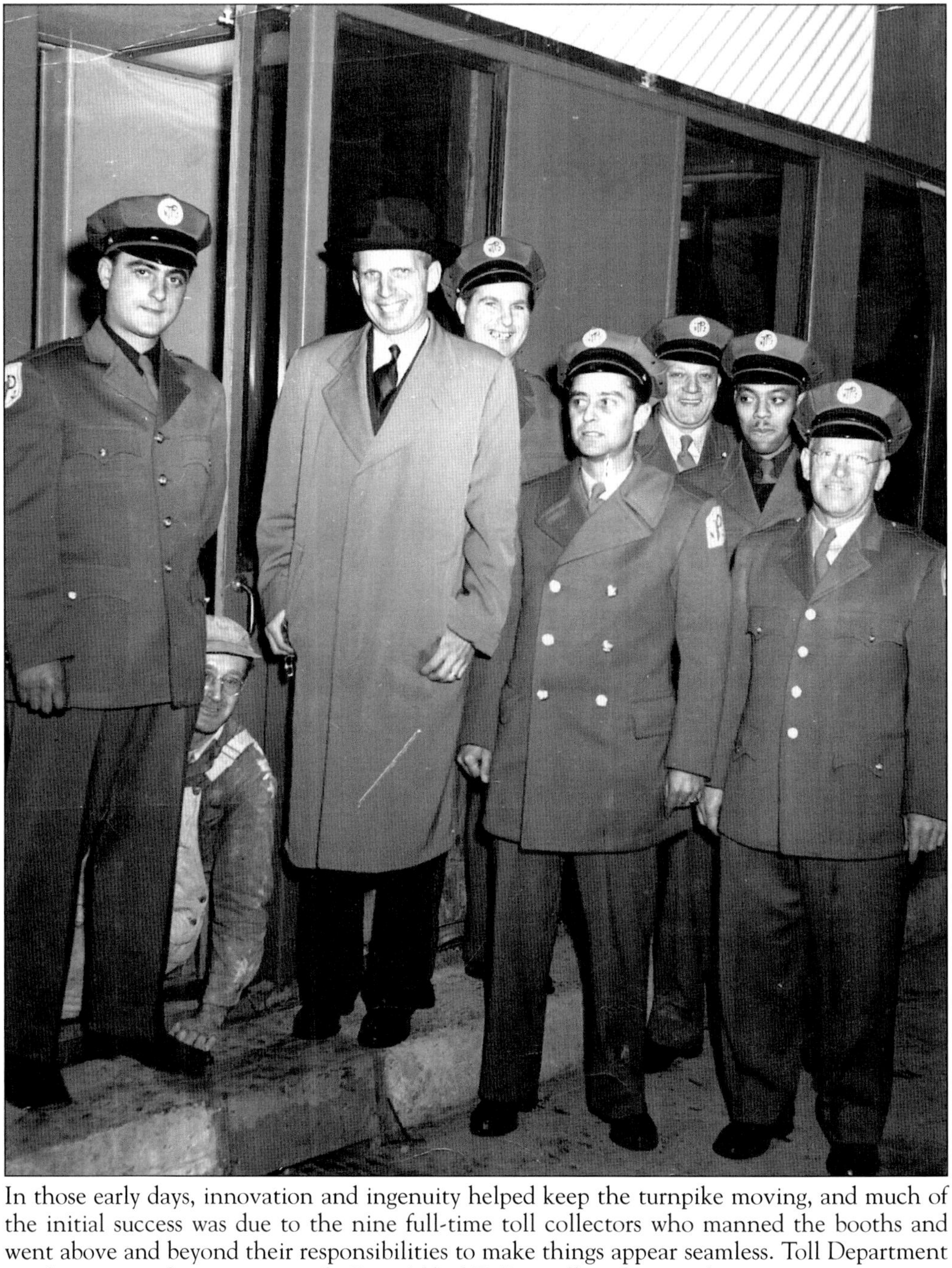

In those early days, innovation and ingenuity helped keep the turnpike moving, and much of the initial success was due to the nine full-time toll collectors who manned the booths and went above and beyond their responsibilities to make things appear seamless. Toll Department employees pose for a picture with Gov. Alfred E. Driscoll at the grand-opening ceremonies at Interchange 18 in Ridgefield Park on January 12, 1952. At the official preview of the turnpike on October 31, 1951, Governor Driscoll himself said: "This turnpike job demonstrates the great reserve strength that rests in our states. It has been designed and built to make our economy secure and to promote the general welfare of our people." Individuals shown are, from left to right, Joe Viola, unidentified, Governor Driscoll, unidentified, Jack Colons (assistant section chief), Charly Maiscee, Will Galloway, and Steve Marco.

Two

The Next 25 Years 1951–1976

With the success of achieving their goal of turnpike completion in 1951, officials at the New Jersey Turnpike Authority soon set out to deal with the next major issue facing them: being victims of their own success.

Apparently, providing motorists with all the conveniences and comforts that would revolutionize their traveling experience drew traffic far beyond the initial expectations of planners. By 1953, traffic volume on the New Jersey Turnpike had already reached levels projected for 1975—22 years ahead of schedule—and revenues from tolls were more than double what had been anticipated. While additional revenue is usually a welcome by-product, the numbers continued to exceed expectations for years. Though this was clear evidence of the success of the roadway and its vision, the increased patronage brought with it its own pitfalls.

With hardly enough time to savor their accomplishments in the construction of the turnpike, Authority officials were quickly back in planning mode to accommodate the increasing traffic volume.

In order to maintain the turnpike's record of safety and commitment to drivers, immediate steps were taken to bolster the road's state police personnel, which grew exponentially to meet increased traffic volume. Also, plans were quickly undertaken to construct the Pennsylvania Turnpike Extension and Newark Bay Extension, both of which were completed in 1956.

By 1961, only 10 years after its completion, the New Jersey Turnpike had established itself as one of the most successful and safest roads in the country, with annual traffic in excess of 141 million vehicles. Portions of the turnpike quickly became the most heavily traveled sections of any roadway in the country. So, in keeping with their tradition of leading the way in innovative transportation practices, in the late 1960s, Turnpike Authority officials set out to construct the nation's first dual-dual highway system to expand the roadway's capacity in the areas that were most highly traveled.

The roadway was expanded to make six lanes available in each direction over a total of 26 miles and was widened to 10 lanes over another 10 miles. Additionally, a western spur of the roadway was constructed north of Interchange 15 to cut directly through the Meadowlands and provide more-direct access to the turnpike from rapidly growing communities.

Completed in January 1971 at a cost of $407 million, the new enhancements to the road also provided improved connections with Route 287 and the Garden State Parkway, and they helped complete a transportation network that far exceeded the expectations of its original planners.

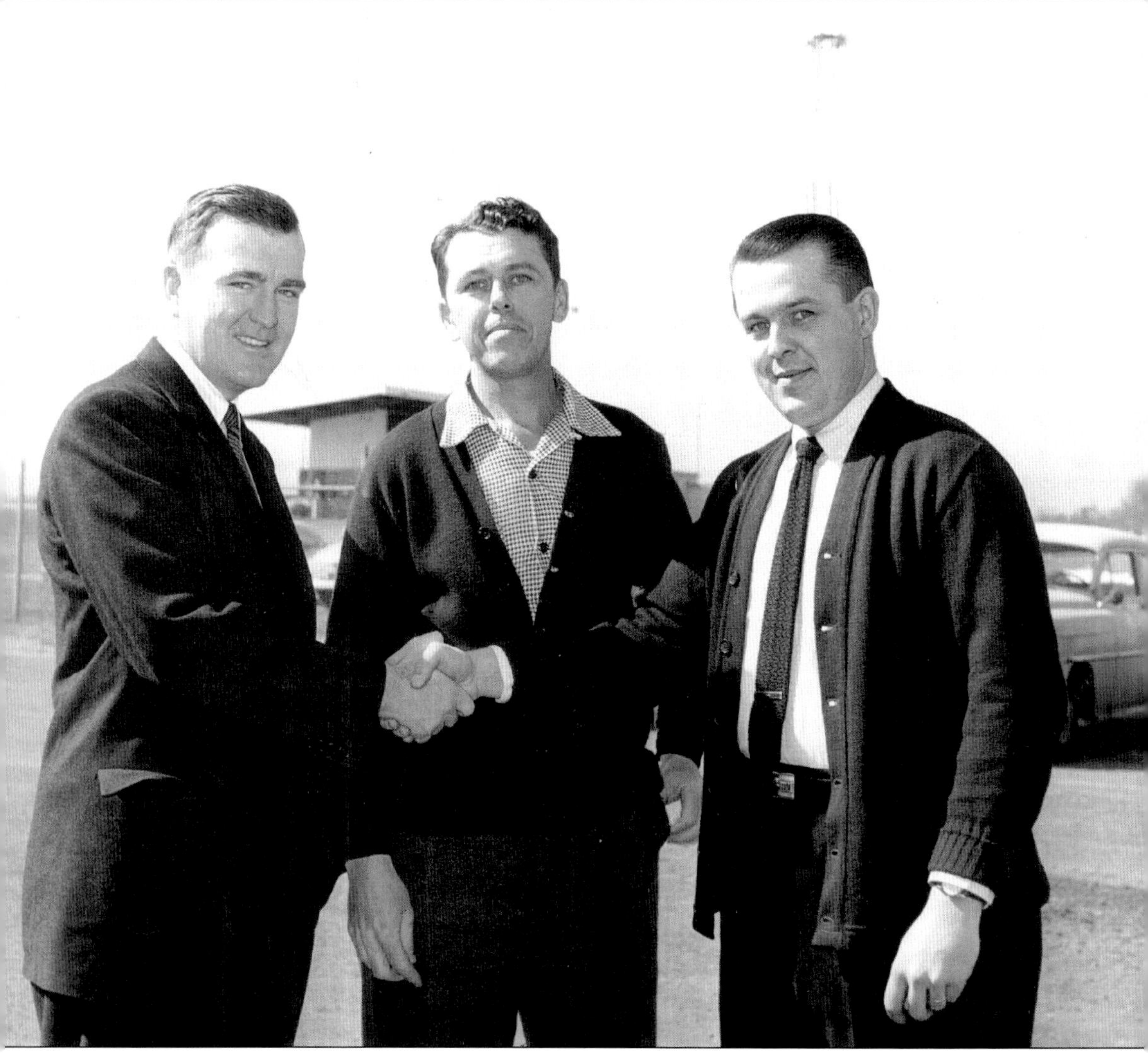

Commissioner and Vice Chairman Cornelius E. Gallagher (1956–1960) presents five-year awards to Sam Troxell (center) and Richard Walley (right) at the Central Shops Maintenance District in 1956. Both Troxell and Walley started their careers on the turnpike on December 3, 1951, just days after the roadway opened. Troxell retired in 1984 after 30 years in the Maintenance Department, while Walley, who retired in 2002, became the first 50-year employee of the New Jersey Turnpike.

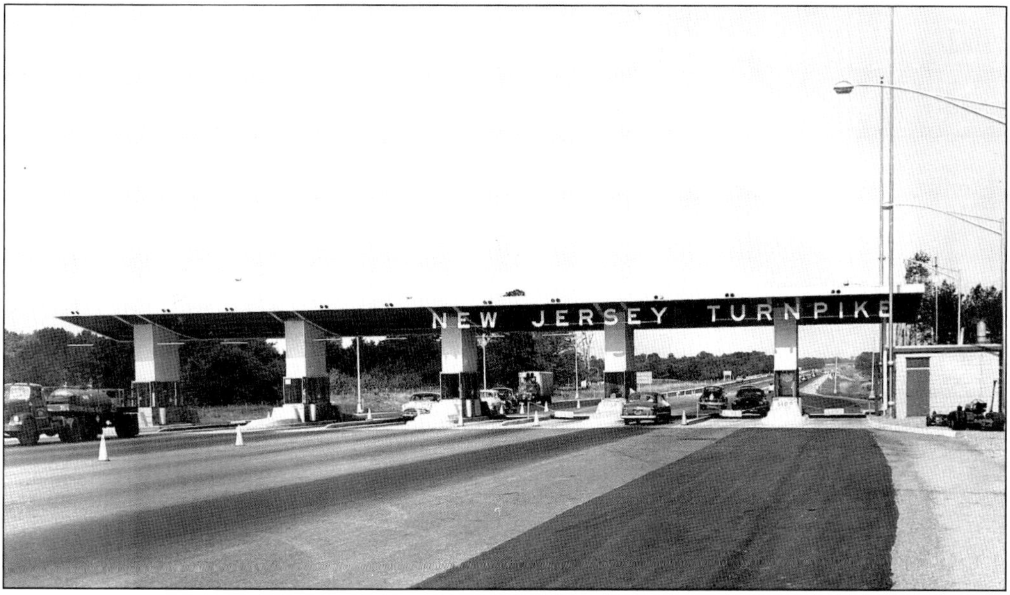

This photograph shows Interchange 1 on the New Jersey Turnpike. The Delaware Memorial Bridge, which opened in August 1951, furnishes adequate facilities at the southern terminus of the New Jersey Turnpike for motorists wishing to continue southwest across the Delaware River.

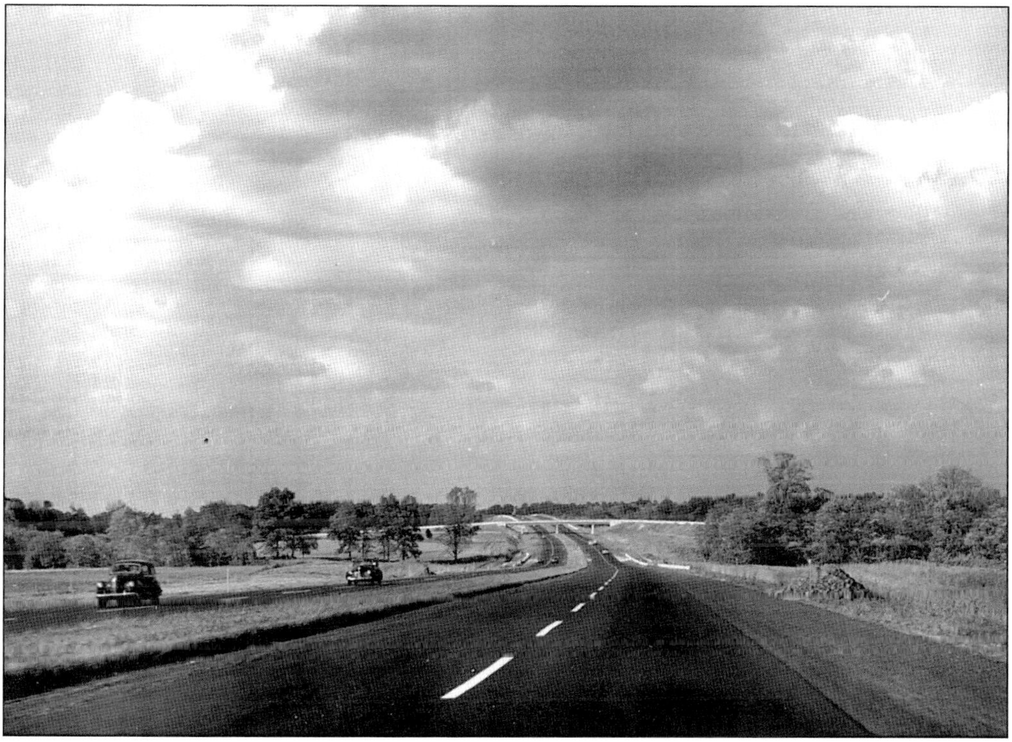

This photograph shows light traffic on the southern end of the New Jersey Turnpike. (Courtesy of Homer R. Hill/Collection of Mitchell E. Dakelman.)

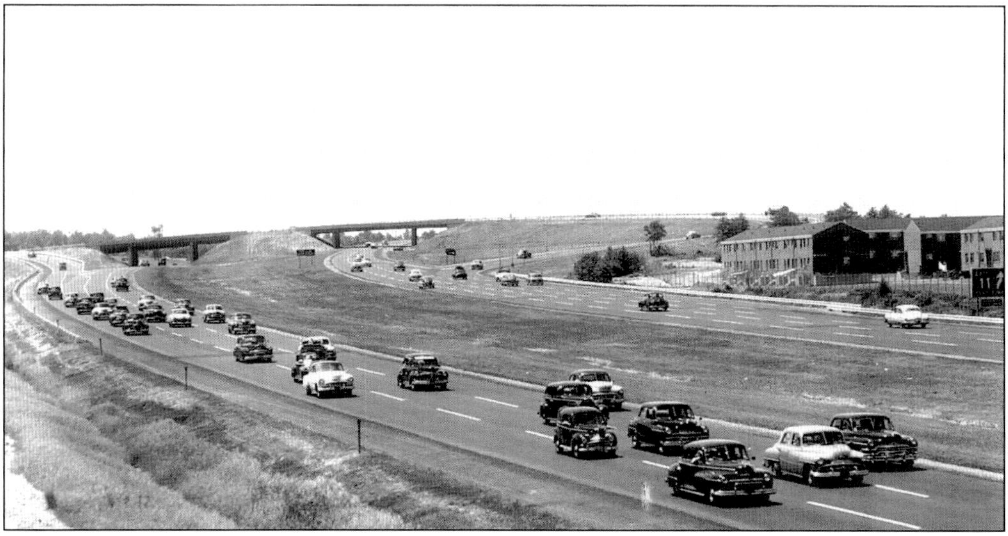

The original construction of the New Jersey Turnpike near Interchange 11 consisted of three lanes of travel in each direction. Today, there are a total of 12 lanes on the turnpike in the Woodbridge area.

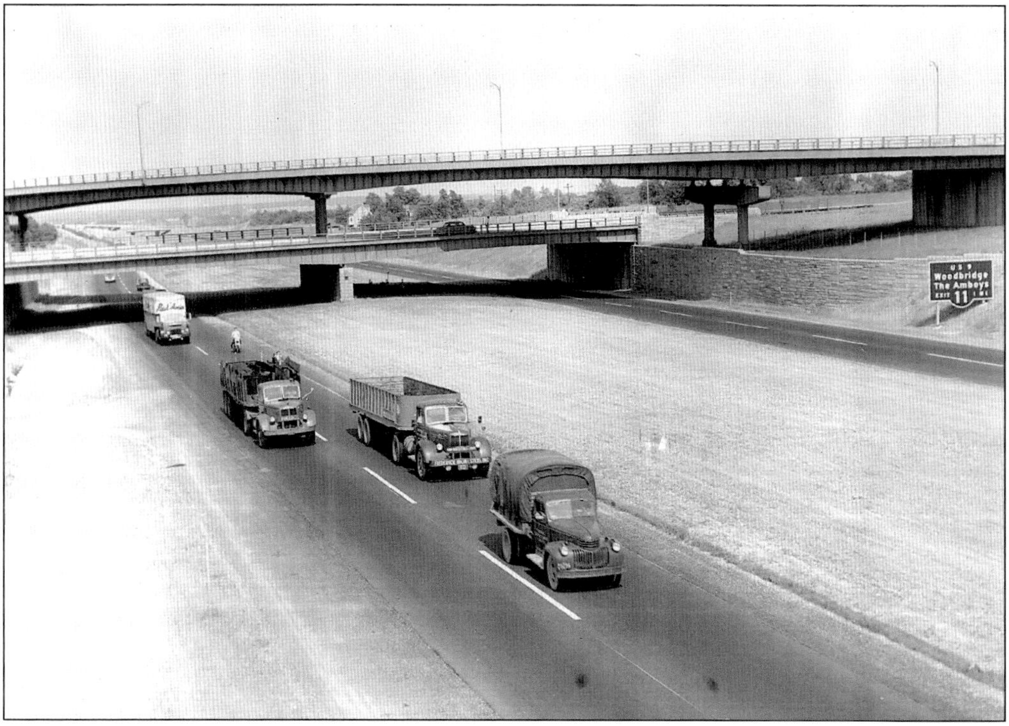

In his article on the New Jersey Turnpike and the state's defenses, Maj. Gen. Edward C. Rose stated: "The New Jersey Turnpike's strategic location in the north—it begins on the New Jersey side of the George Washington Bridge—gives it top priority for emergency movements. The bridge and the turnpike would be the No. 1 route for movement of supplies and equipment from New York south, or from the south to New York and the New England region."

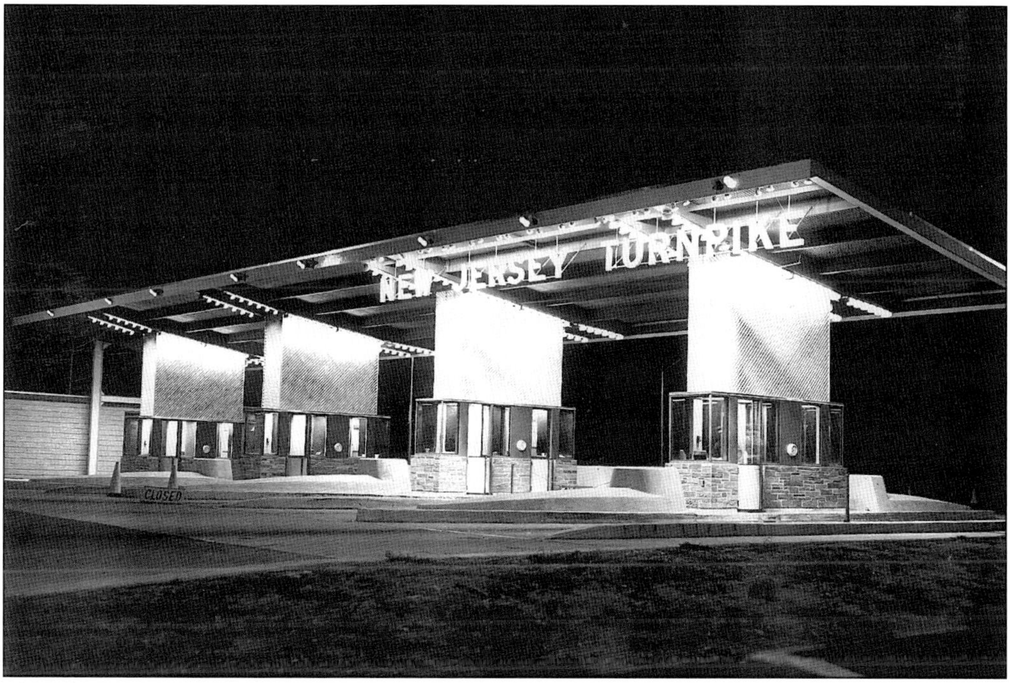

The photograph above shows a night view of a typical toll plaza on the New Jersey Turnpike. Operations of the turnpike in 1952 surpassed the most optimistic expectations and far exceeded the 1949 estimates made by the traffic and revenue engineers. A total of 18,239,527 vehicles used the turnpike in 1952, an average of 49,834 vehicles daily.

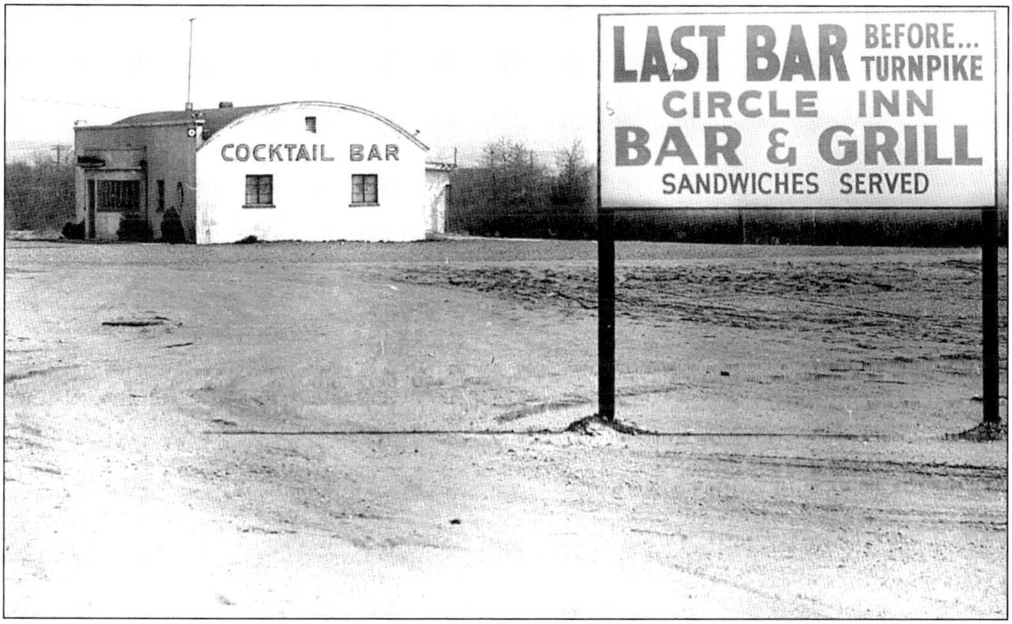

The sign in this photograph advertises the last bar before entering the New Jersey Turnpike. On May 3, 1952, *Middlesex News* bureau manager Harry A. Edwards sent a letter along with this photograph to inform the Authority that Alcoholic Beverage Control acting director Edward J. Dorton ordered that the sign be removed "under a penalty of revocation of the license."

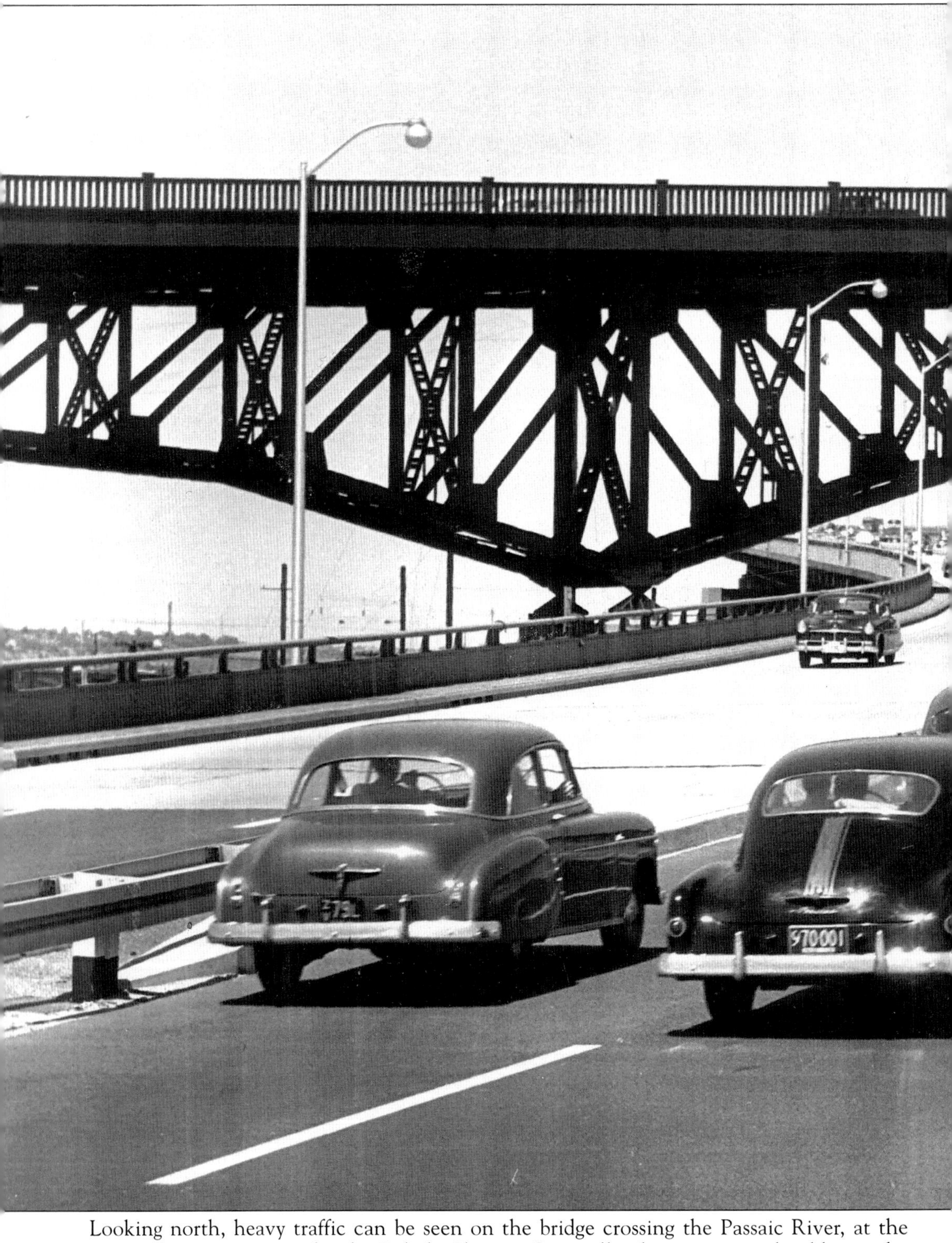

Looking north, heavy traffic can be seen on the bridge crossing the Passaic River, at the point where it passes under the Pulaski Skyway. Originally, there were no shoulders and a

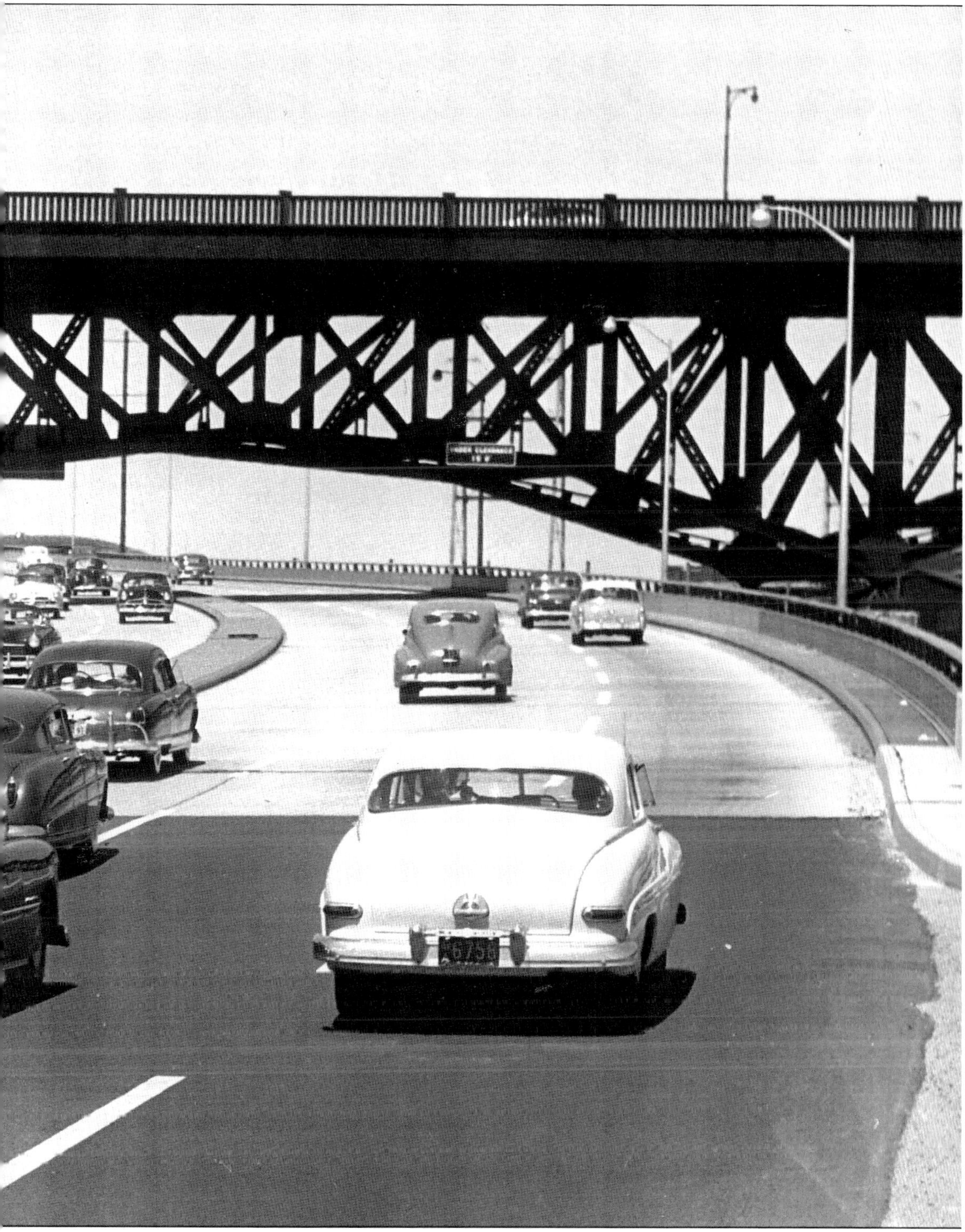

minimal median on this bare concrete roadway.

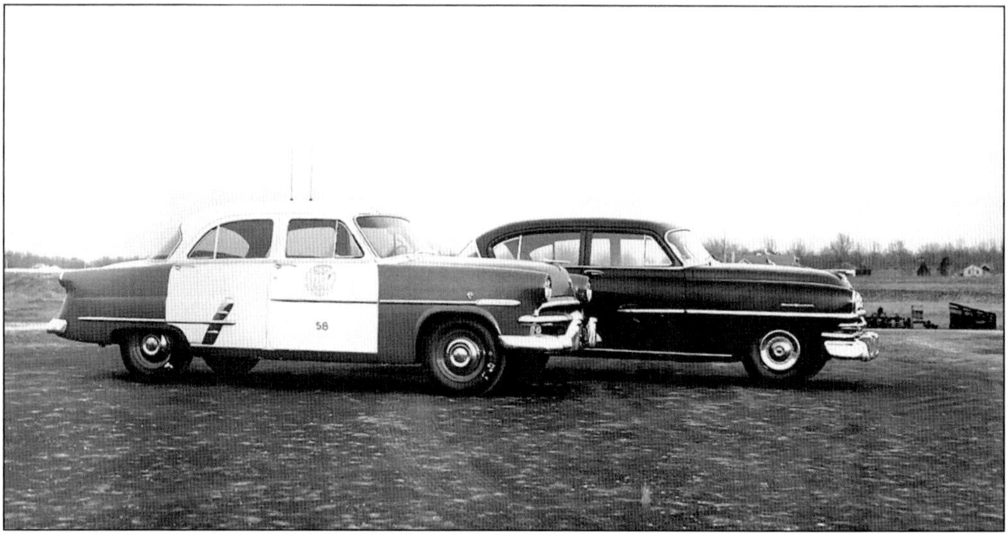

These are two types of police vehicles used on the turnpike. On the left is a blue-and-white car, and on the right is a black unmarked car.

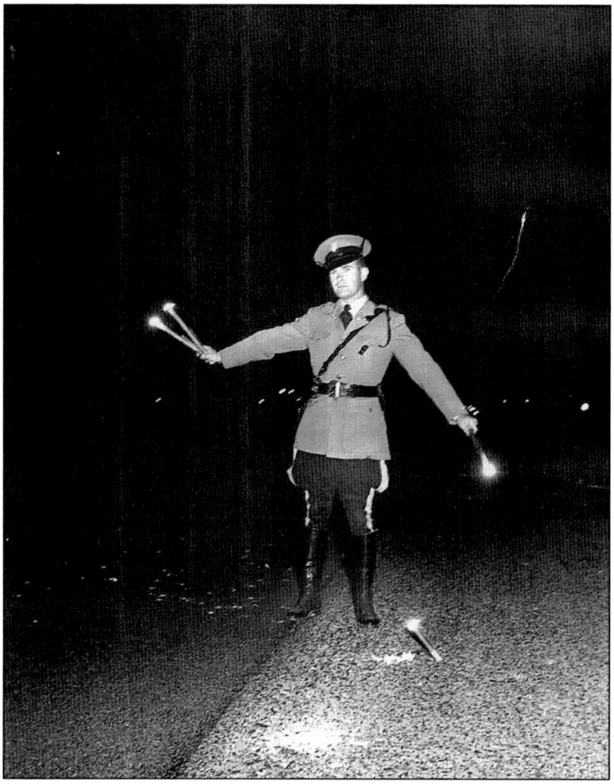

Here, a state trooper uses flares to guide motorists through areas of low visibility.

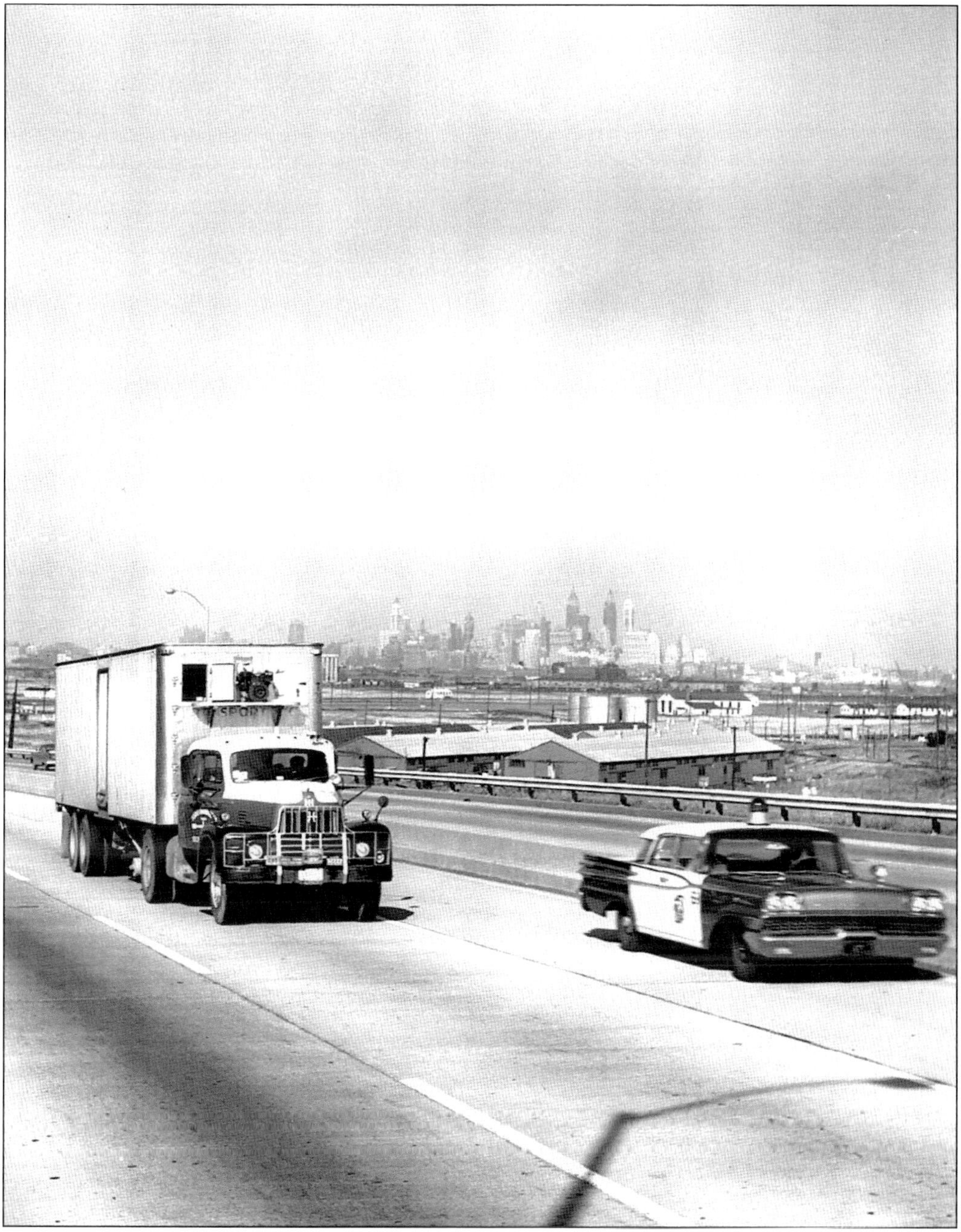

An original photograph from April 22, 1959, shows state police patrolling on the Holland Tunnel Extension of the New Jersey Turnpike.

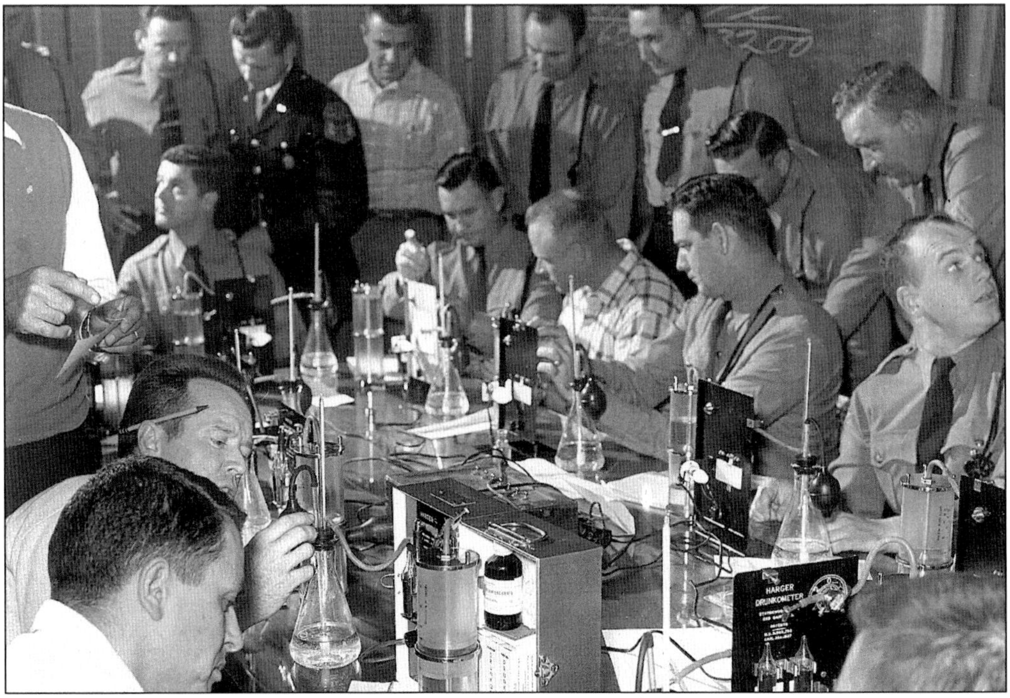

In this photograph, state police officers assigned to the turnpike are studying the proper use of drunkometers. This device is used to measure drivers' blood alcohol content.

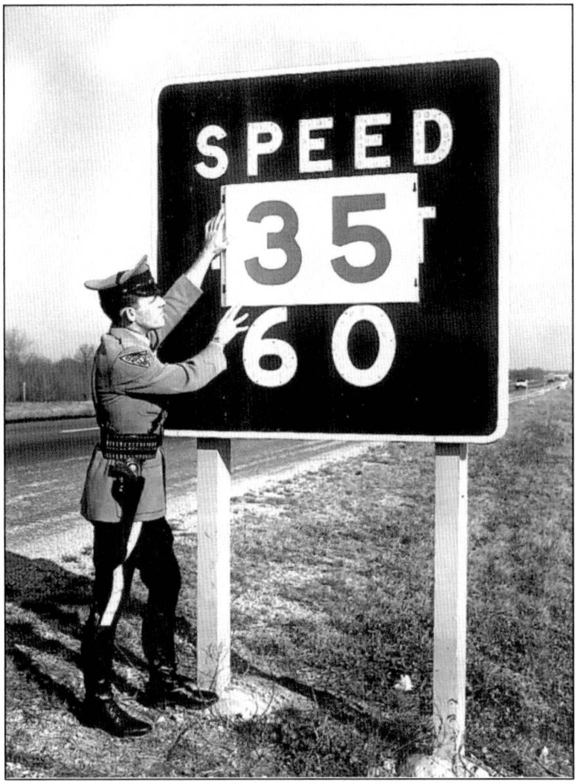

New Jersey State Police patrolmen had to change the speed limit signs by hand during the early years of the turnpike's operation.

The biggest haul in a series of five pickups for possession of marijuana was New Jersey State Trooper John Billick's discovery of 795 pounds of pure marijuana, valued at over $7 million, on November 1, 1968, at the Interchange 6 toll plaza. On October 19, 1968, Trooper Billick intercepted a vehicle loaded with 220 pounds of marijuana. But the November 1 grab was the biggest ever reported in the state.

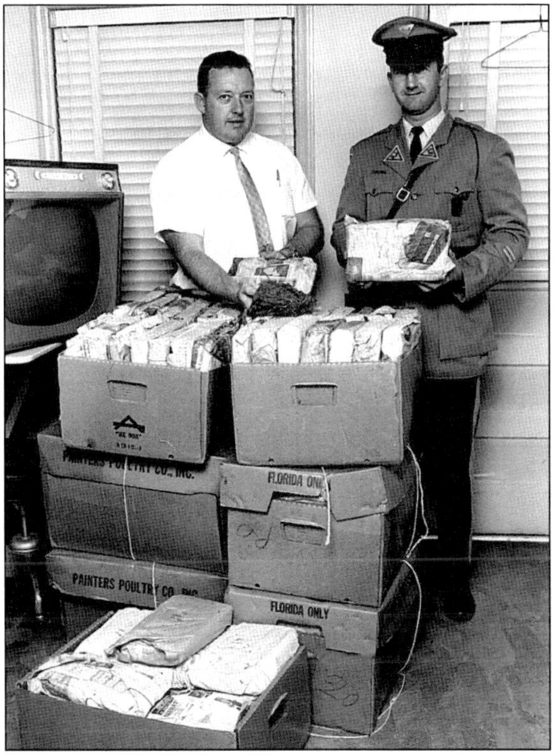

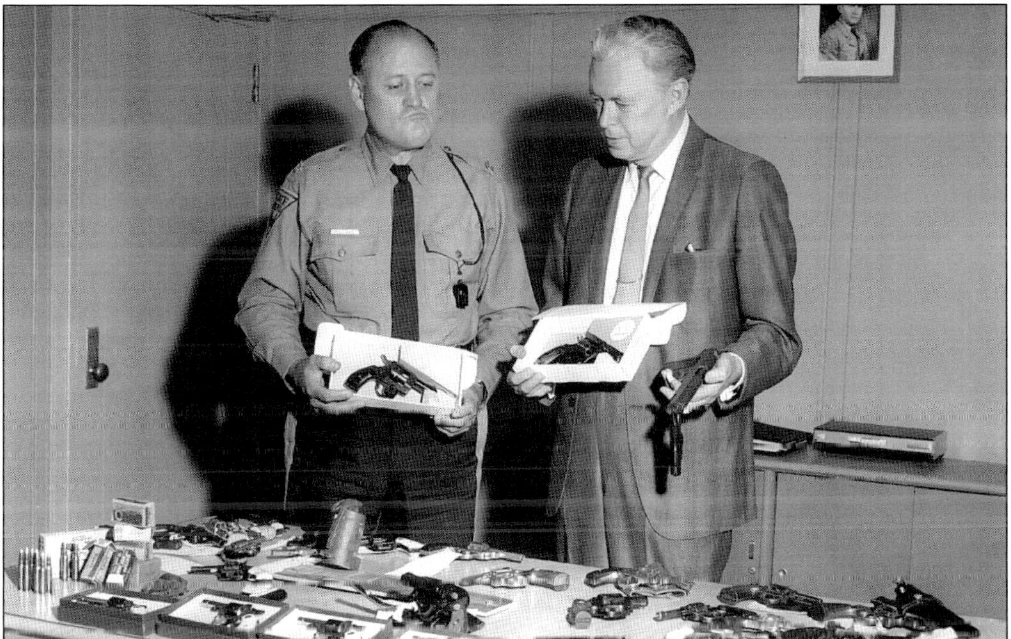

Capt. William J. Kennedy (left), commander of the New Jersey State Police Troop D on the New Jersey Turnpike, and William J. Flanagan, executive director of the Authority, look over a collection of 30 handguns and a hand grenade seized from vehicles by troopers during a one-month span in a drive against illegal gun traffic.

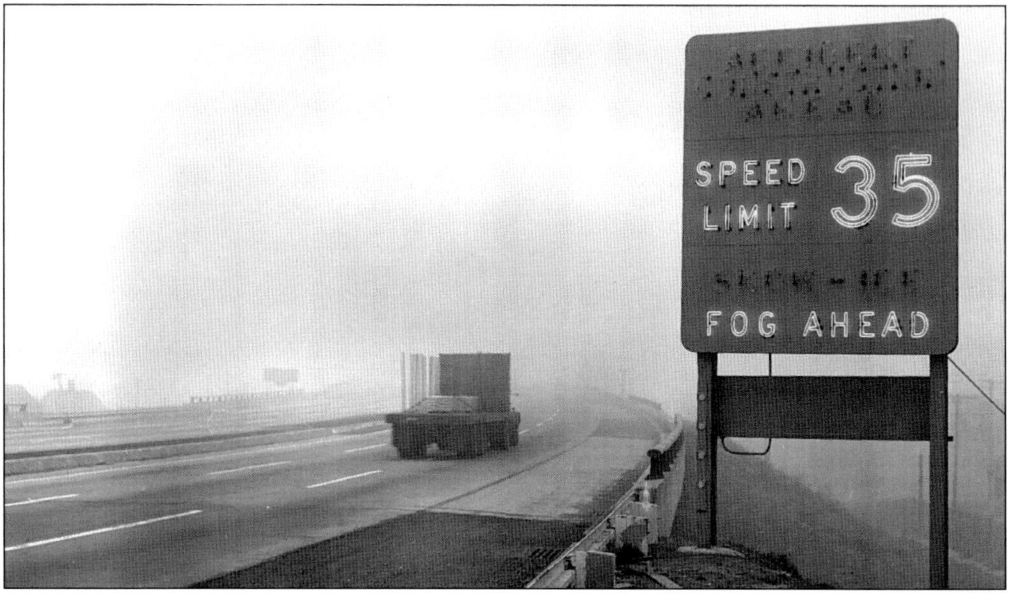

This photograph shows a new type of neon-lit sign erected to give motorists advance notice of the roadway conditions ahead. The turnpike was a leader in providing motorists with warnings about weather and traffic conditions.

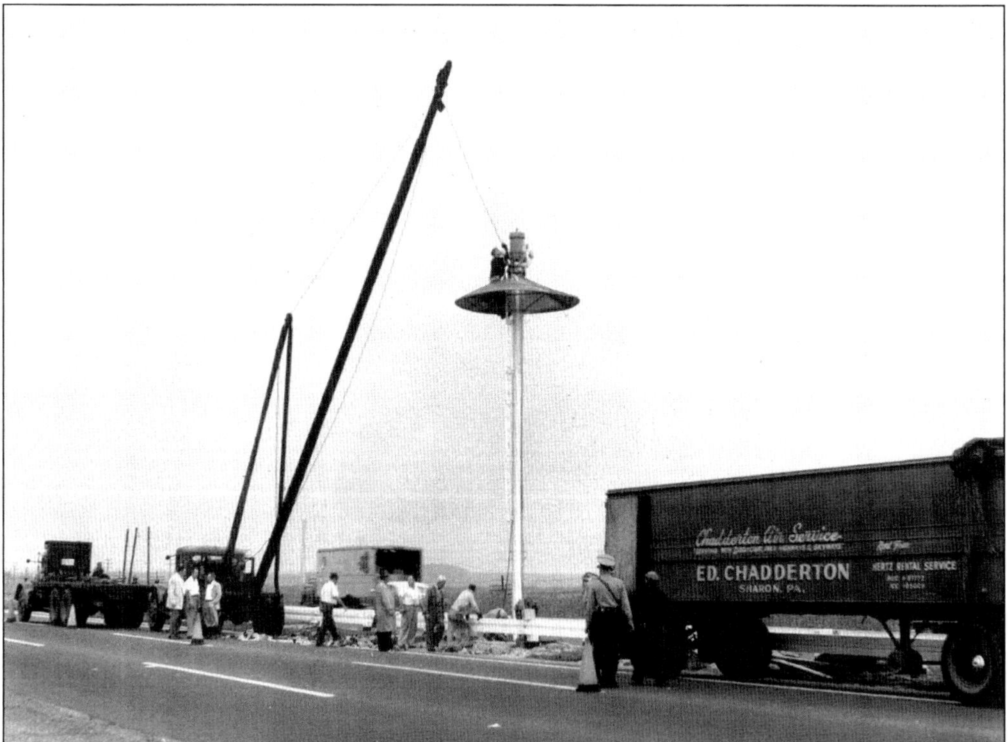

In the 1950s, four Weathermaster fog-dispersal units were erected in specifically selected locations on the northern half of the turnpike to test their value in detecting and dispersing shallow ground fog peculiar to this area.

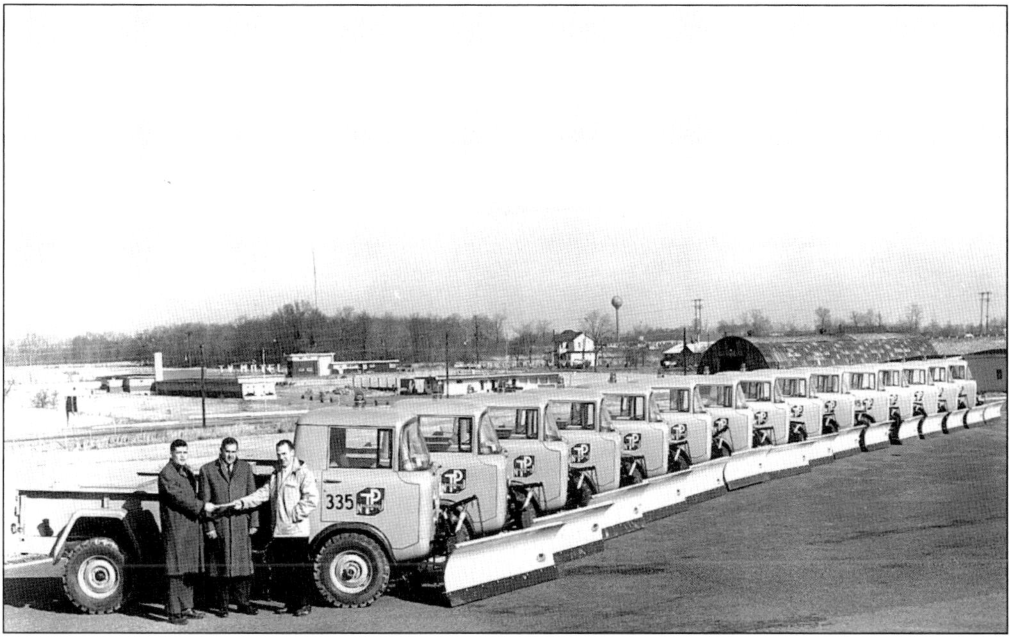

These 15 brand-new Jeeps were lined up in "go formation" at central shops in Hightstown in January 1962, to augment the rolling equipment for the New Jersey Turnpike Maintenance Department. Howard S. Heydon, director of Maintenance (right), is shown receiving the bill of sale from Joseph R. Rainear, treasurer of Rednor and Rainear, a Trenton Jeep dealer. In the center is Barry Rednor, vice president of the firm. The Jeeps, featuring hydraulic reversible plows, were used for snow removal at service areas and to move stalled cars at interchanges.

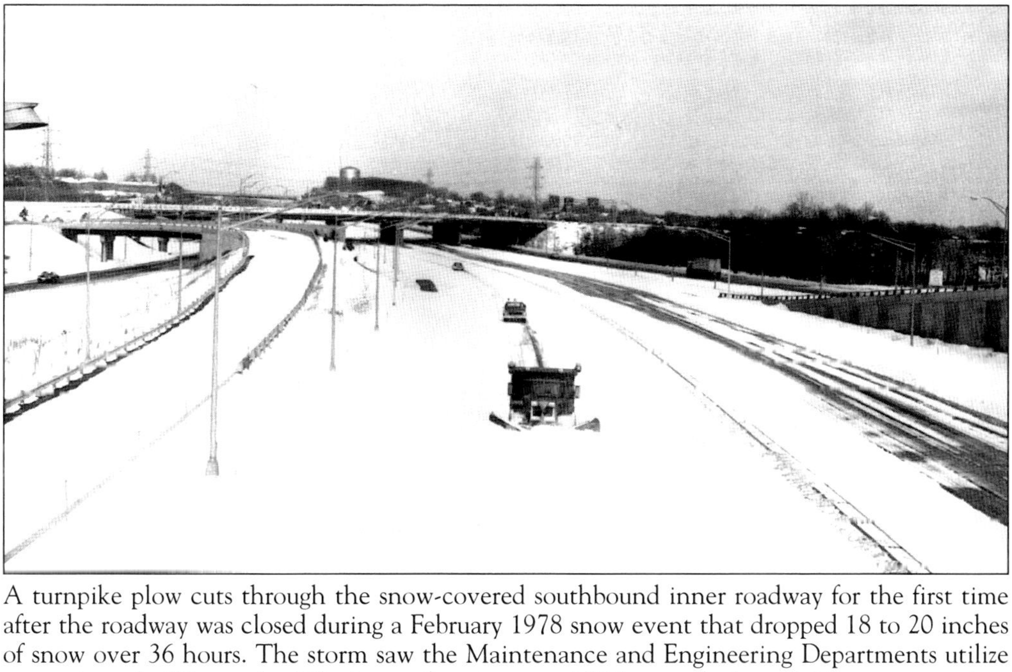

A turnpike plow cuts through the snow-covered southbound inner roadway for the first time after the roadway was closed during a February 1978 snow event that dropped 18 to 20 inches of snow over 36 hours. The storm saw the Maintenance and Engineering Departments utilize approximately 275 people, 180 pieces of equipment, 4,000 tons of salt, and 14 contractor plow teams at a cost of about $500,000 in an effort to keep the roadway open.

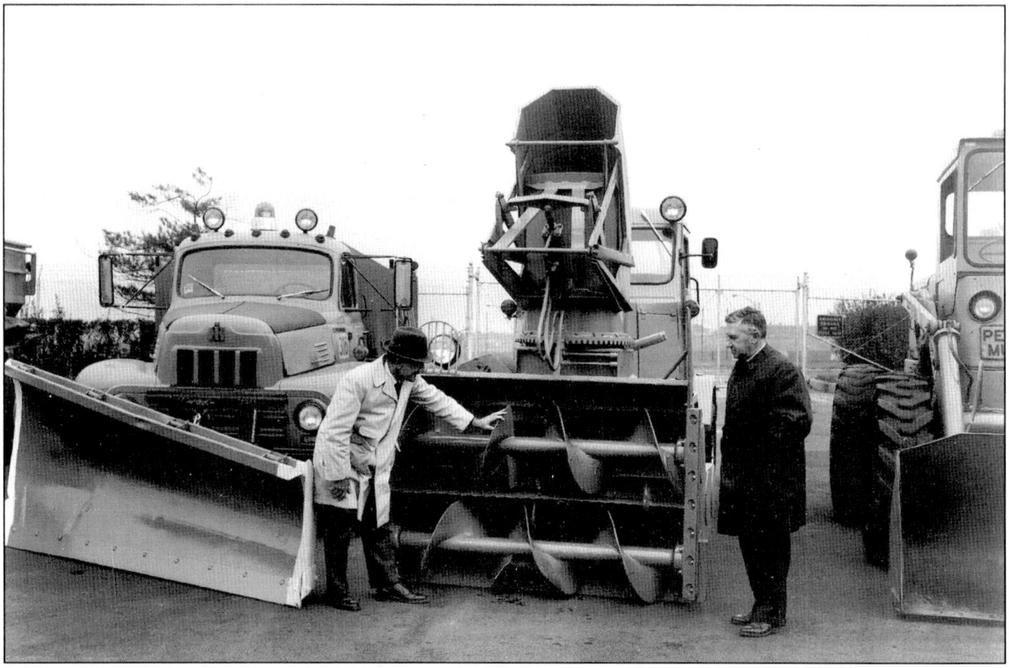

In the 1960s, the turnpike sought to return the roadway to "clear and black" pavement as soon as possible after snowstorms. The Maintenance Department implemented innovative equipment such as snow blowers and snow melters.

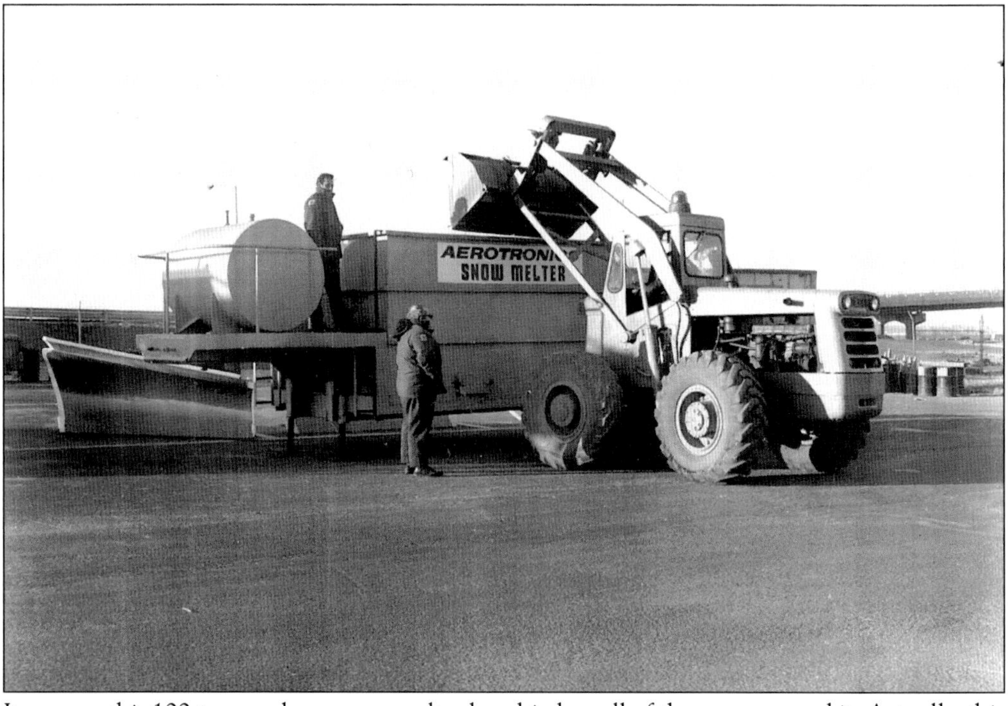

It appears this 100-ton-per-hour snow melter has dried up all of the snow around it. Actually, this is the scene of a dry run right after the equipment has arrived at the District 5 maintenance yard. From left to right are employees Orlando Chirico, Paul Cancro, and Sam Bardach (on loader).

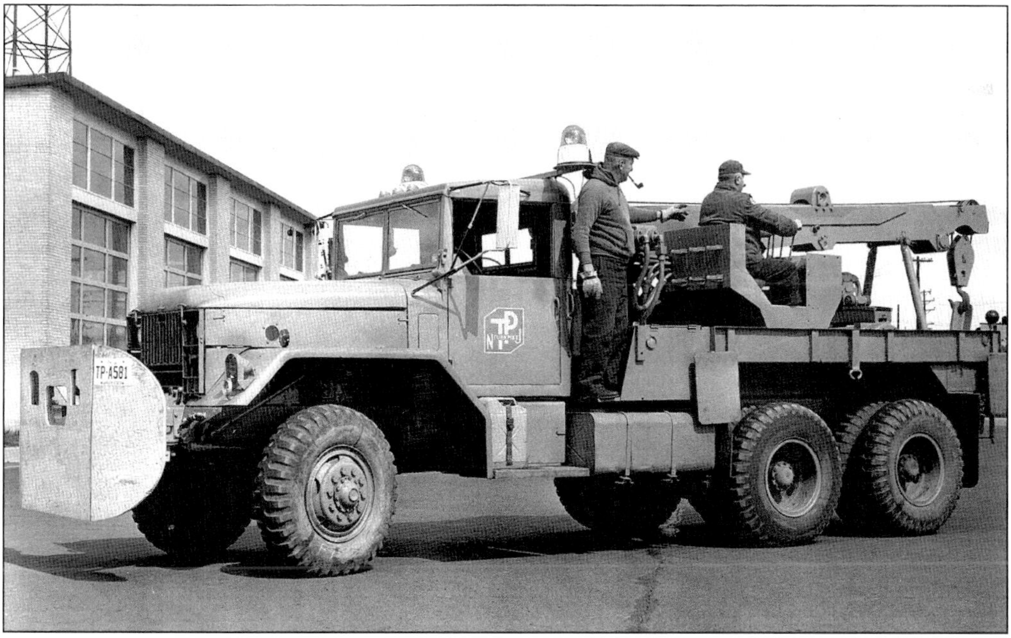

This vehicle, a completely rebuilt army wrecker weighing 16 tons, has been assigned to patrol the Hackensack and Passaic River Bridges during hours of peak traffic in order to avoid congestion and prevent accidents. Disabled vehicles were towed off the bridges to a safe place at the Authority's expense.

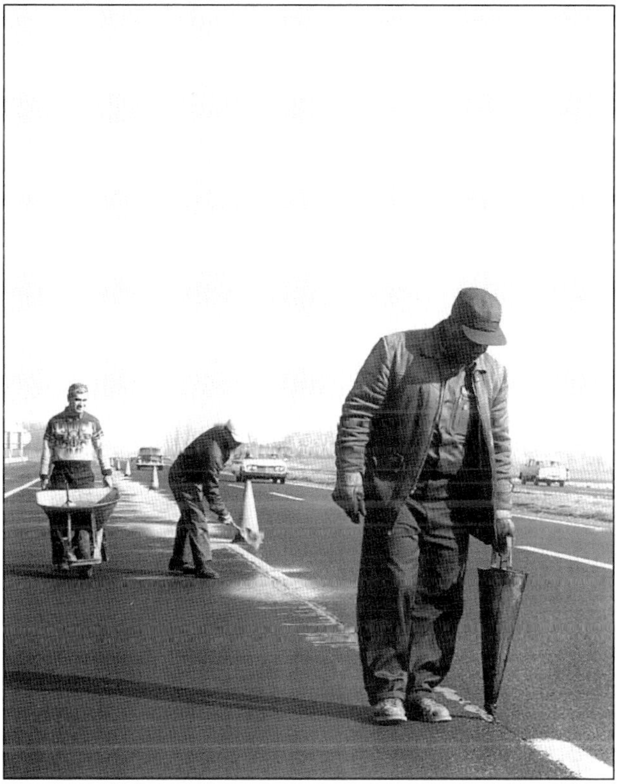

Turnpike Authority maintenance crews can be seen filling cracks in the roadway.

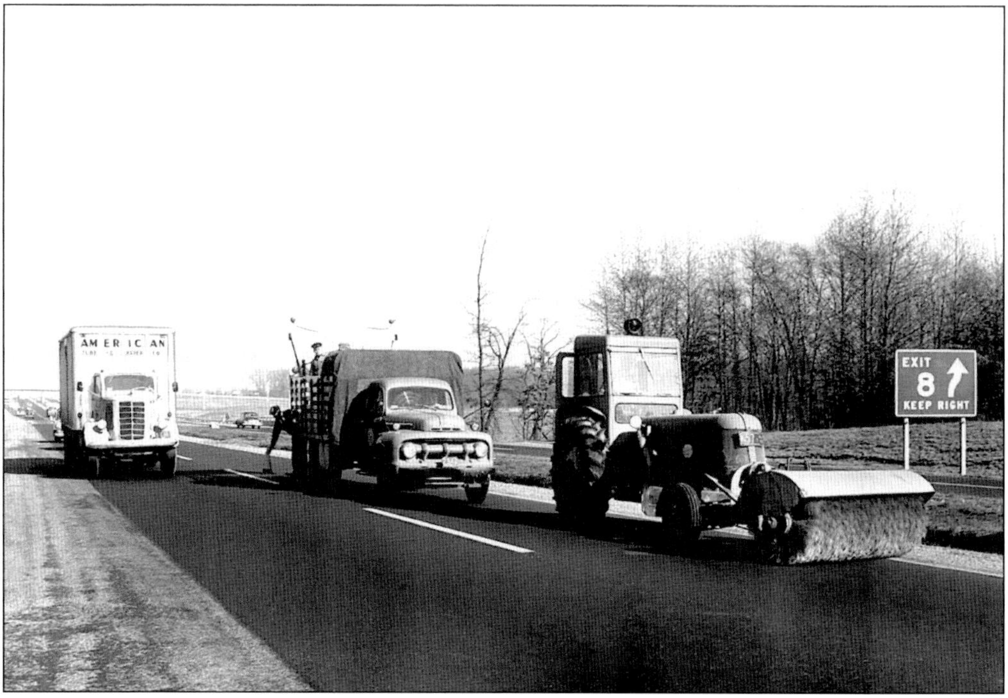

A tractor with a large sweeper on the front is used to clear roadway debris. A maintenance vehicle follows closely behind as workers place cones to indicate a lane closure.

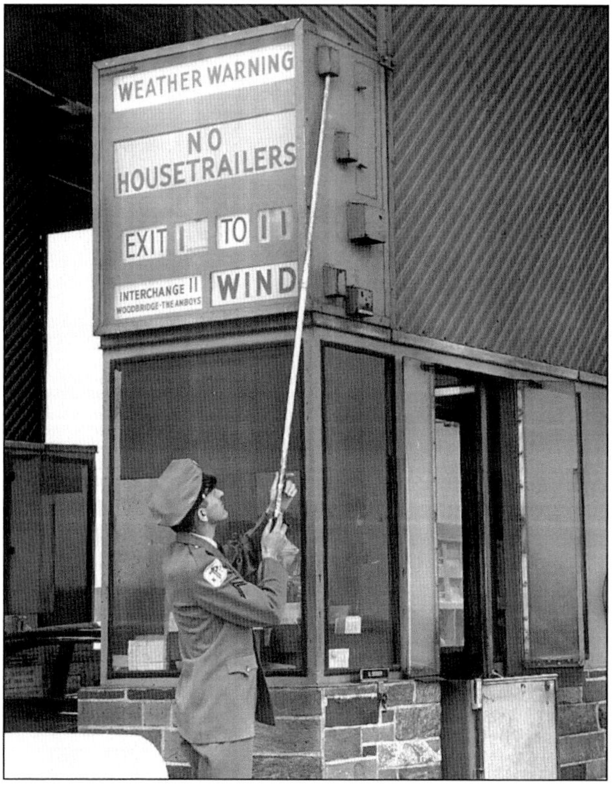

A toll collector at Interchange 11 changes a weather warning sign at the toll plaza to advise motorists of high-wind conditions on the roadway.

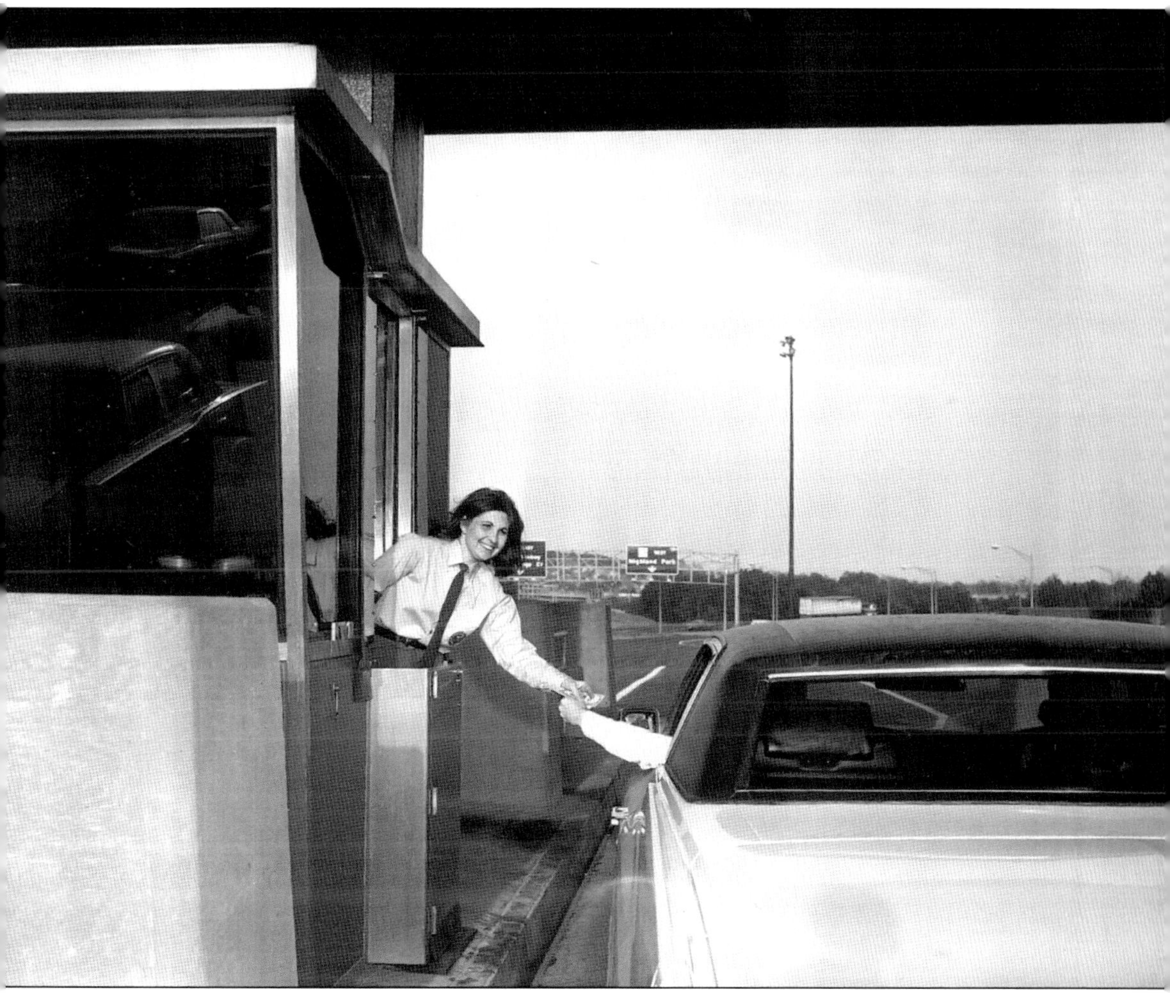

One of the first female toll collectors to be hired by the Turnpike Authority is former Engineering file clerk Bonnie Stafford. Here she is eagerly awaiting her next patron at Interchange 10. Bonnie first joined the turnpike in June 1973, and she became the first of 12 female toll collectors.

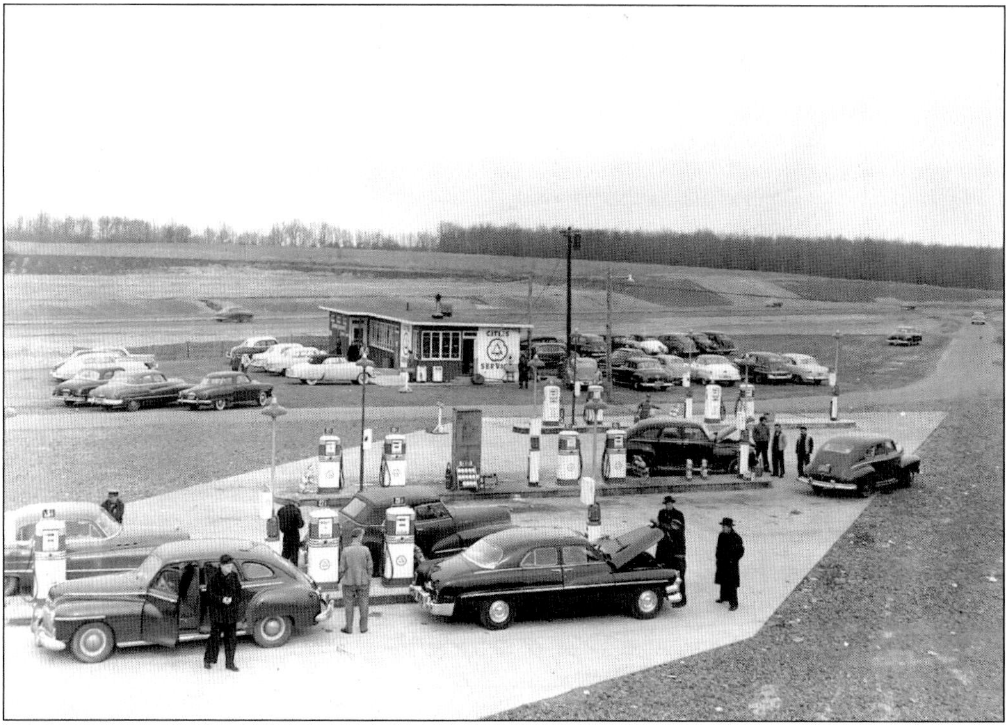

Howard Johnson's and Cities Service were awarded contracts to operate the turnpike's 10 service areas. The service areas were strategically located on high ground for better visibility and to aid in the deceleration and acceleration of vehicles while exiting from or returning to the roadway. Cities Service trained 150 men to offer bumper-to-bumper service to turnpike motorists.

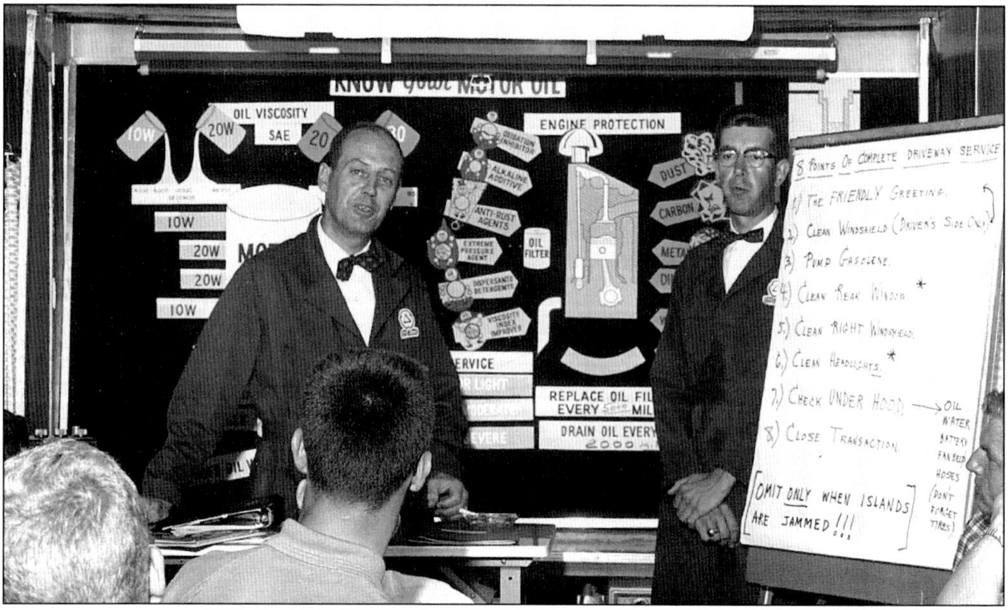

Ernest Stutz (left) and Harry Kels Swan instruct Cities Service trainees on the eight points of complete driveway service.

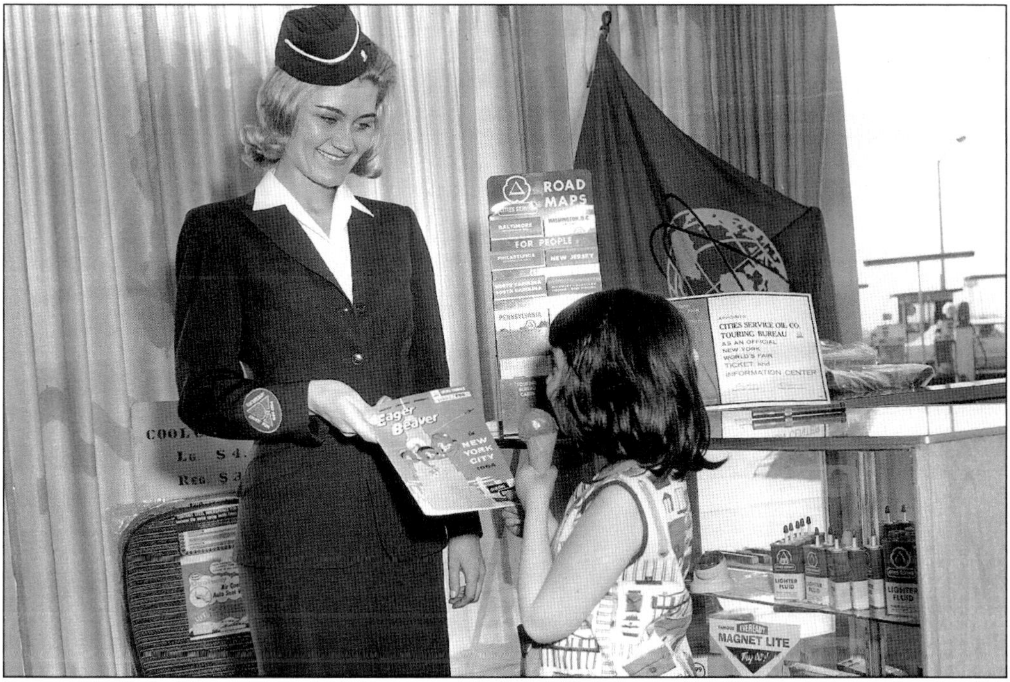

In order to maintain a high level of customer service for turnpike patrons, "Pikettes" were trained to assist motorists with travel plans and general information about the newly opened turnpike.

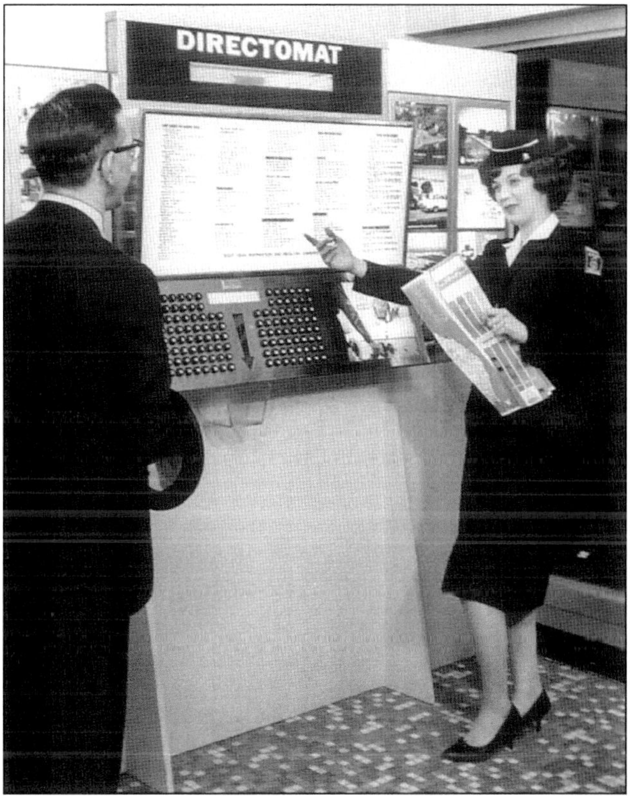

A New Jersey Turnpike Pikette assists a patron by using a Directomat on the New Jersey Turnpike. These travel aids were installed by Cities Service Oil Company at information booths located at service stations along the roadway.

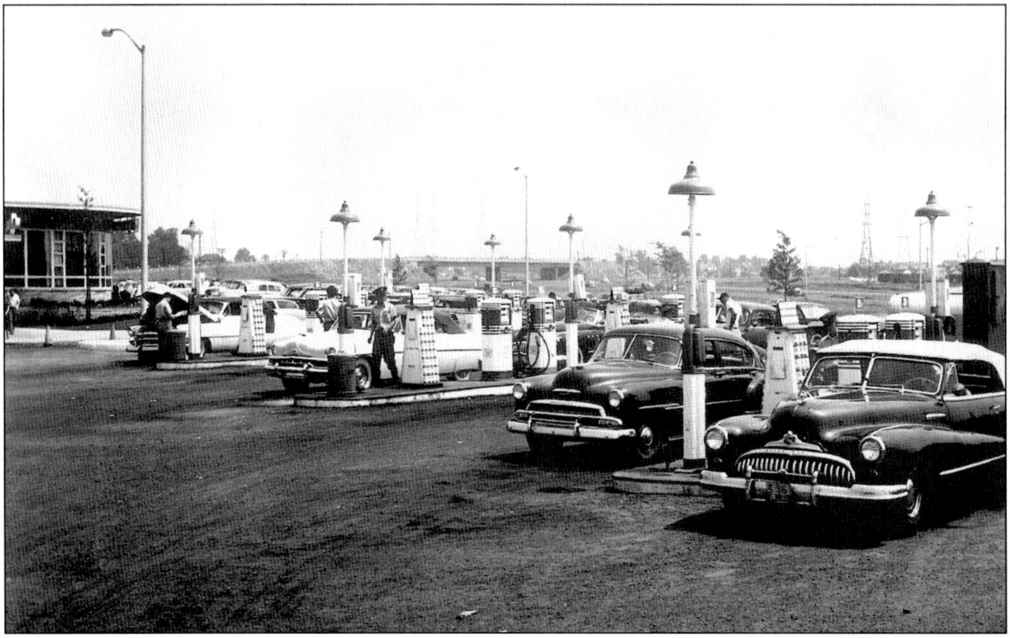

In this view, cars line up at the Cities Service rest area for fuel and routine vehicle maintenance.

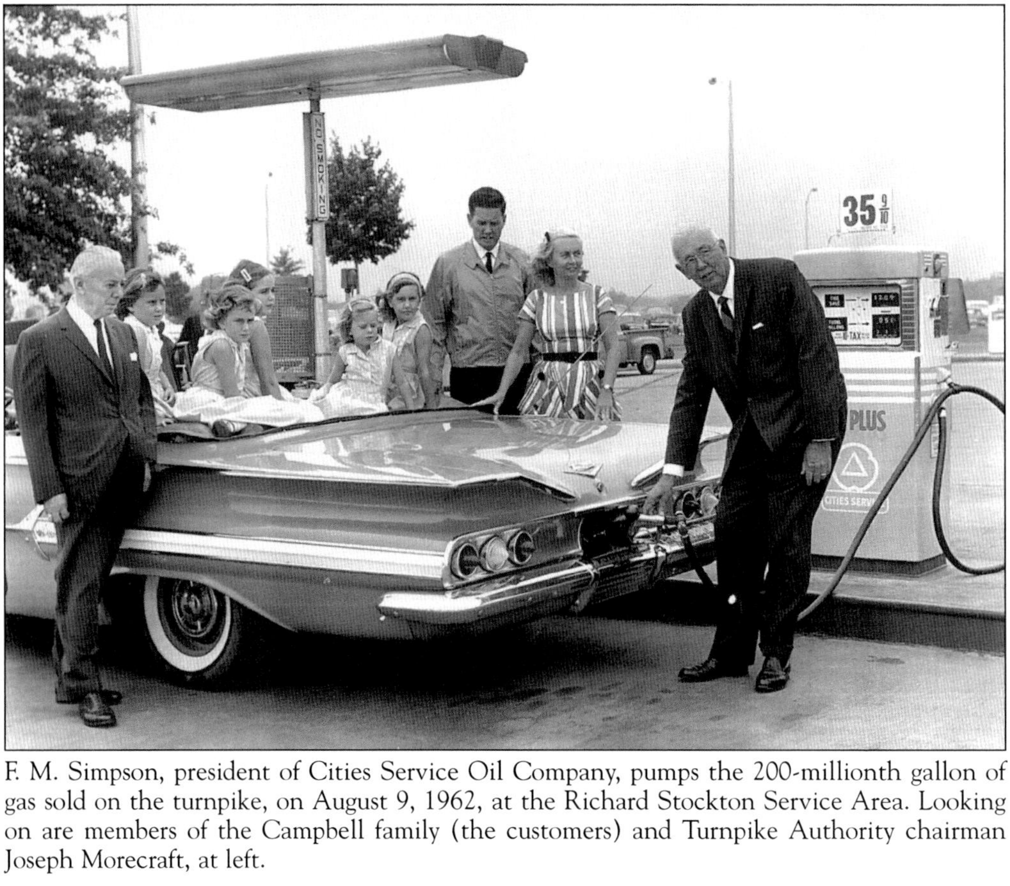

F. M. Simpson, president of Cities Service Oil Company, pumps the 200-millionth gallon of gas sold on the turnpike, on August 9, 1962, at the Richard Stockton Service Area. Looking on are members of the Campbell family (the customers) and Turnpike Authority chairman Joseph Morecraft, at left.

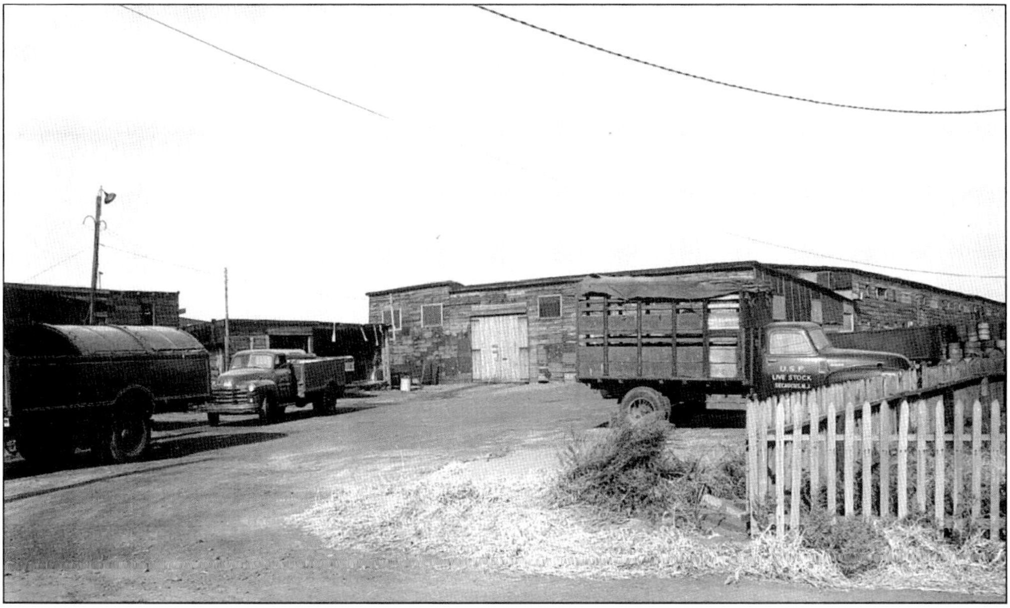

This photograph shows one of the remaining pig farms along the turnpike in Secaucus.

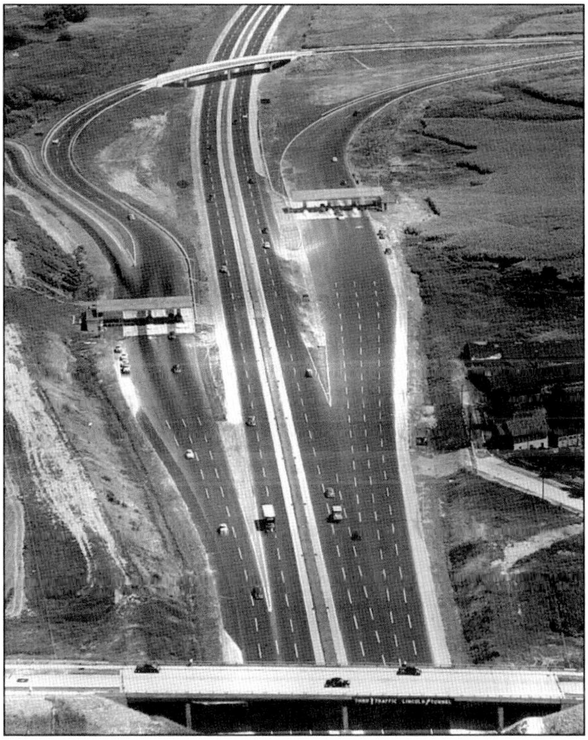

This early view of a split entry/exit toll plaza at Interchange 16 is from a photograph taken prior to the construction of the Interchange 16E/18E complex that was completed as part of the turnpike-widening project.

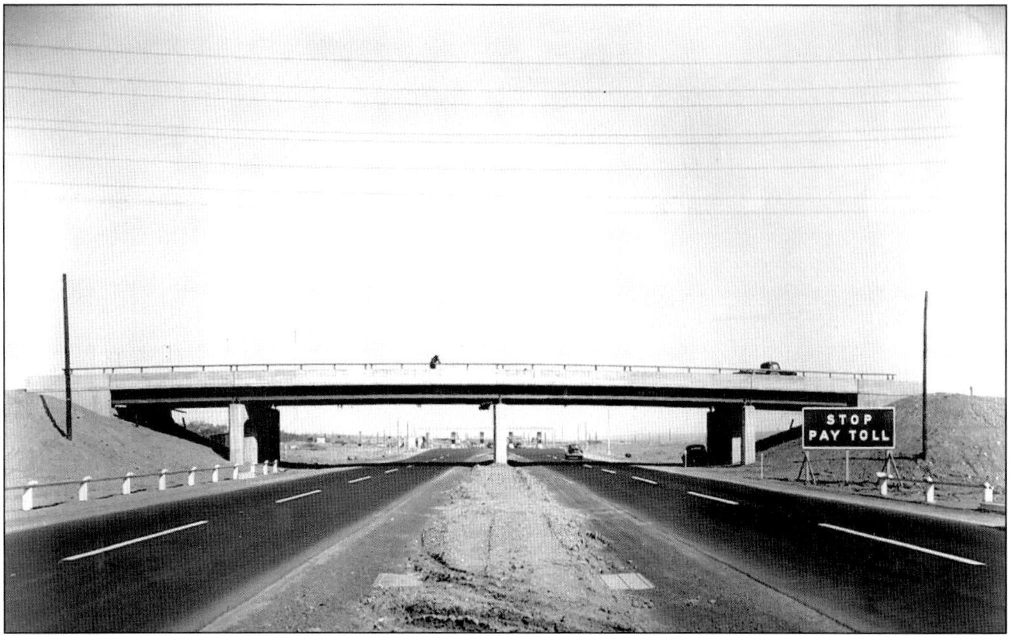

An original photograph dated February 15, 1952, looking north, shows a general view of motorists approaching Interchange 18 beneath the Bergen Turnpike underpass.

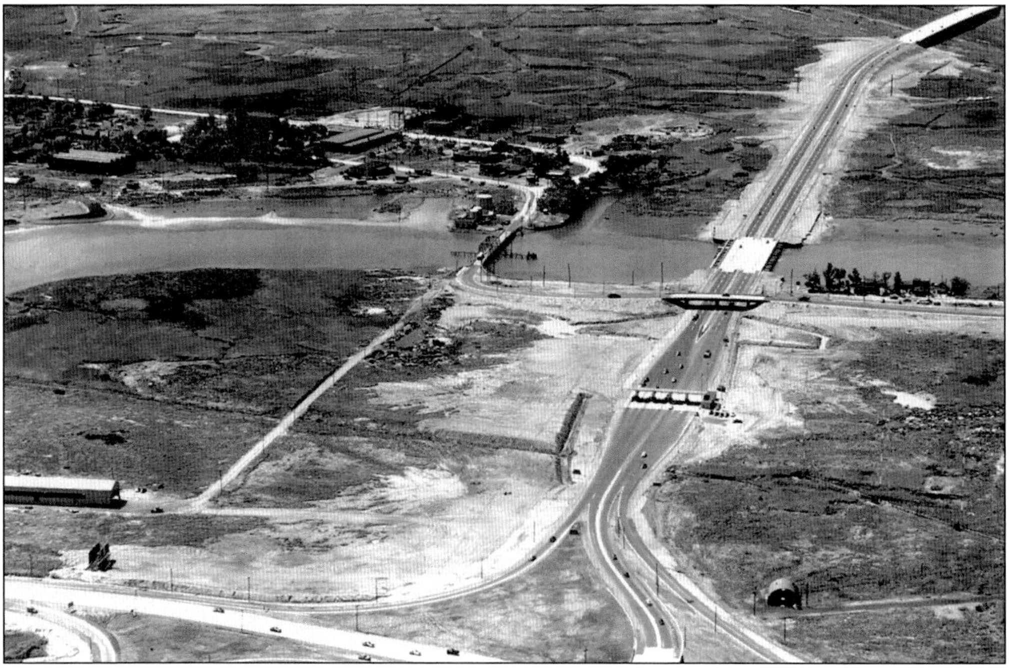

This is a photograph of the northern terminus of the turnpike at Interchange 18. This exit leads traffic northward to the George Washington Bridge and Route 95. The original design of the interchange served two cars in either direction. Today, the combined interchanges of 18E and 18W contain 21 entry and exit lanes, eight of which are dedicated E-ZPass lanes. In addition, Interchange 18W has four Express E-ZPass lanes. On a recent weekday, these combined toll plazas handled more than 140,000 vehicles.

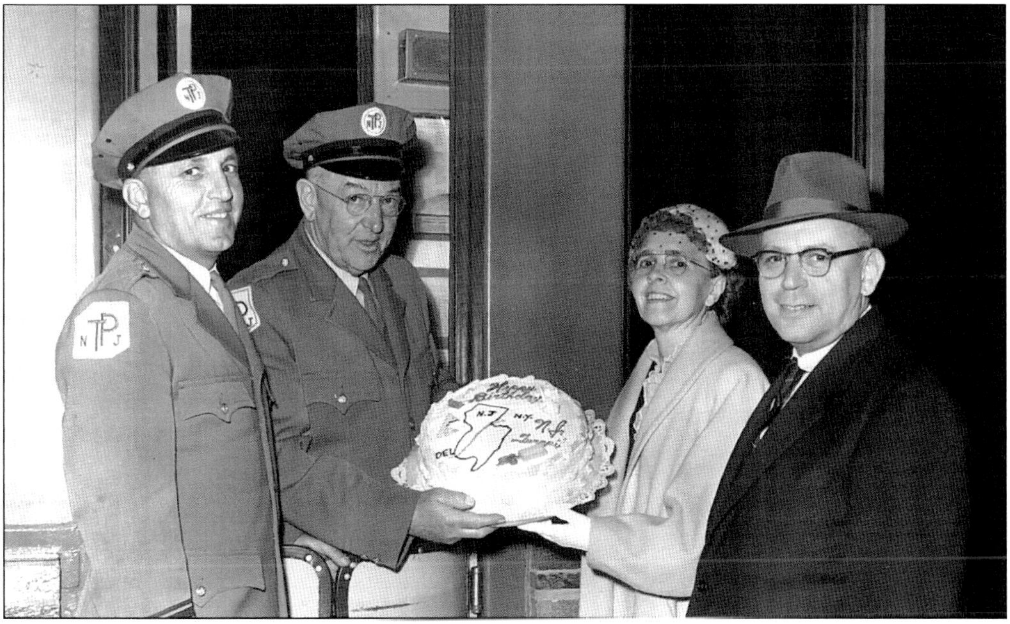

Mr. and Mrs. Elmer F. Zeigenfus (on right), frequent patrons of the New Jersey Turnpike, present Toll Collectors Frank Ford and Thomas Sawyer with a birthday cake celebrating the one-year anniversary of the roadway on November 11, 1952.

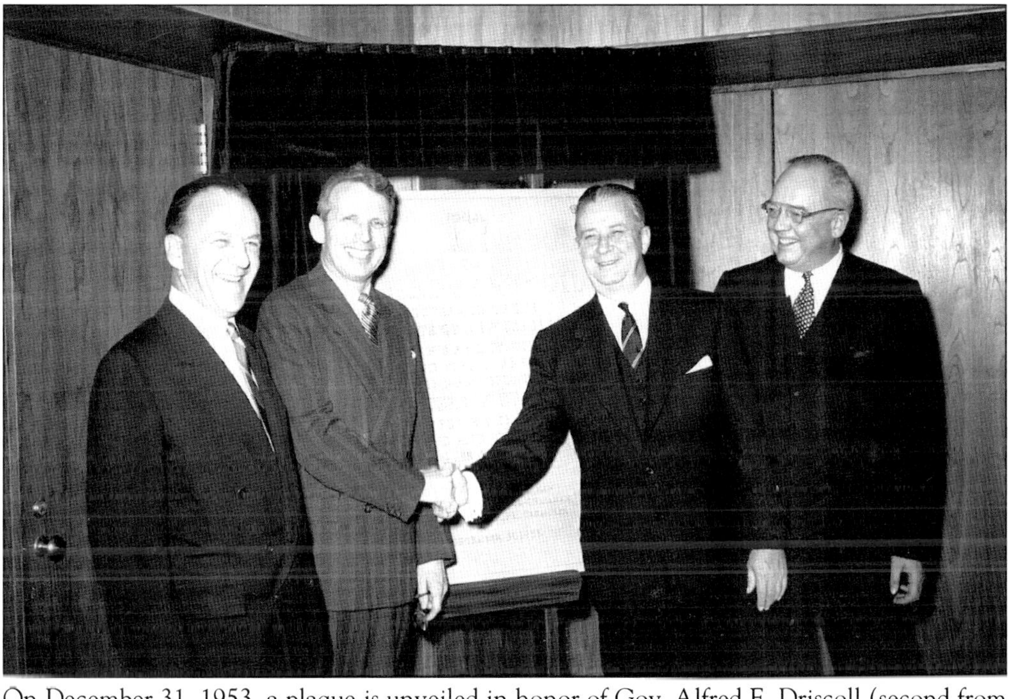

On December 31, 1953, a plaque is unveiled in honor of Gov. Alfred E. Driscoll (second from left) "for his ability, vision, and statesmanship in initiating and sponsoring the New Jersey Turnpike and for his unfailing aid and support during its construction and operation." Pictured with the governor are, from left to right, former commissioner George F. Smith, Chairman Paul L. Troast, and Treasurer Maxwell Lester Jr.

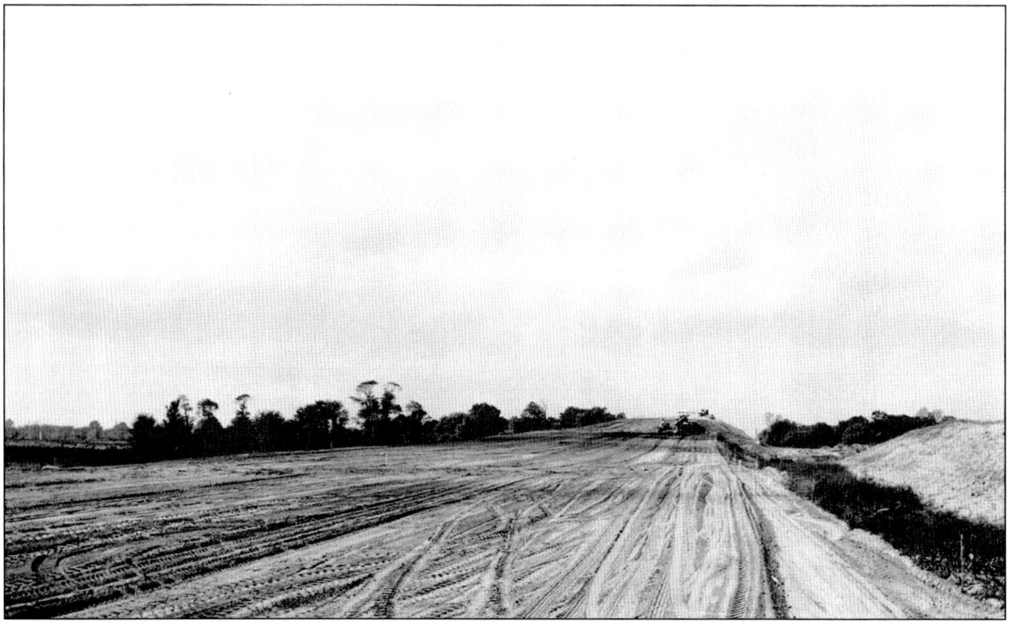

As with the Newark Bay–Hudson County Extension, mention of creating an extension between the New Jersey Turnpike and Pennsylvania Turnpike began in 1949. However, it was not until 1951 that numerous discussions were held with members of the Pennsylvania Turnpike Commission concerning a direct connection to the Pennsylvania Turnpike at a point south of Trenton. The project would require a new interchange south of the Bordentown Interchange, the construction of five miles of new road, an eastern extension in Pennsylvania from King of Prussia to the Delaware River, and the participation of the Pennsylvania Turnpike Commission in the cost of a new bridge across the Delaware River. The New Jersey Turnpike Authority and Pennsylvania Turnpike Commission collaborated on the project because it allowed motorists and truckers safe and rapid transportation to and from the New York area and to areas as far west as the Ohio border. The interconnections developed new traffic and revenues, and they aided in the relief of congestion on the public highways in these states.

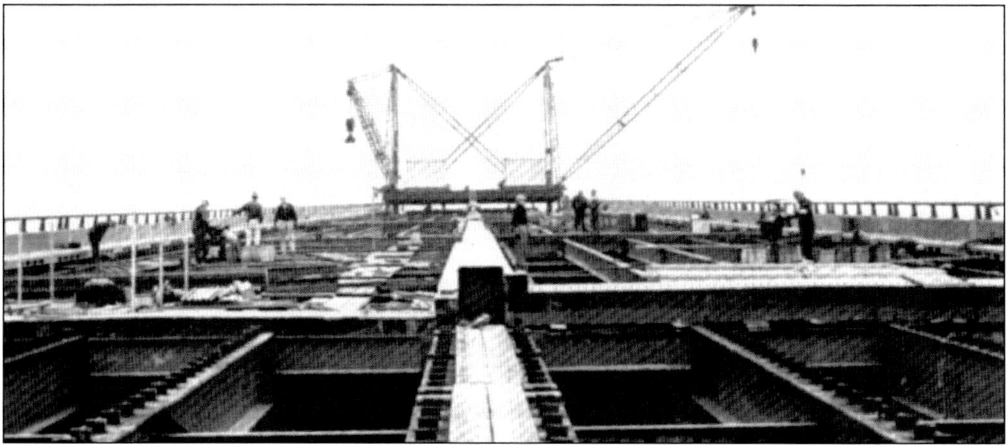

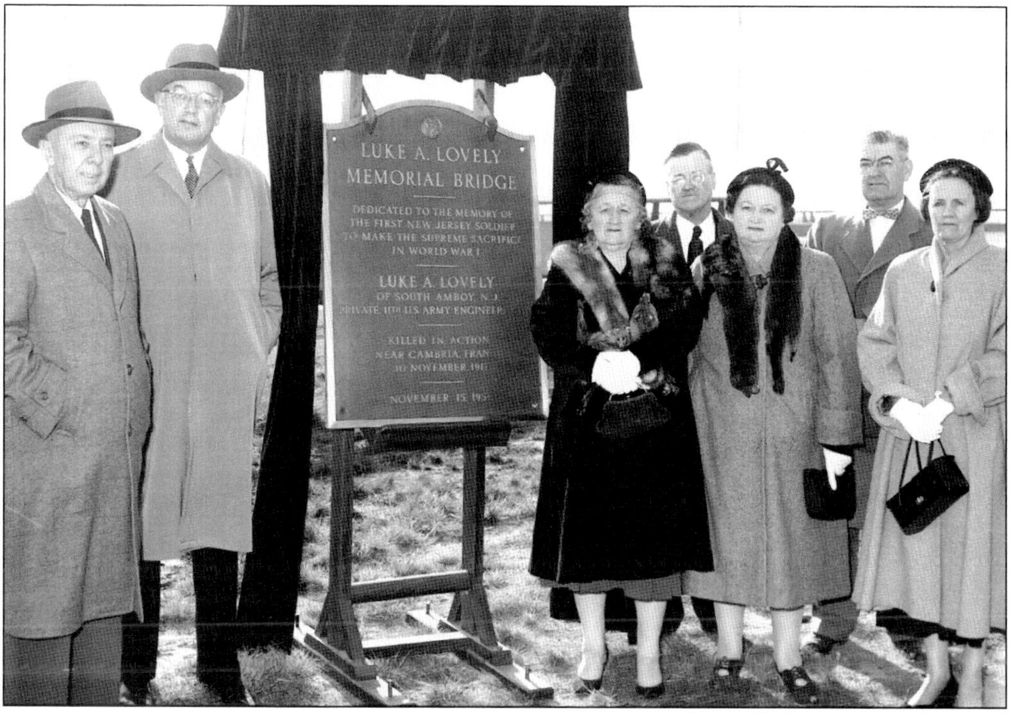

On November 15, 1954, the Rahway River Bridge was dedicated to the late Pvt. Luke A. Lovely of South Amboy. Private Lovely was the first New Jersey soldier to lose his life in World War I, on November 30, 1917, in France.

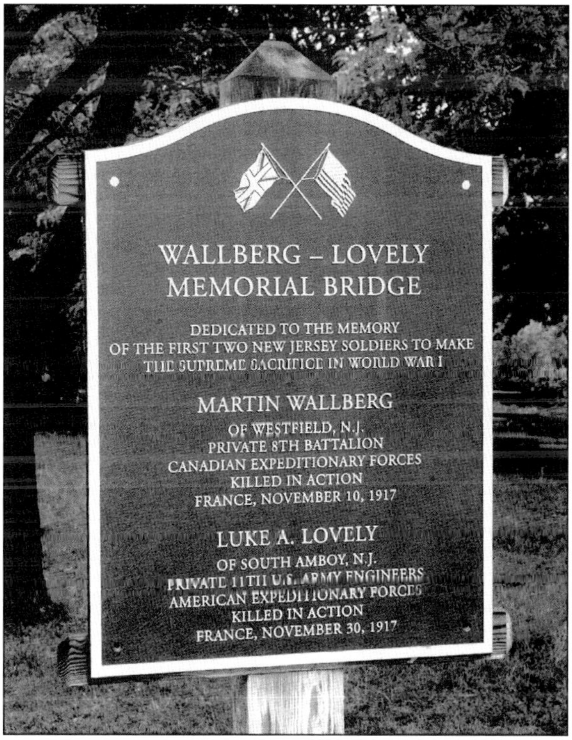

Turnpike Authority officials recently received a letter from one of its patrons with information that Pvt. Martin Wallberg of Westfield was killed in action on November 10, 1917, while fighting with the 8th Battalion Canadian Expeditionary Forces in France. The Authority subsequently rededicated the Rahway River Bridge as the Wallberg-Lovely Memorial Bridge in honor of the first two New Jersey soldiers to make the supreme sacrifice in World War I.

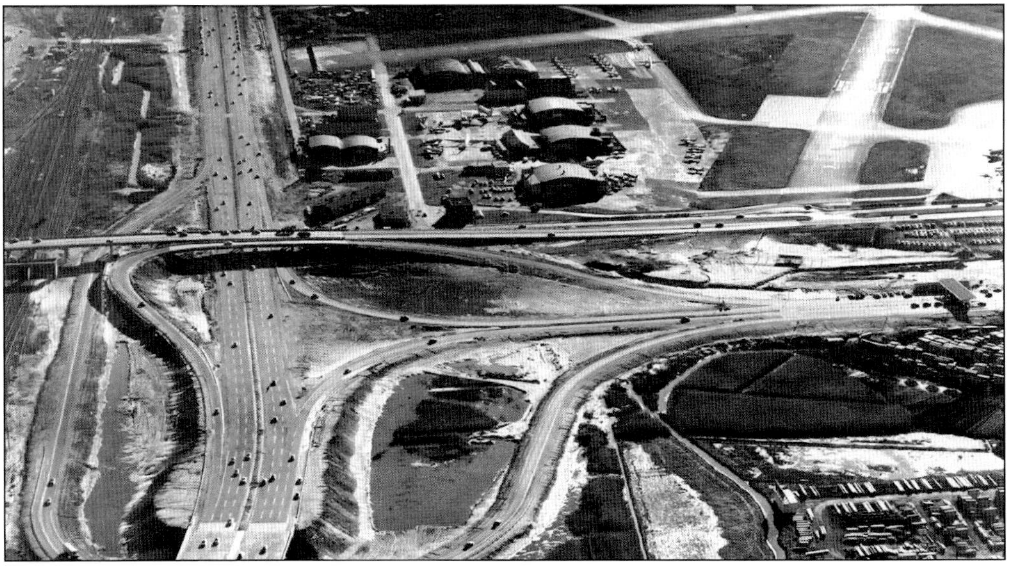

Originally explored in 1949, construction for the Newark Bay–Hudson County Extension did not begin until 1953. The idea of the extension was a bridge across Newark Bay, which allowed access to the Newark Airport Interchange with a direct link to the Hudson County peninsula and an expressway through Jersey City to connect with the Holland Tunnel Plaza. The Authority believed the extension would relieve the traffic congestion along the local streets and highways in Jersey City and Bayonne, and provide a more convenient and faster route for traffic moving between Route 1, the New Jersey Turnpike, the Holland Tunnel, Jersey City, and Bayonne. In addition, the extension allowed for a new and direct route from New York City to Newark Airport. This photograph, looking north, shows early views of the turnpike mainline, Interchange 14 near the emerging Newark Airport. A new ramp for the Newark Bay–Hudson County Extension is visible at center left of the photograph, parallel to Port Street.

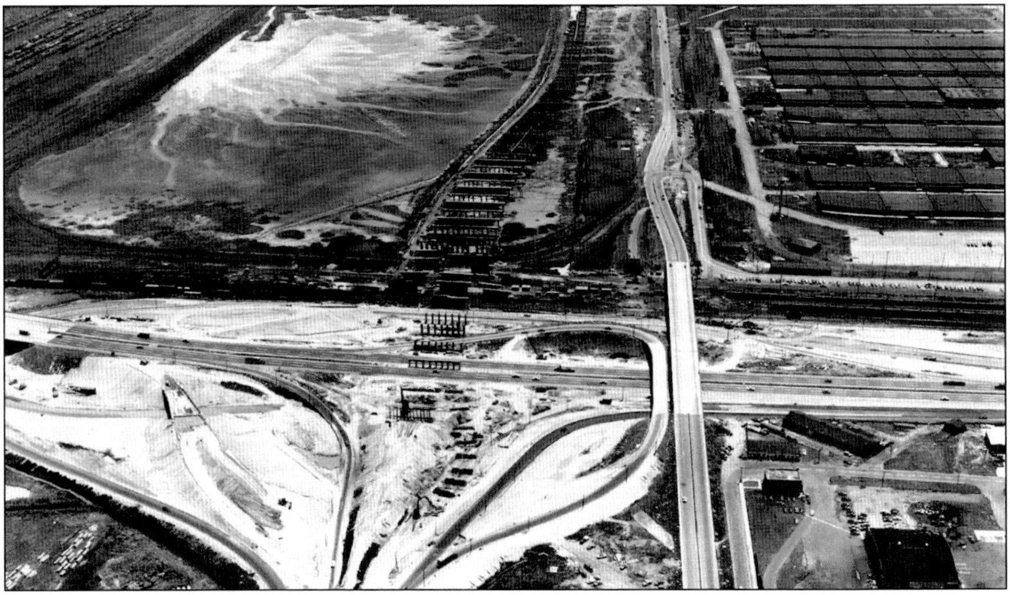

Looking east from Interchange 14, this photograph shows bridge piers being constructed to carry traffic over the turnpike mainline along Port Street, June 29, 1955.

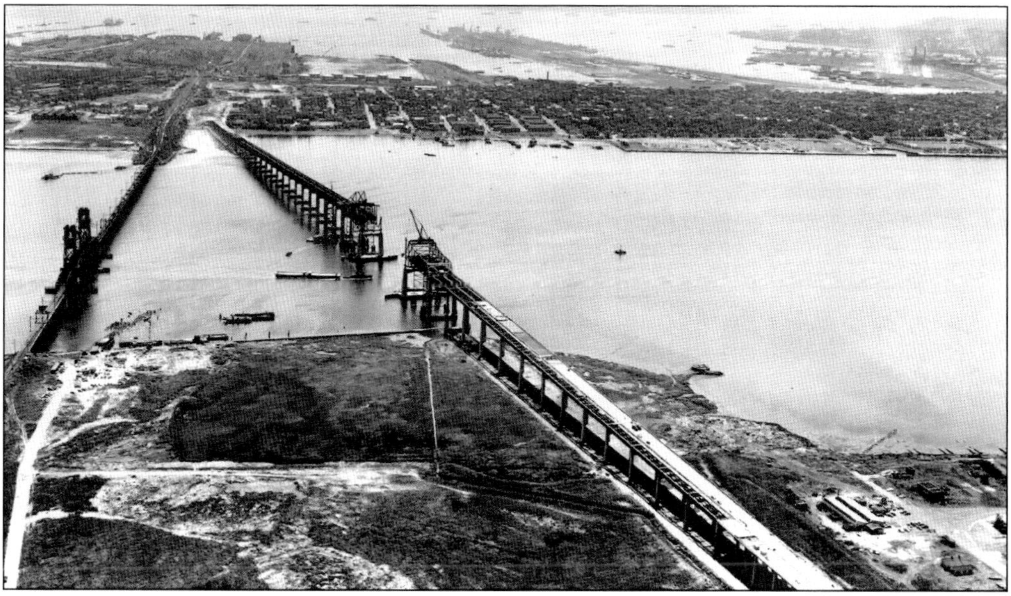

Looking east toward Jersey City and Bayonne, the bridge over Newark Bay awaits construction of the center span. Sixty-eight percent of the extension was built as a viaduct structure, with small sections involving roadway in Bayonne and Jersey City. This was primarily due to the extension's challenge in design and construction, providing formidable problems involving railroad yards, existing streets, and public utilities.

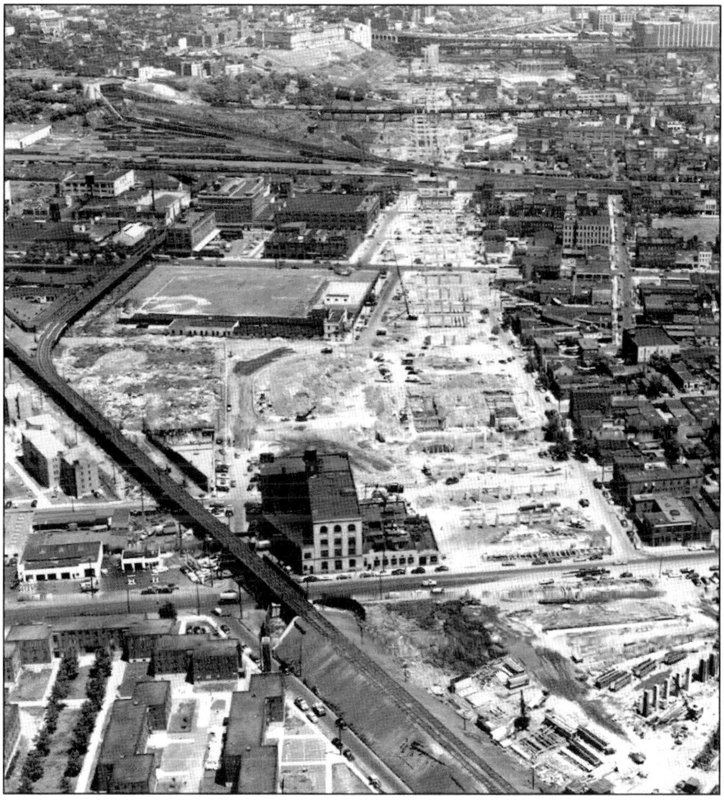

This photograph, looking east toward the Holland Tunnel, shows the construction of the elevated portion of the Newark Bay–Hudson County Extension through downtown Jersey City. Dickinson High School is visible in the upper left of this view. During 1956, difficulties encountered in procurement of materials, especially steel, had an effect upon deliveries and influenced primarily the construction of the final section of the Newark Bay–Hudson County Extension in Jersey City. The completion and opening of the extension was delayed by several months.

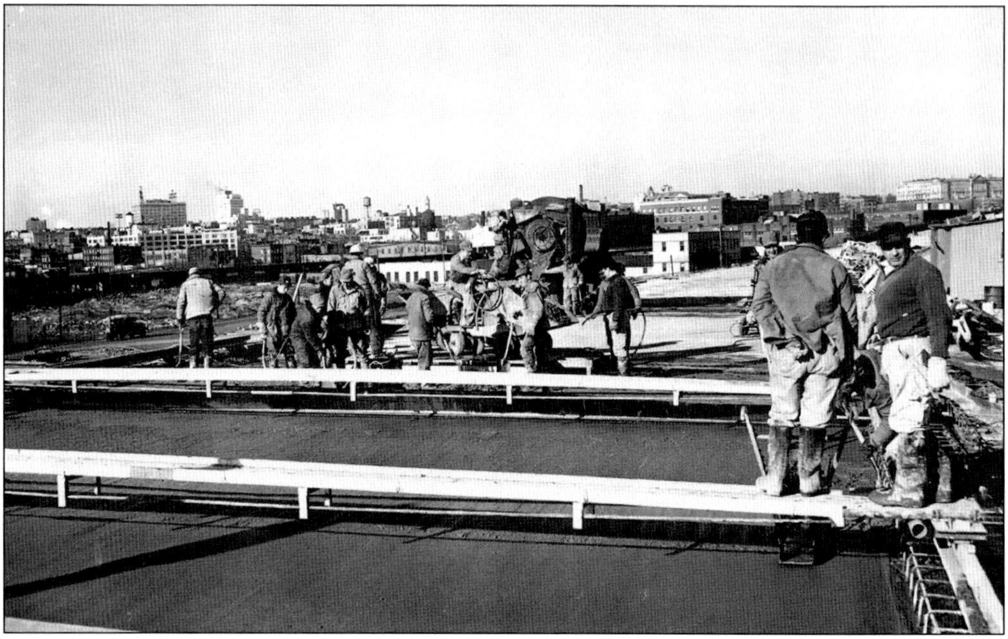

Looking north from the centerline of the Newark Bay–Hudson County Extension, workmen are seen pouring concrete as part of the deck paving operation. This photograph was taken on January 5, 1956.

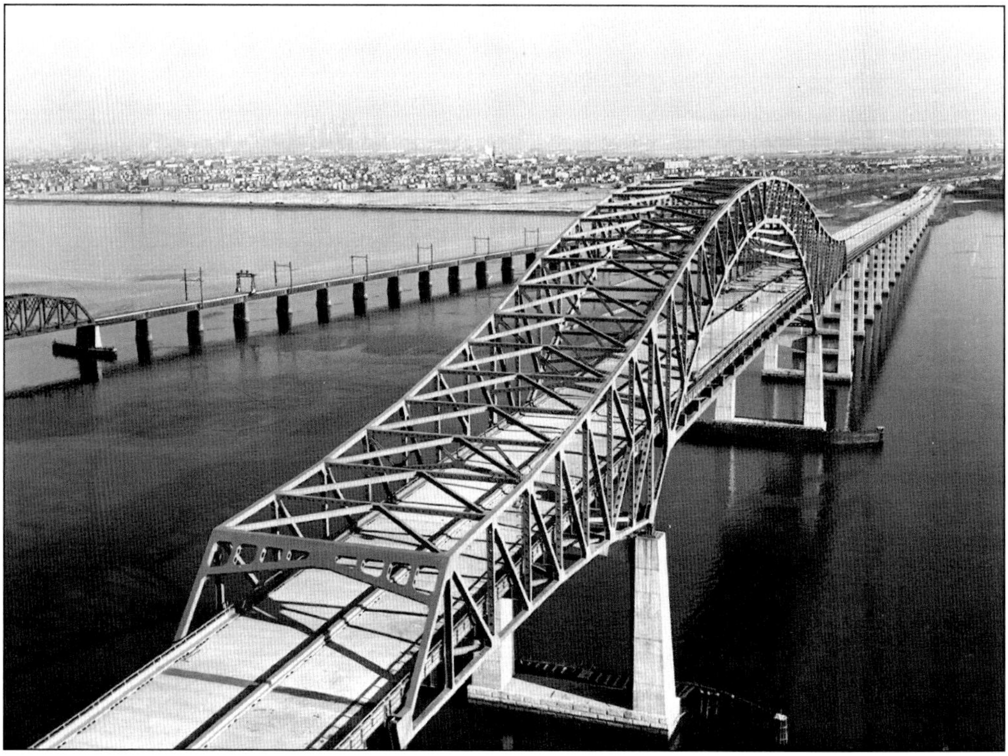

This photograph, looking east, shows the completed Newark Bay–Hudson County Extension Bridge. The New York City skyline is visible in the background.

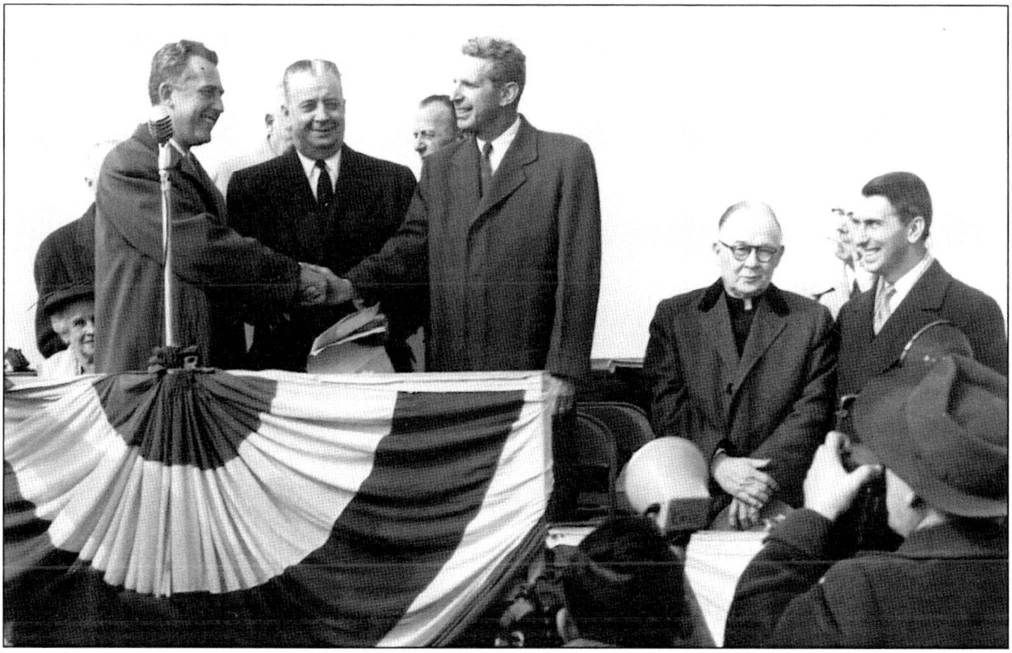

Above, posing for a photograph on the podium are New Jersey governor Robert Meyner (left), Turnpike Authority chairman Paul L. Troast (center), and former governor Alfred E. Driscoll, as they take part in the Newark Bay Bridge dedication ceremonies on April 5, 1956. In the photograph below, Troast and Governor Meyner are joined by Commissioners Joseph Morecraft and Lester Maxwell, among others, as they cut the ribbon on the Newark Bay Bridge.

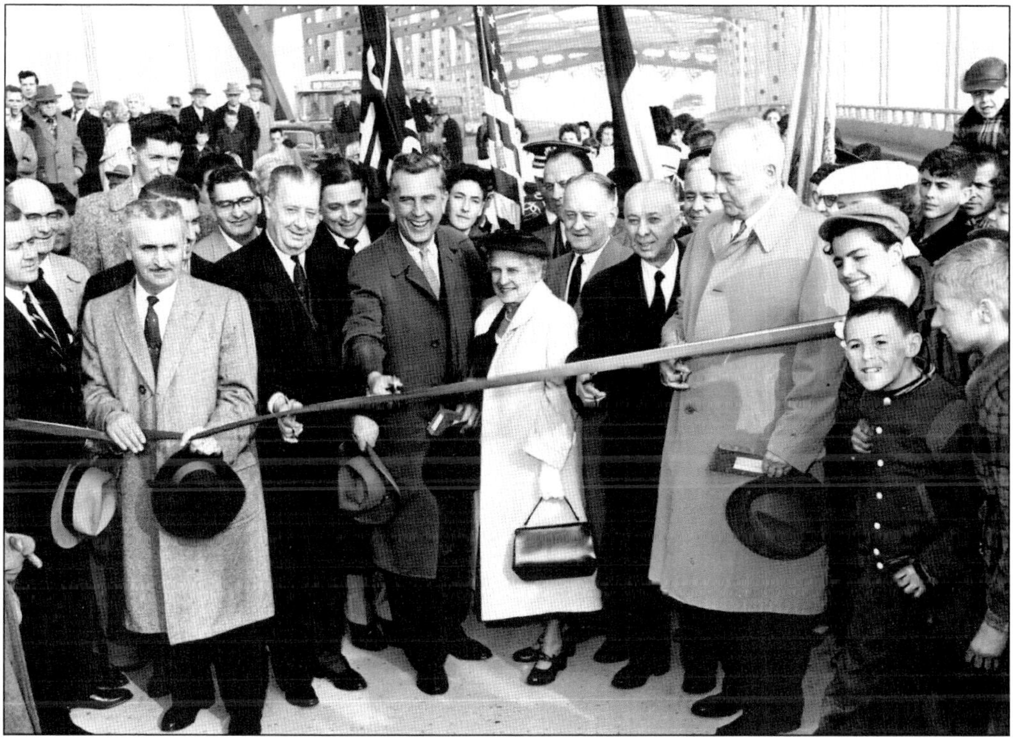

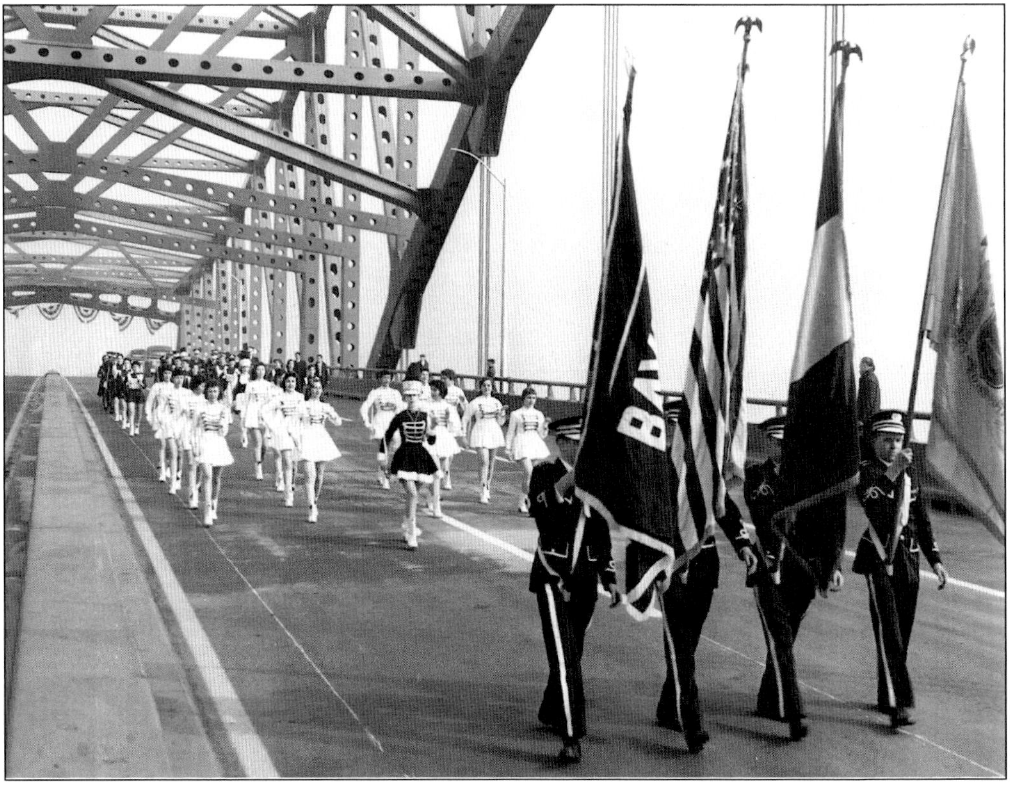

The Bayonne High School color guard, majorettes, and marching band are among the first to cross the Newark Bay Bridge on opening day.

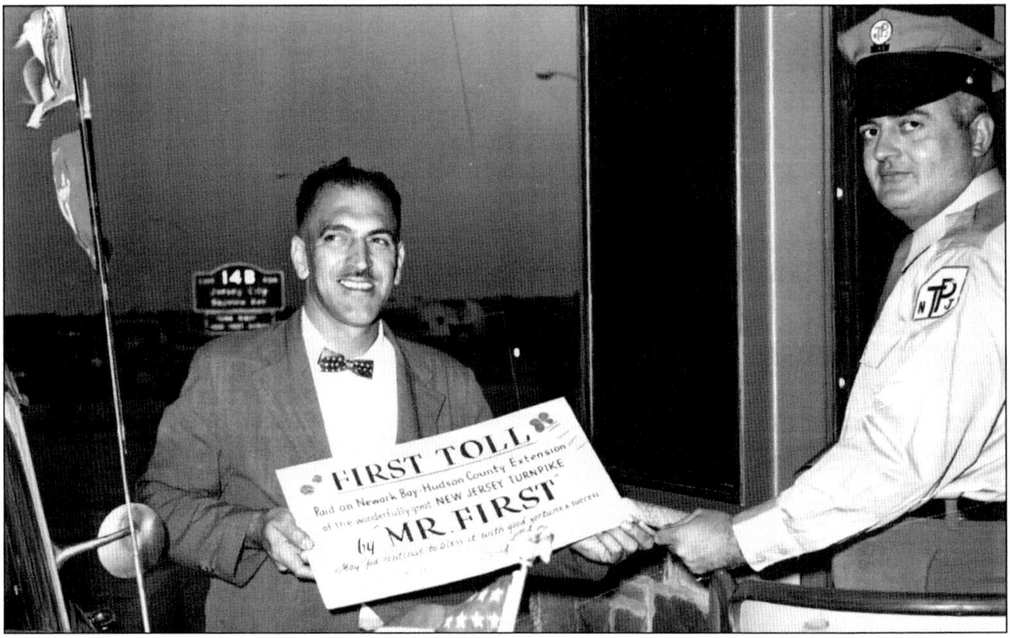

On September 15, 1956, Omero C. Catan—"Mr. First"—paid the first toll on the Newark Bay–Hudson County Extension.

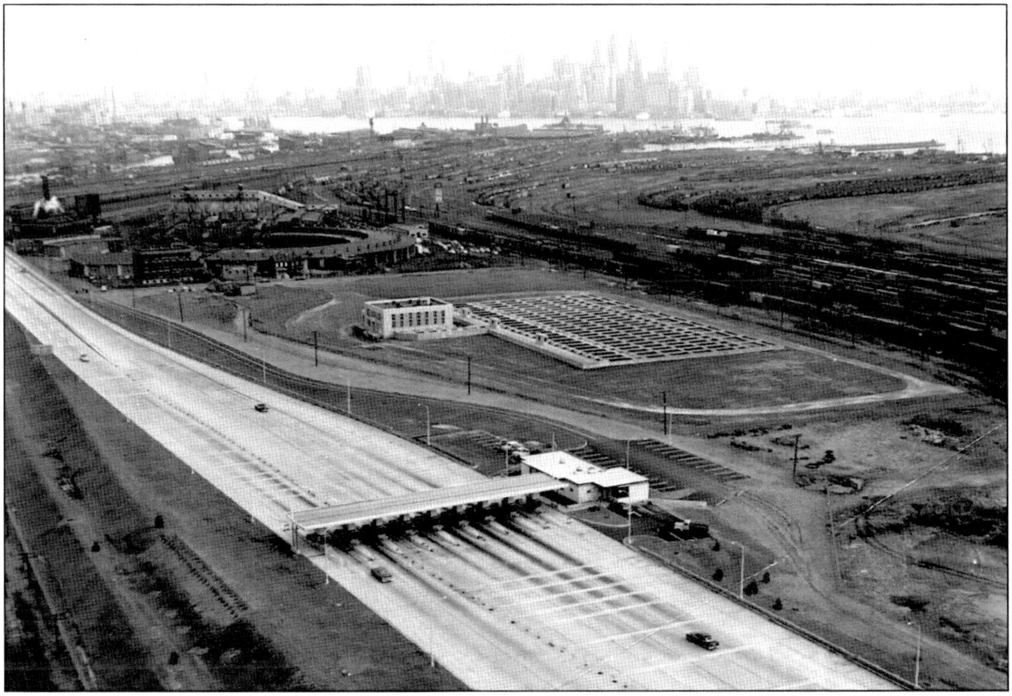

This photograph shows Interchange 14C, downtown Jersey City, with a world-class view of the Lower Manhattan skyline. The crossing of the main lines of the Erie Railroad in Jersey City posed several major problems. These included the relocation of the railroad's principal car and coach repair shops and yard, a signal tower, the "pick-a-back" freight trackage yard, and essential utilities such as telephone and telegraph lines, steam and water lines, and others.

This view shows cars traveling eastbound on the Hudson County Extension after paying the toll at Interchange 14C. Motorists could either exit at the Grand Street ramp into Jersey City or continue to the entrance of the Holland Tunnel to downtown Manhattan.

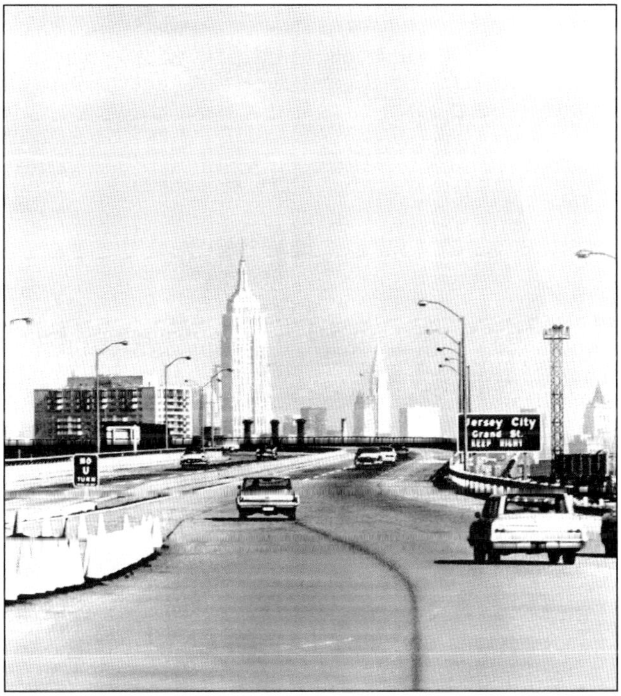

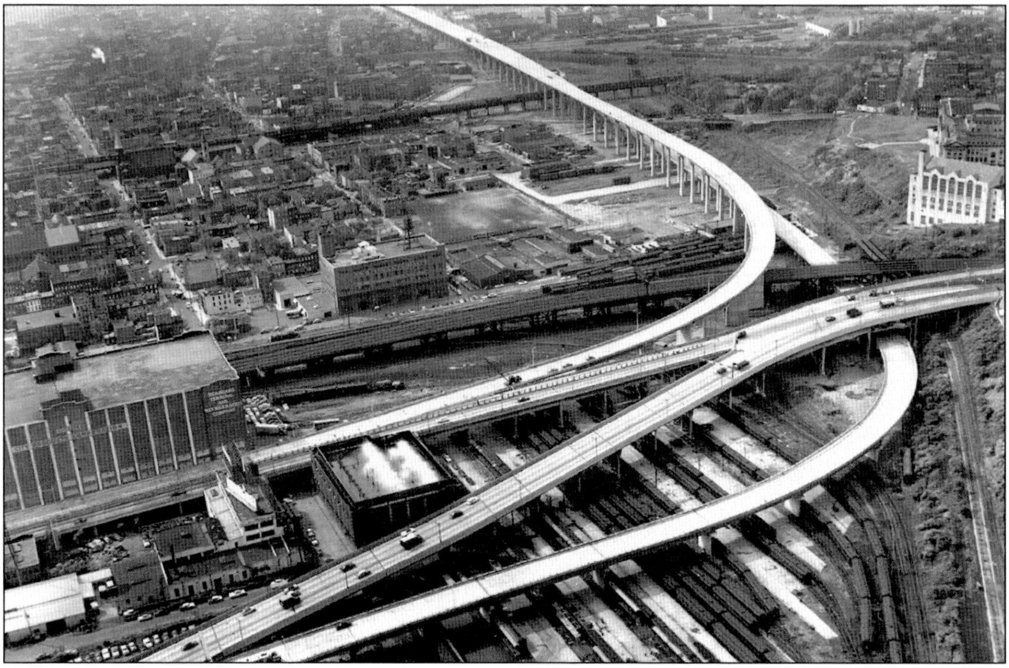

This view of the north terminal ramps of the Newark Bay–Hudson County Extension shows the entry and exit ramps from the turnpike to downtown Jersey City, Hoboken, and the Holland Tunnel.

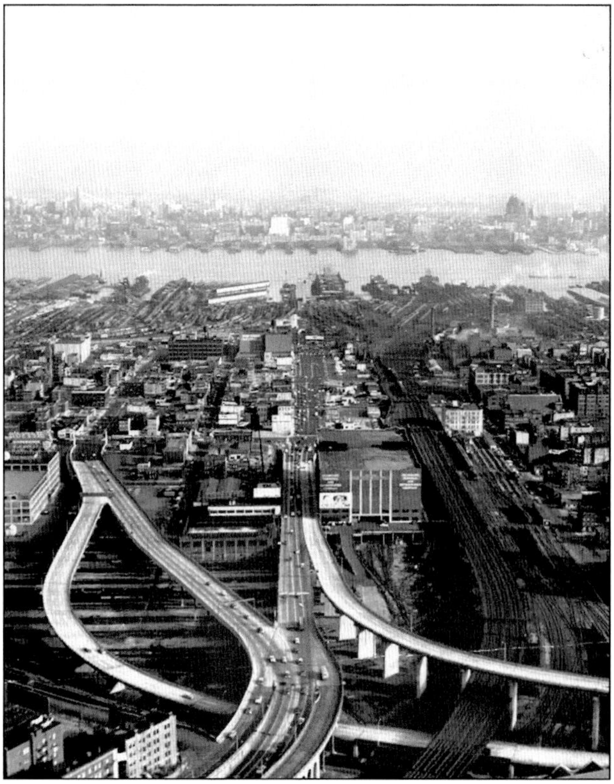

This 1950s aerial photograph shows the entrance and exit ramps from the New Jersey Turnpike to the Holland Tunnel, as well as a view of the New Jersey waterfront on the Hudson River, and the mid-Manhattan skyline.

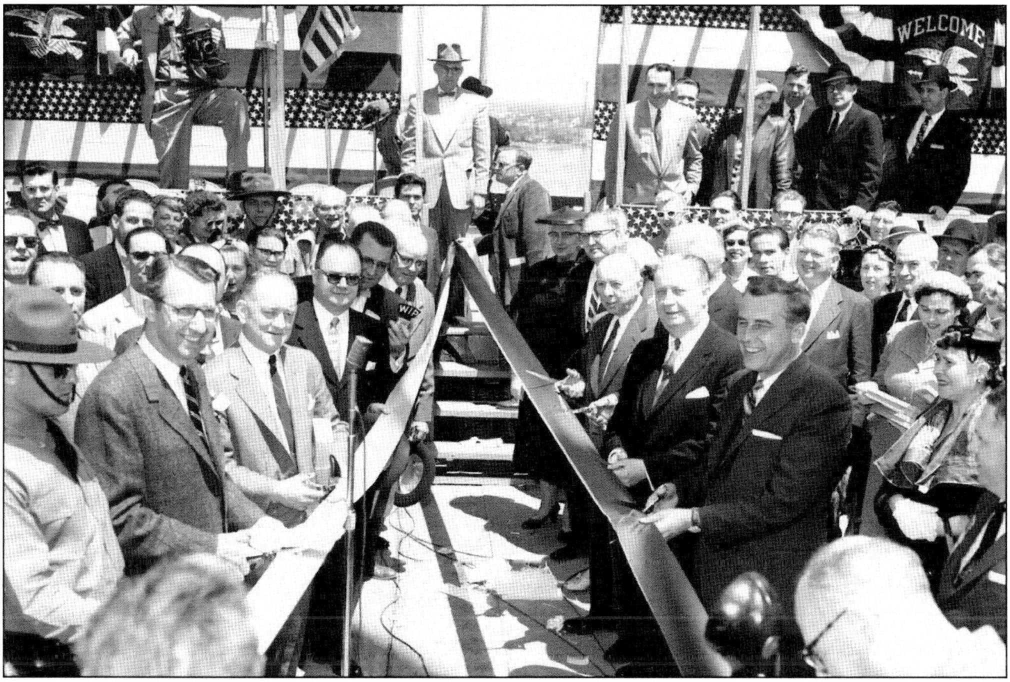

Above, the delegations from New Jersey and Pennsylvania meet at the centerline of the Pennsylvania Extension Bridge on May 25, 1956. Ready to cut the ribbon, state officials pose for a picture during the bridge dedication ceremonies. In the photograph below, a motorcade of vehicles and invited guests are some of the first to travel the newly opened bridge.

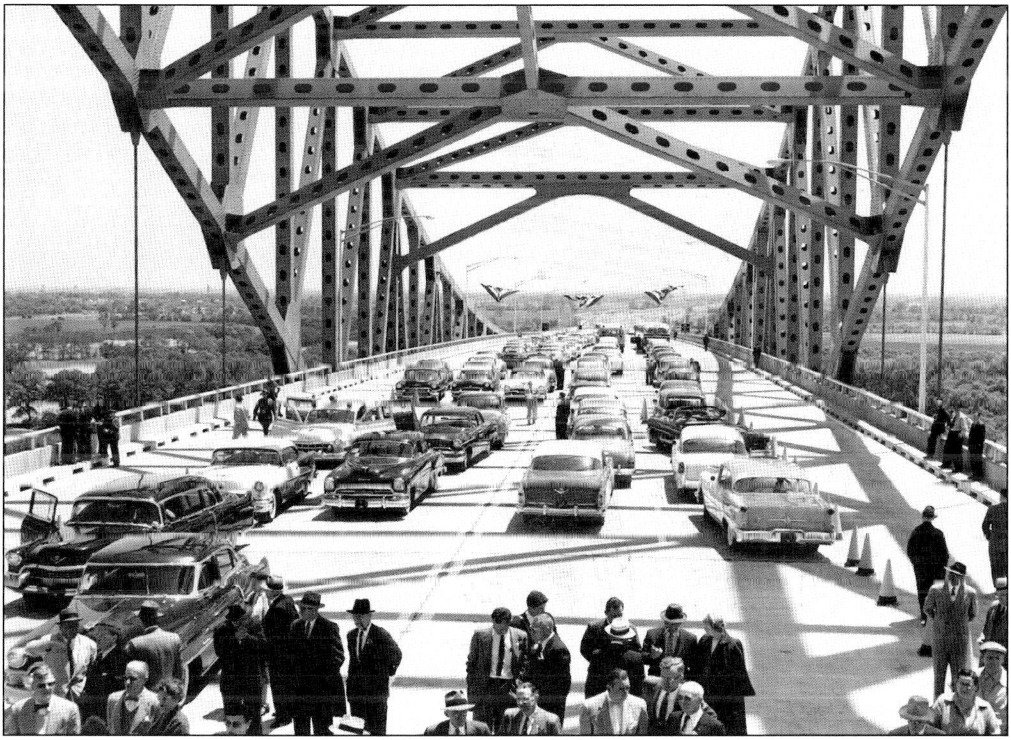

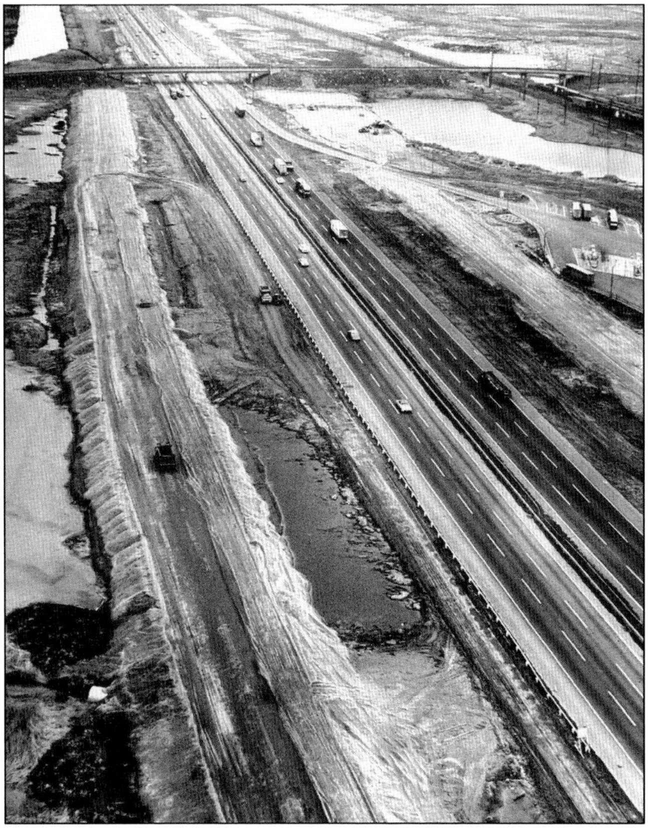

When the first 53 miles of the New Jersey Turnpike, from Deepwater to Bordentown, were opened to the public on November 5, 1951, no one imagined that 15 years later men and machines would again be assembled for another great construction effort on the state's first toll highway of modern times. On December 17, 1964, the New Jersey Turnpike Authority, led by Executive Director William J. Flanagan, placed in the hands of then governor Richard J. Hughes plans for the greatest expansion program in the turnpike's history: a project to widen the northern stretch of the road from six to twelve lanes. In this view, a ribbon of newly spread sand flanks the New Jersey Turnpike main line just south of North Avenue in Elizabeth, as the highway-widening program progresses on April 6, 1967.

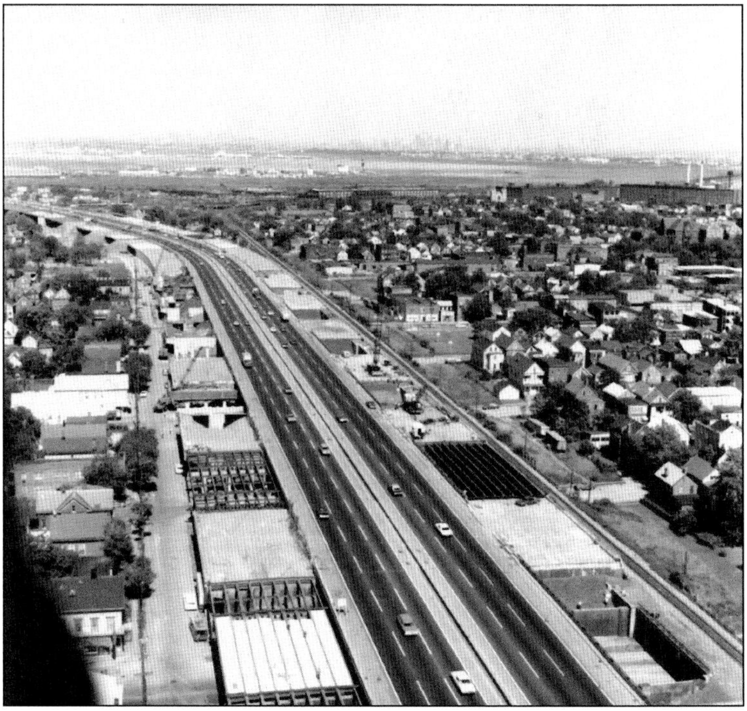

This photograph shows the new overpasses for the dual-dual roadway being built over local streets in Elizabeth.

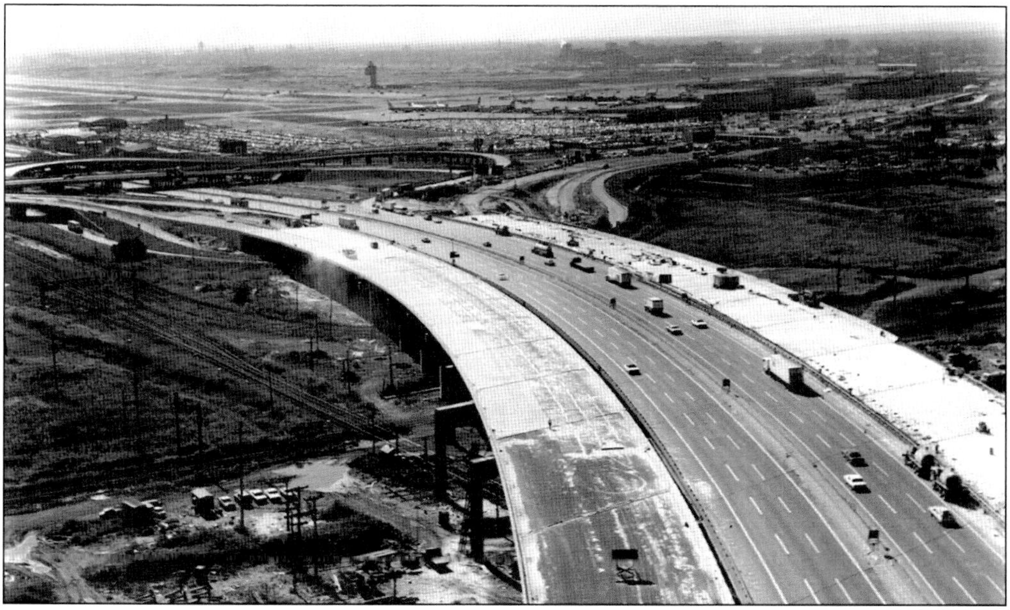

The main line of the turnpike is flanked by the nearly completed bridges erected during the construction of the dual-dual roadway, in this photograph, looking southwest, on October 16, 1969. The roadway to the left accommodates northbound traffic, while the lanes to the right accommodate southbound traffic. Newark Airport can be seen in the background.

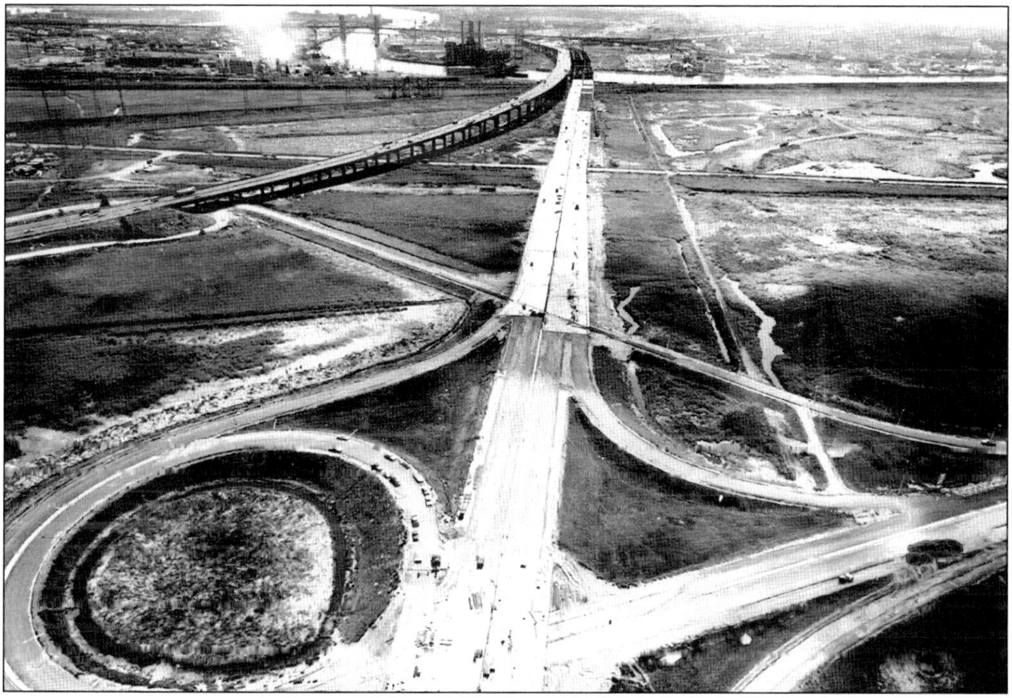

Farther north, where the widened turnpike branches off into the new Meadowland spur of six and four lanes, paralleling the west bank of the Hackensack River, the Laderman Bridge begins to rise. The bridge consists of 60 piers and is the largest structure of the widening project. Named after the late Harry Laderman, toll collector, the bridge runs parallel to the Passaic River Bridge.

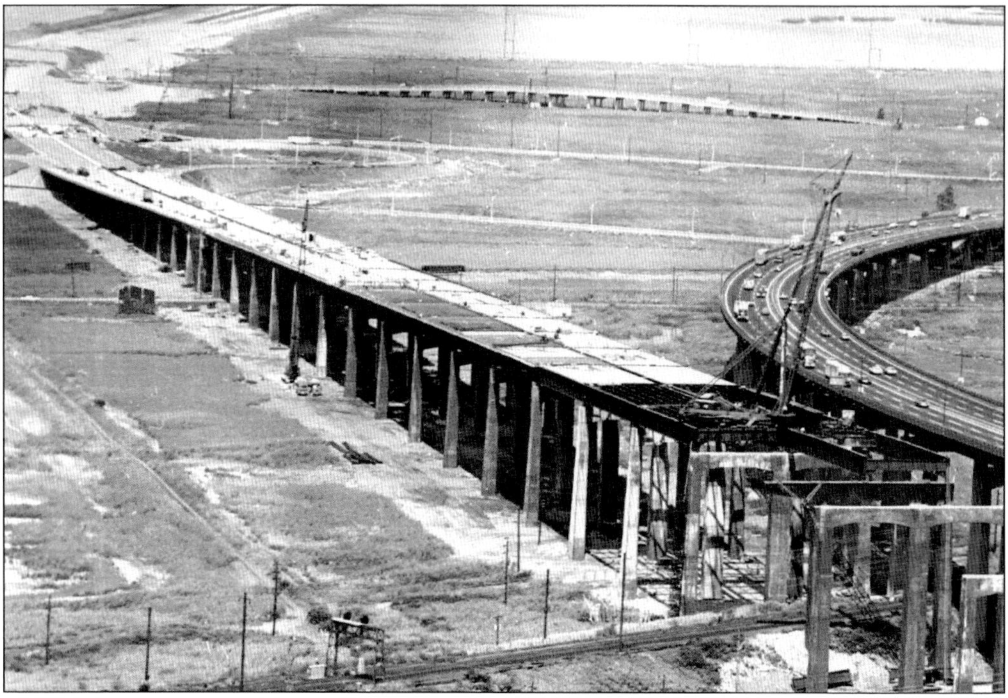

Traveler cranes can be seen erecting steel girders on the westerly alignment bridge.

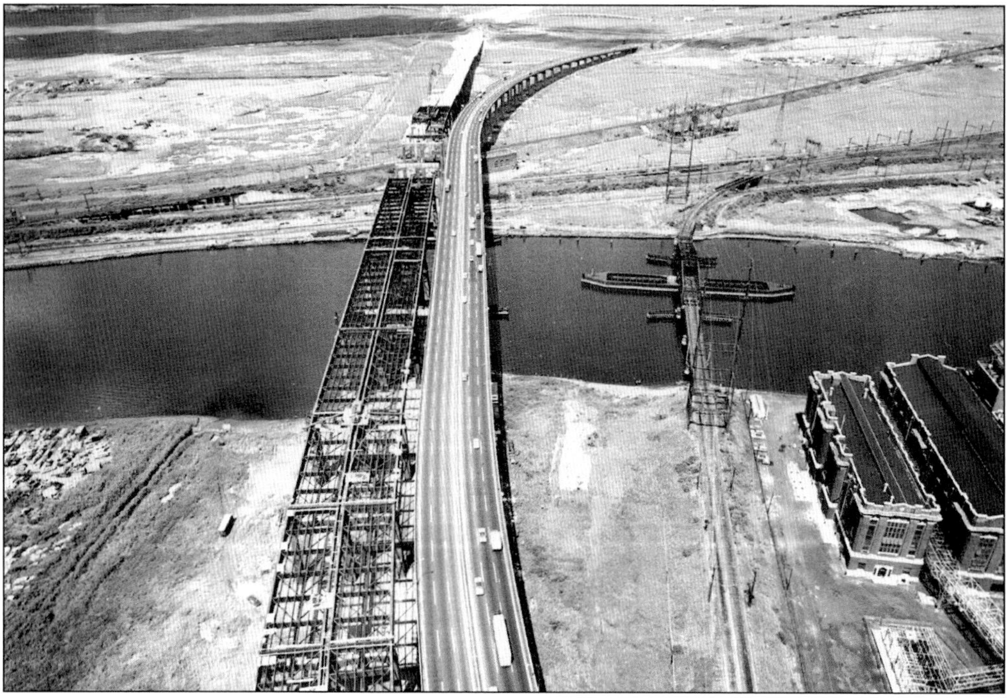

Steel girders are being placed across the final two spans of the Passaic River on the westerly alignment bridge. The Harry Laderman Bridge is key to the new westerly route of the expanded turnpike. It is the second major span over the Passaic River and features full shoulders, as does the new Hackensack River span.

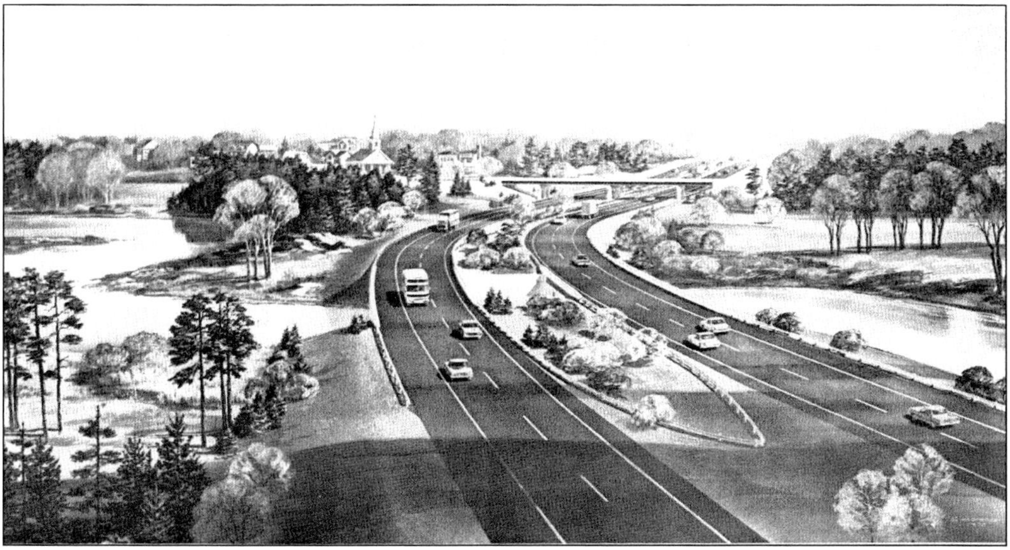

A 1972 turnpike employee newsletter states the following about the proposed Driscoll Expressway: "The Expressway will be more than an extension of Turnpike travel facilities. It will be an extension of the Turnpike's beautification program, placing a 'parkway within a turnpike' along the 38 miles of the new road's alignment from Toms River to South Brunswick." The above is a artist's rendering of the expressway by Howard, Needles, Tammen, and Bergendoff, the Turnpike Authority's consulting engineers. The Driscoll Expressway project was not undertaken by the Authority and was therefore never built. Below, a public hearing regarding the proposed Driscoll Expressway is held at a new information center in Manalapan.

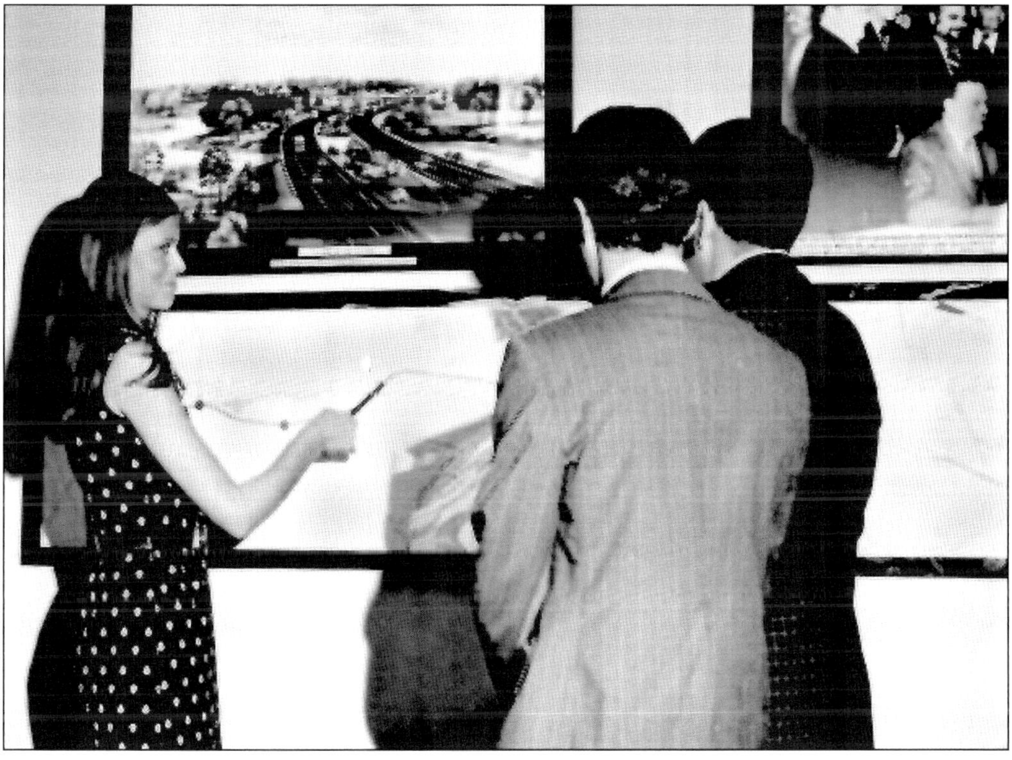

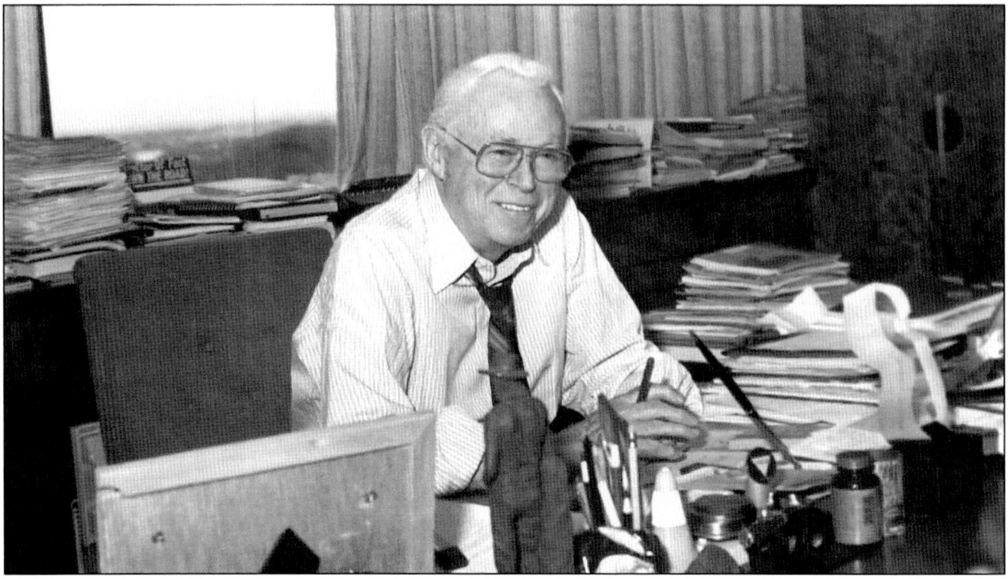

William J. Flanagan began his career as a journalist, became the deputy mayor of Jersey City, and once held the powerful position of Hudson County sheriff. President-elect John F. Kennedy also asked him to join his new administration in Washington. It was an invitation Flanagan was honored to receive, but declined to accept because of commitments to his family. For nearly 26 years (1962–1988), Executive Director Flanagan guided the turnpike through a period of intense development and innovative improvements. He had a grand and glorious public career, but through it all he retained the humility of a simple, devoutly religious family man. He had more of an impact on the New Jersey Turnpike than any man before him in the turnpike's first 45 years of existence. Flanagan is best remembered for his efforts in establishing the turnpike family and his determination in enforcing Authority policy on speeding foreign diplomats, which received national and international press coverage.

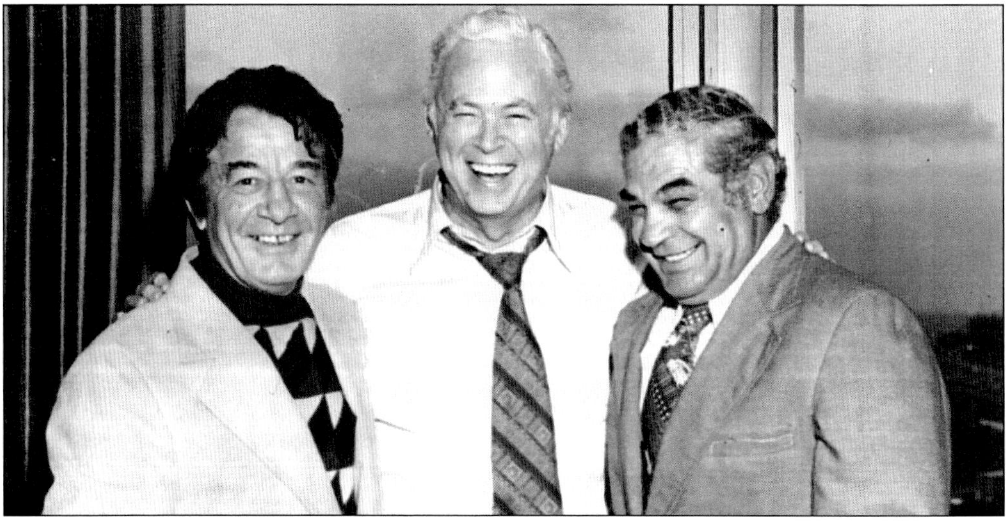

En route to the Camden area to promote an amateur boxing card to benefit the Bethlehem Baptist Church in Woodbury, former middleweight champion Rocky Graziano (left) and the turnpike's own middleweight contender, Armando "Ernie" Durando (right), stop off to share recent developments with Turnpike Authority executive director William J. Flanagan.

Executive Director Flanagan (kneeling, center) listens as a diver explains how he cuts sheeting with an underwater torch at a cofferdam on the site of the new Laderman Bridge over the Passaic River.

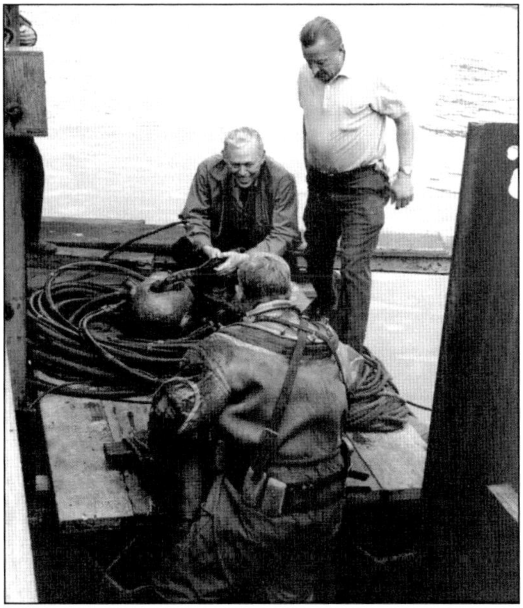

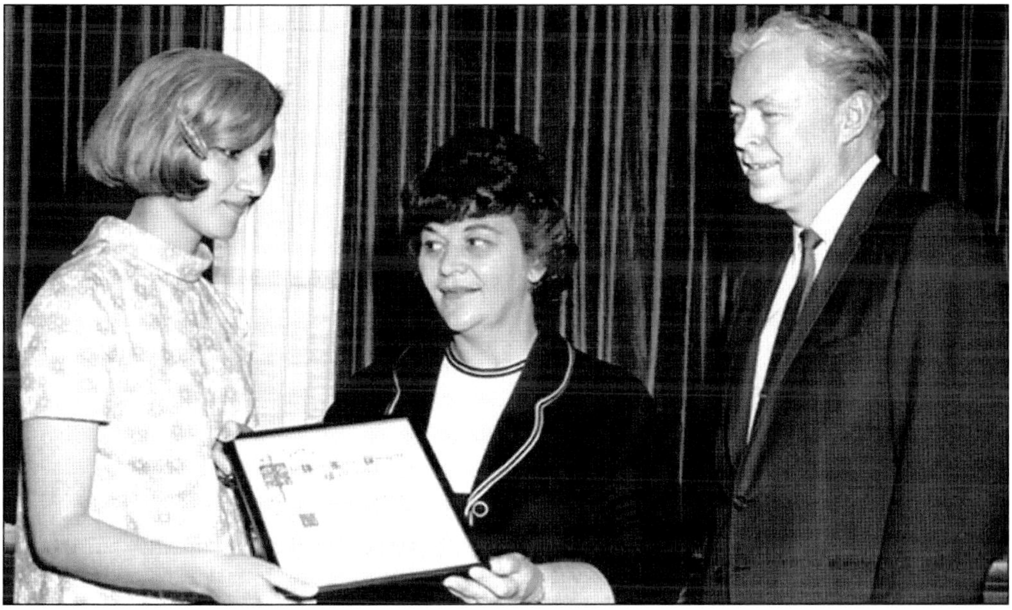

The Harry Laderman Scholarship fund honors Toll Collector Harry Laderman, who, on February 2, 1967, was the first turnpike employee to lose his life in the line of service, when a truck struck his toll booth at the Lincoln Tunnel Interchange. The scholarship, the first-ever award of its kind made by a public agency in the state of New Jersey, has assisted more than 34 recipients since its establishment. The scholarship is available to students who are children of New Jersey Turnpike Authority employees and who demonstrate exceptional scholastic ability and achievements. Karen Jo Beck, a 17-year-old senior at Woodbridge Senior High School, was the first recipient of the award in 1968. She was a member of the National Honor Society and was ranked 44th in her class of 720. Her father, Walter G. Beck, was a landscaper for 20 years, before retiring in 1985. Pictured here are Karen Jo Beck (left), an unidentified woman, and Turnpike Authority executive director William J. Flanagan

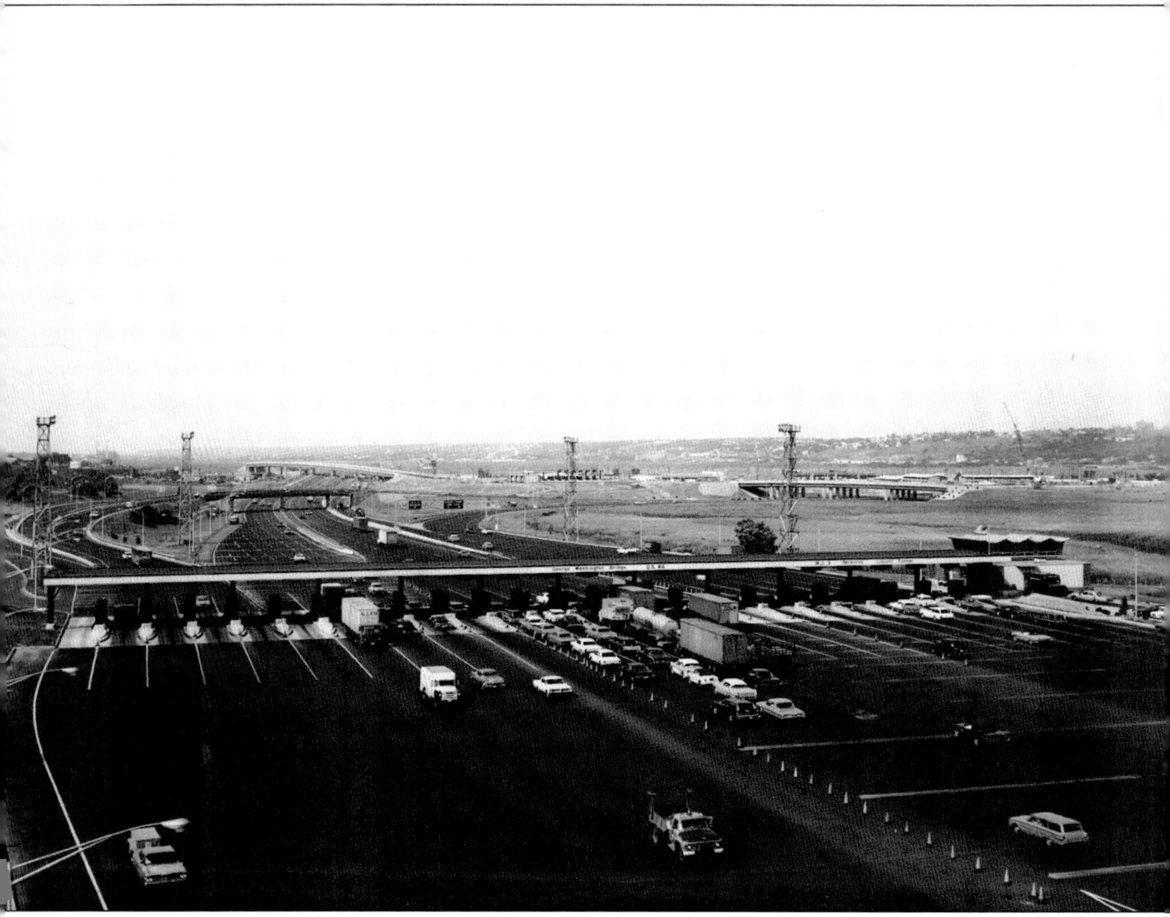

The Lincoln Tunnel Complex, completed February 25, 1964, with its 24-lane toll plaza was, at that time, the largest of its kind on any toll road in the world.

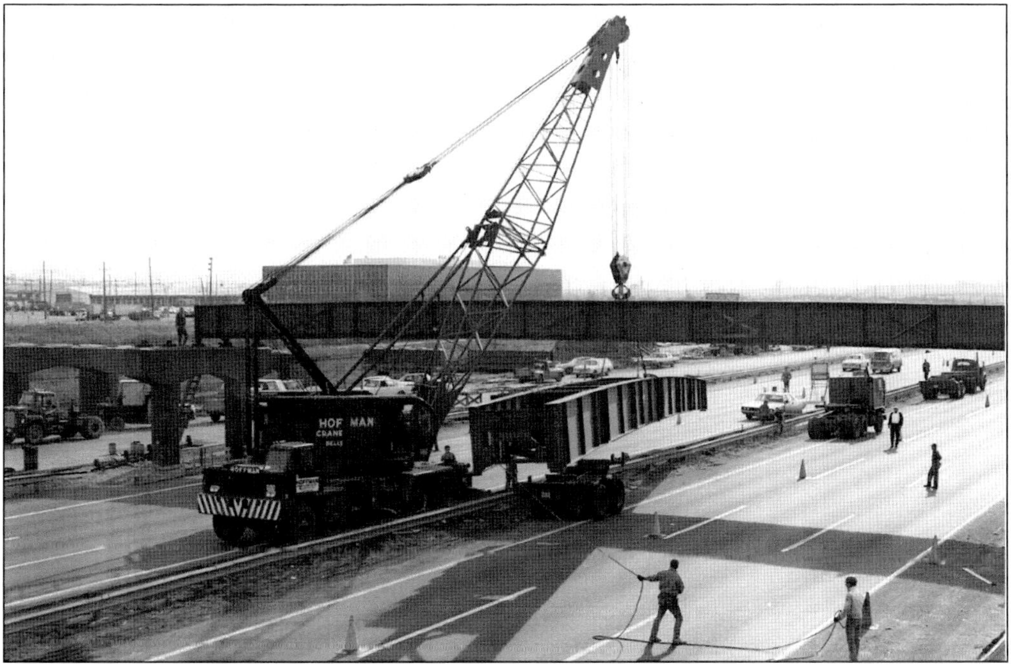

On November 4, 1969, traffic is temporarily stopped while a truck crane erects steel for a U-turn overpass across the widened turnpike.

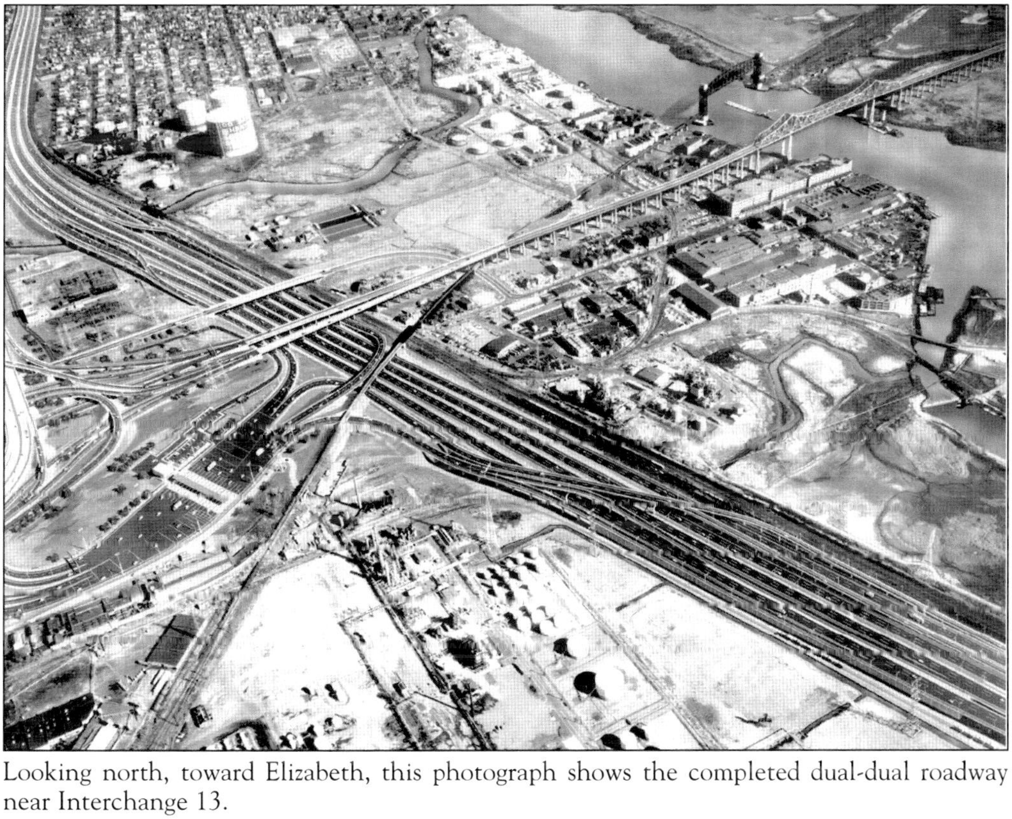

Looking north, toward Elizabeth, this photograph shows the completed dual-dual roadway near Interchange 13.

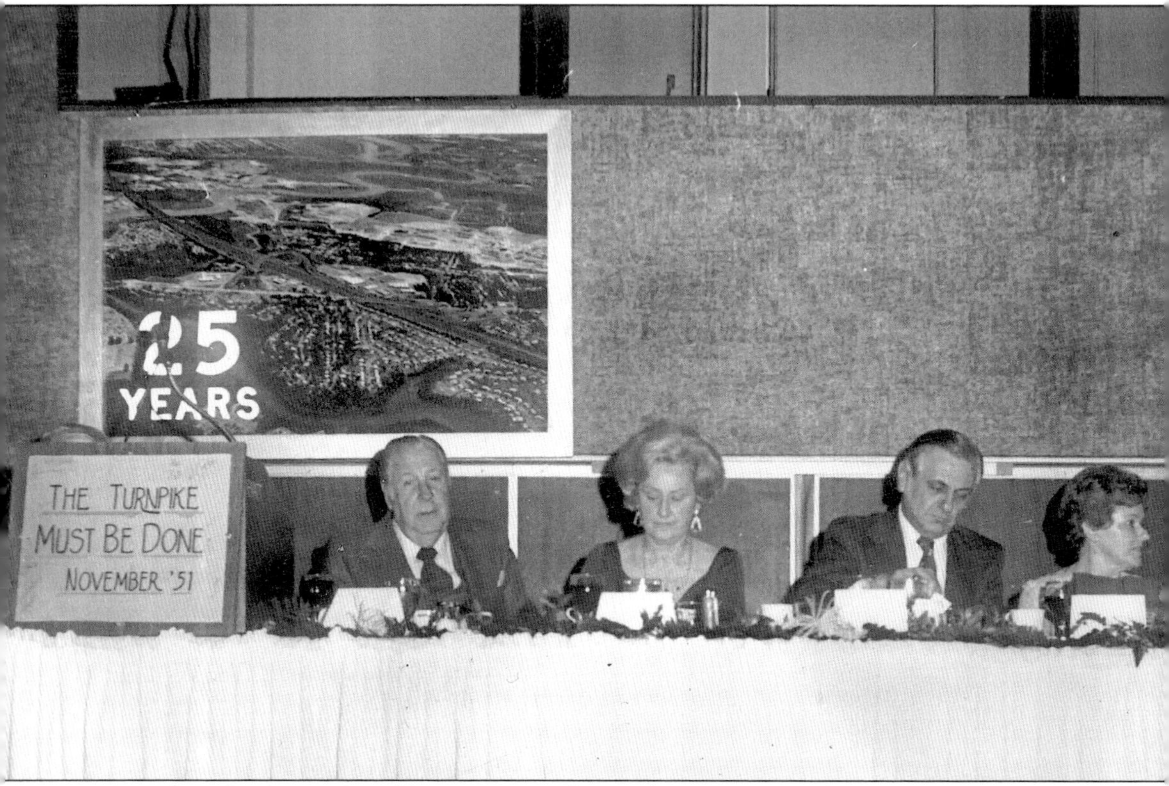

Seated on the dais at the 25th-anniversary dinner-dance on November 13, 1976, are, from left to right, New Jersey Turnpike Authority chairman Francis G. Fitzpatrick and his wife, Marion, and commissioner Richard D. Ilnicki and his wife, Helen. In his remarks at the turnpike celebration Chairman Fitzpatrick said: "What a difference 25 years makes! . . . It would take a long time to recite all the engineering advances made since the New Jersey Turnpike opened its lanes to the public 25 years ago. But with all of that—all that the Authority can boast of, all the great achievements of a quarter century of progress—all that would not have been realized if it had not been for the turnpike people, the Authority's forces in the field and in the offices—the toll collectors, the maintenance crews, the engineers, the whole army of talent at work every day from Deepwater to Ridgefield Park, and all the stations at the 27 interchanges. Including, of course, 14A in Bayonne. You are the people who deserve to take a bow."

Three

The Potter's Field Project

The Turnpike Authority's proposed Secaucus Interchange, currently under construction and scheduled to open in late 2005, required the disinterment of a Potter's Field cemetery on property originally owned by the County of Hudson. From 1880 to 1962, Hudson County owned and operated several institutions on the site originally known as Snake Hill and presently referred to as Laurel Hill in the town of Secaucus. Maps dating back to the late 1800s and early 1900s showed the location of an almshouse, a penitentiary, an asylum for the insane, infectious-disease hospitals, and three separate cemeteries.

In 1950, during the original construction of the turnpike, one of the three cemeteries was active and in the direct path of the proposed roadway's alignment. In order to avoid construction delays, it was decided to bridge the cemetery rather than undertake the time-consuming and costly process of disinterring the cemetery's remains. Only a small number of disinterments were performed at that time to facilitate the construction of the bridge's piers. Those disinterred individuals were reburied in a location within the cemetery that was not impacted by the roadway's construction.

During the 1960s, Hudson County attempted to have all the remains removed from the cemeteries, but the project ended with the indictment of some officials, and it is still uncertain whether any bodies were actually moved. For nearly two decades the cemeteries were neglected, to the point of being unrecognizable, and in the 1980s, the county authorized construction of a temporary correctional facility on the parcel containing the third cemetery, herein referred to as Potter's Field.

The first of two substantive attempts to verify the cemetery's location and quantify the number of burials in Potter's Field occurred in 1992, when the Turnpike Authority began assessments for the construction of a new interchange on the Eastern Spur, known as the Secaucus Interchange. In 1996, additional archaeological investigations, including the use of remote sensing techniques and the excavation of trenches, determined that human remains were in fact buried within the cemetery. However, over the decades of neglect, virtually all of the cemetery's original wooden grave markers had burned in brush fires, and the ceramic cylinders used to mark the locations of graves had disappeared.

Based on the results of these two preliminary site investigations and the limited records available through the county, it was anticipated that the site contained between 600 and 900 burials. However, in the spring of 2002, as the Authority was preparing to engage an archaeological firm to perform the disinterments and subsequent reinterments, county officials identified burial ledgers that indicated there could be as many as 3,500 burials at the site. The handwritten ledgers showed that the burials, which had been performed by the county between the years of 1920 and 1962, were interred in this Potter's Field cemetery.

In the fall of 2002, the Authority began the legal process to obtain an order permitting the disinterment of the remains. A public notice was issued through local, state, and national newspapers listing the names recorded in the burial ledgers and notifying any descendants of the legal proceedings. Three additional court hearings were held in November and December 2002 and January 2003 to review evidence and hear oral arguments in support of or in opposition to the Turnpike Authority's application.

Also in the fall of 2002, the Authority solicited proposals from archaeological firms to perform the disinterment and reinterment activities associated with the Potter's Field project. At the October 2002 commission meeting, the Louis Berger Group of East Orange was issued an order of professional services for the disinterment and reinterment of Potter's Field. The Berger Group assisted the Authority with the preparation of the project's disinterment and reinterment plans, which were then filed with the court. In January 2003, the court approved the final order and judgment, and the following month, after an on-site ecumenical service that paid respects to the thousands of lost souls buried in the forgotten cemetery, disinterment activities on the project known as the Potter's Field Disinterment/Reinterment project commenced.

After almost nine months of intensive field efforts, Berger's team of more than 100 archaeologists, osteologists, and field technicians exhumed the last of 4,571 sets of human remains. This project is believed to be the largest single disinterment contract ever performed in the United States. As part of the disinterment activities, more than 20,000 cubic yards of soil were excavated, moved, and graded to allow for the identification of 2,686 grave shafts extending over a two-acre parcel.

A total of 113,544 artifacts or non-skeletal objects were recovered, of which over 50 percent were coffin nails. Other personal effects or "grave goods" included dentures, glass eyes, coins, clay smoking pipes, embalming bottles, whiskey and wine bottles, combs, over 4,500 buttons, more than 500 ceramic fragments, clothing remnants, shoes, hats, jewelry, military medals, religious items, and medical devices or prosthetics, all of which were photographed and documented by the Louis Berger Group. All artifacts were reinterred with the respective individuals.

The on-site osteological analyses at Potter's Field indicated that the causes of death of the interred individuals ranged from infectious diseases, such as smallpox, tuberculosis, cholera, and influenza; to pathologies, including lesions, vertebral fusion, untreated fractures, and developmental defects; to blunt-force traumas. There also was evidence of a number of autopsies and amputations among these individuals.

Using historic maps, original handwritten burial ledgers, osteological examination, background research, and artifact analysis, Berger's team was able to determine possible identities for approximately 900 of the disinterred remains. Of particular note, positive identifications were established for two interments who have living linear descendants. The remains of a woman who died in 1928 and those of a man who was buried in 1949 were returned to their respective relatives for private ceremonies and reburial, ending the families' searches for their long-lost grandparents.

The remaining 4,569 individuals exhumed from Potter's Field, together with their personal effects, were placed in 94 standard, triple-depth precast concrete burial vaults and were reinterred at Maple Grove Park Cemetery located in Hackensack.

In the summer of 2004, a granite memorial monument, approximately 60 feet long and 6 feet tall, with bronze plaques listing the 7,767 named individuals from the burial ledgers was erected at Maple Grove Park Cemetery. This monument stands as a permanent reminder for all those poor, diseased, or nameless individuals who were buried in the Hudson County burial ground. This site will serve in perpetuity as their final resting place and a sanctuary of peace.

—John Keller

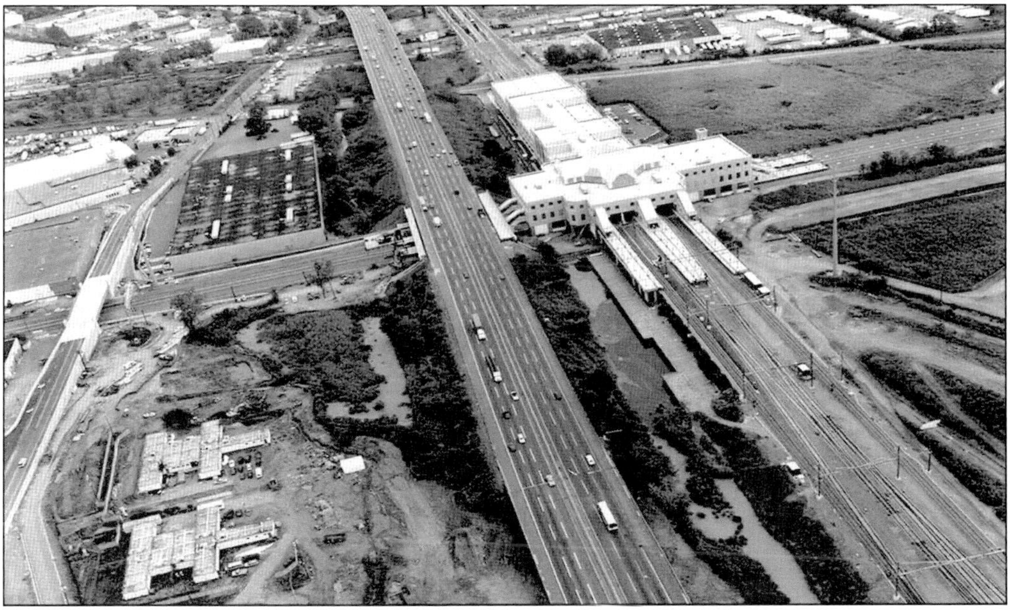

This aerial photograph, taken in October 2003, shows the turnpike's eastern spur and New Jersey Transit's recently constructed Secaucus Rail Station. The Potter's Field Disinterment/Reinterment project was necessitated by the construction of the Authority's proposed Secaucus Interchange project, which, when complete, will provide direct access to the rail station and the Secaucus Warehouse District, seen on the far left. In the lower left corner is the Hudson County Correctional Facility complex that was erected over part of Potter's Field.

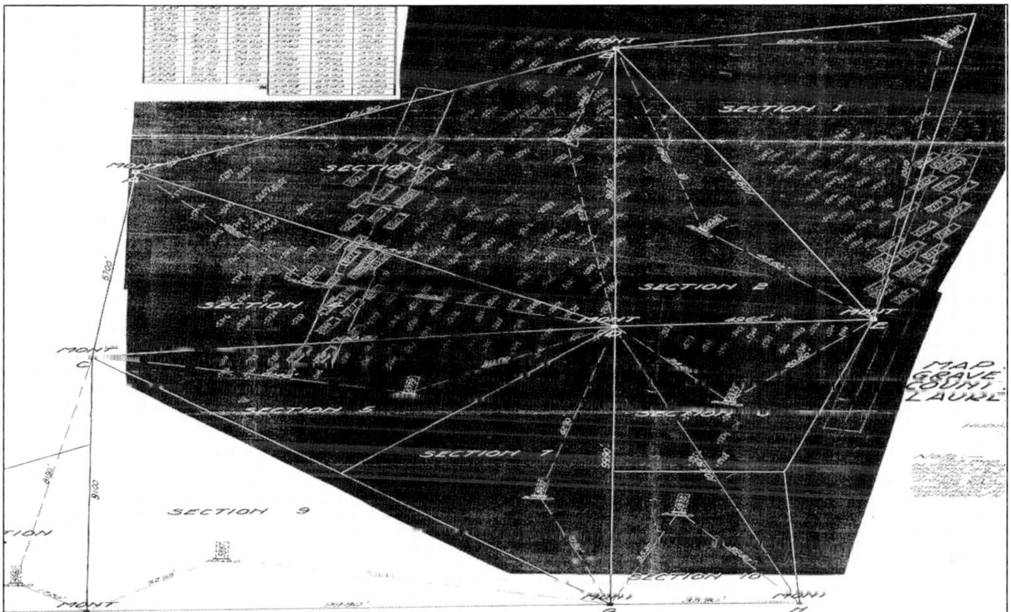

This 1935 map is one of the documents found by Hudson County that depicts the location of the cemetery. Very few of the monuments shown on the plan that establish the cemetery's boundaries were found by the archaeologists. Those that were located were approximately six feet below the existing ground line.

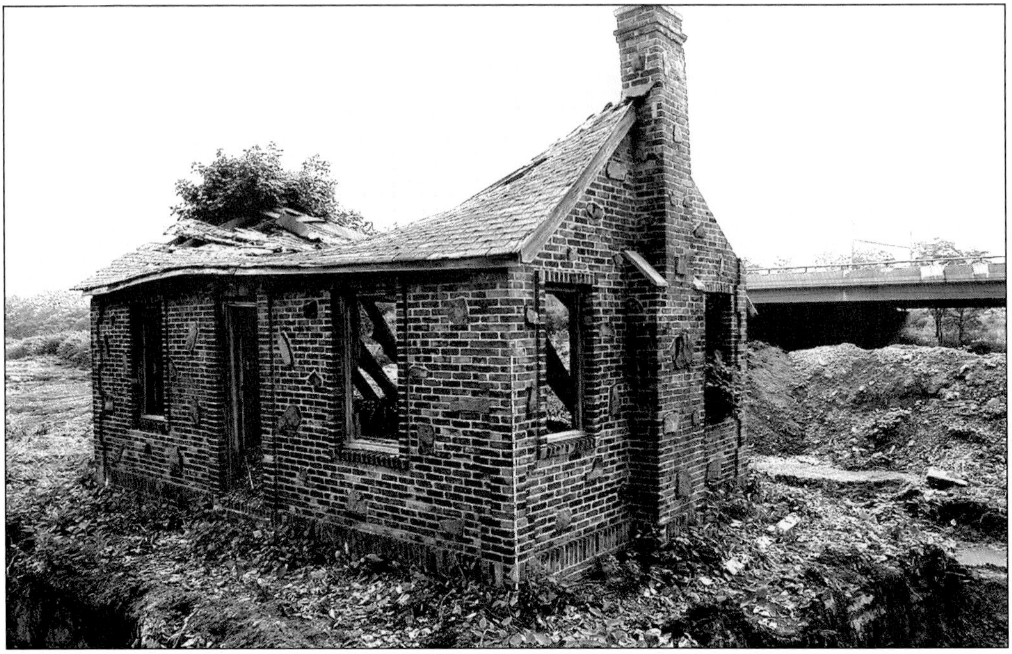

This one-story dilapidated brick building, which served as the cemetery office, was the only means by which to establish the approximate location of the cemetery. One of the plans showed an offset from the building to one of the cemetery boundary monuments. From this one dimension, archaeologists were able to fairly accurately establish the limits of the original cemetery.

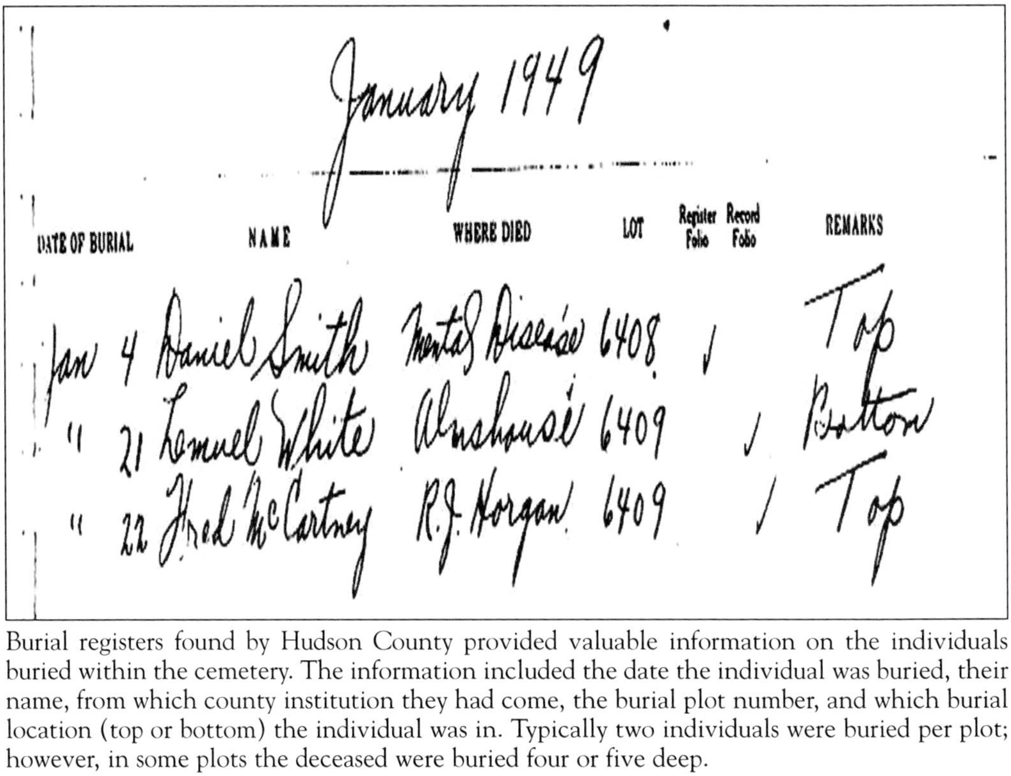

January 1949

DATE OF BURIAL	NAME	WHERE DIED	LOT	Register Folio	Record Folio	REMARKS
Jan 4	Daniel Smith	Mental Disease	6408	/		Top
" 21	Lemuel White	Almshouse	6409		/	Bottom
" 22	Fred McCartney	R.J. Horgan	6409		/	Top

Burial registers found by Hudson County provided valuable information on the individuals buried within the cemetery. The information included the date the individual was buried, their name, from which county institution they had come, the burial plot number, and which burial location (top or bottom) the individual was in. Typically two individuals were buried per plot; however, in some plots the deceased were buried four or five deep.

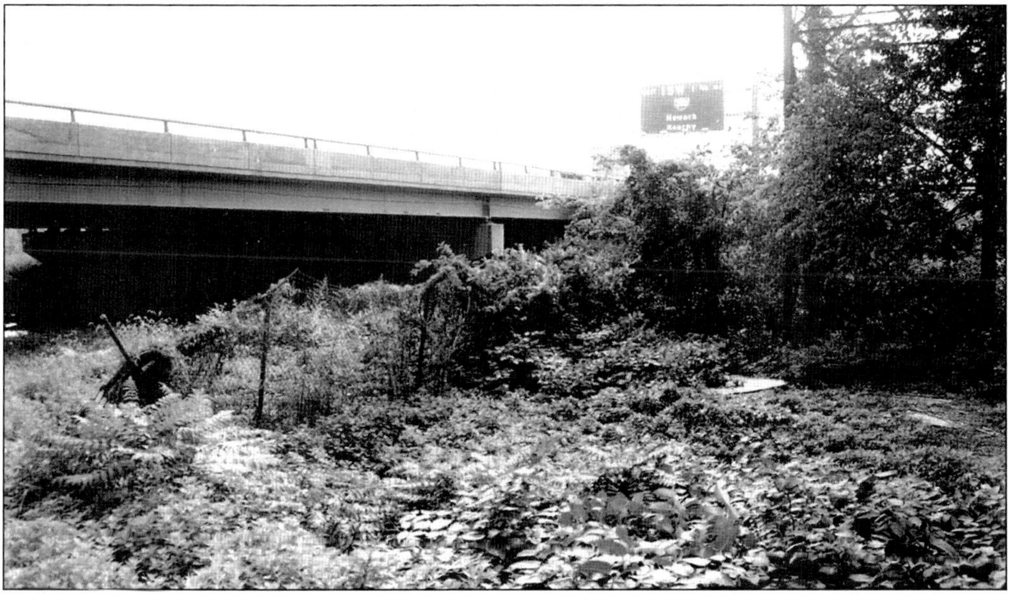

This photograph shows the condition of the site prior to disinterment activities. The dense vegetation and years of neglect made the cemetery unrecognizable. This turnpike bridge, built in 1950 as part of the original turnpike construction, was built solely to span the then-active burial ground. During the construction of the bridge a small number of the graves were disinterred at the locations of the bridge piers and reinterred within the cemetery beyond the roadway's footprint.

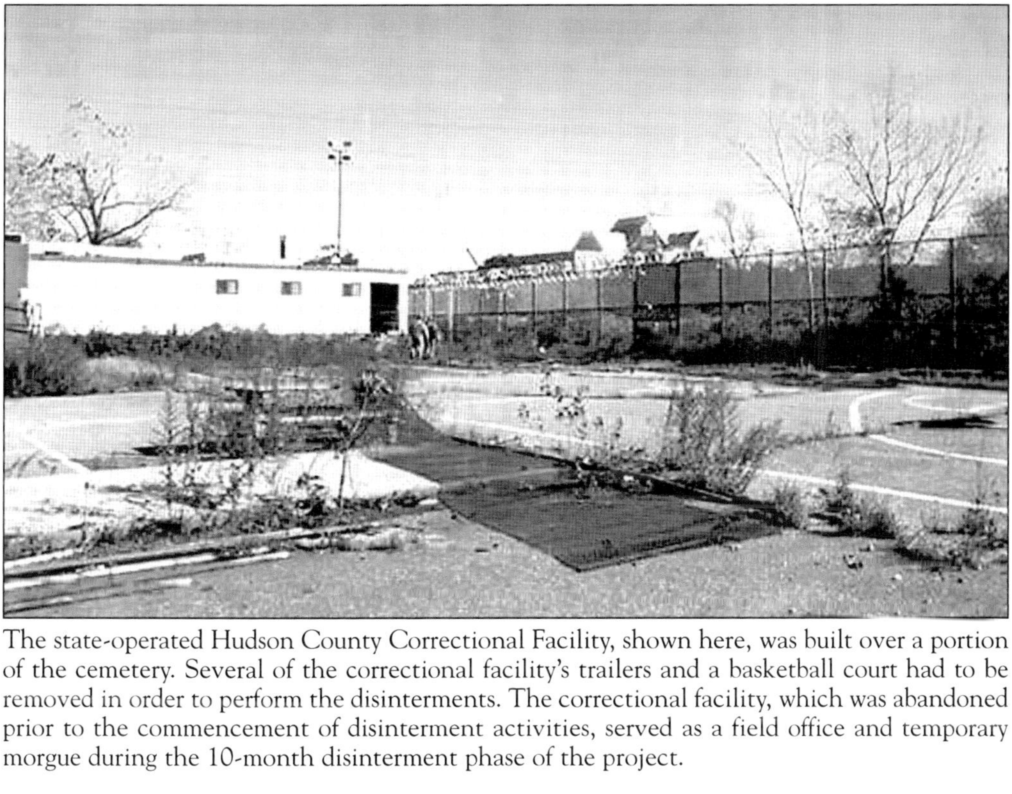

The state-operated Hudson County Correctional Facility, shown here, was built over a portion of the cemetery. Several of the correctional facility's trailers and a basketball court had to be removed in order to perform the disinterments. The correctional facility, which was abandoned prior to the commencement of disinterment activities, served as a field office and temporary morgue during the 10-month disinterment phase of the project.

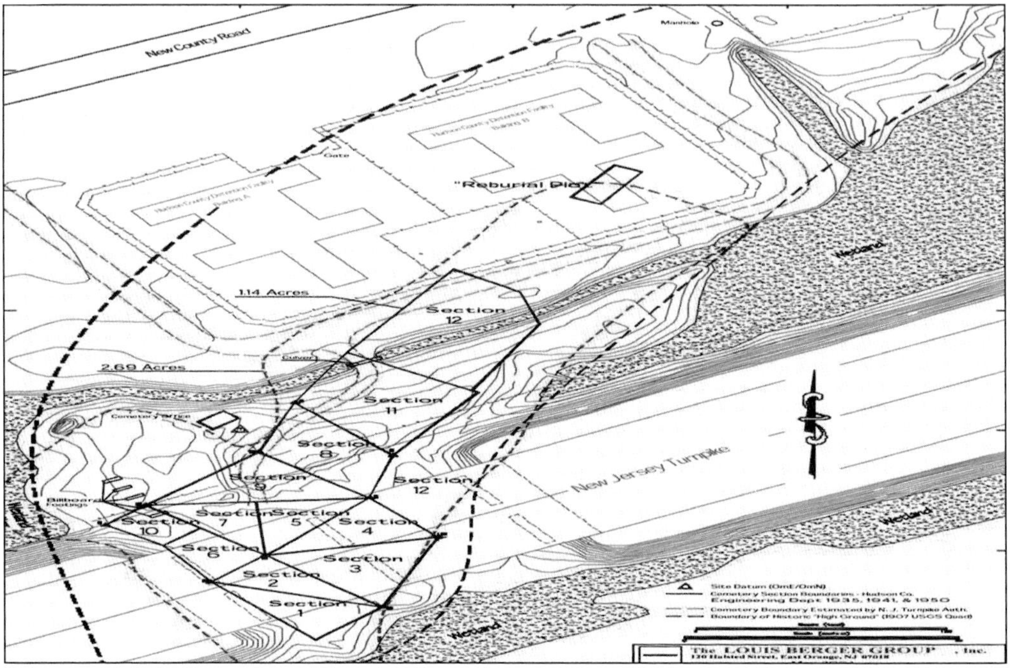

This map, created by the archaeology firm of Louis Berger during the early stages of the project, is a composite of numerous early-to-mid-1900s maps obtained from Hudson County and overlaid on present topography. The available mapping suggested that the original cemetery was composed of 12 sections. The cemetery's southern sections were under the turnpike's bridge, and the northern section was near the correctional facility. This original cemetery was believed to be approximately 1.2 acres; however, during the performance of the project the cemetery was found to occupy a greater area and the project acreage doubled, extending northward to include a significant portion of the correctional facility grounds and other points well to the north.

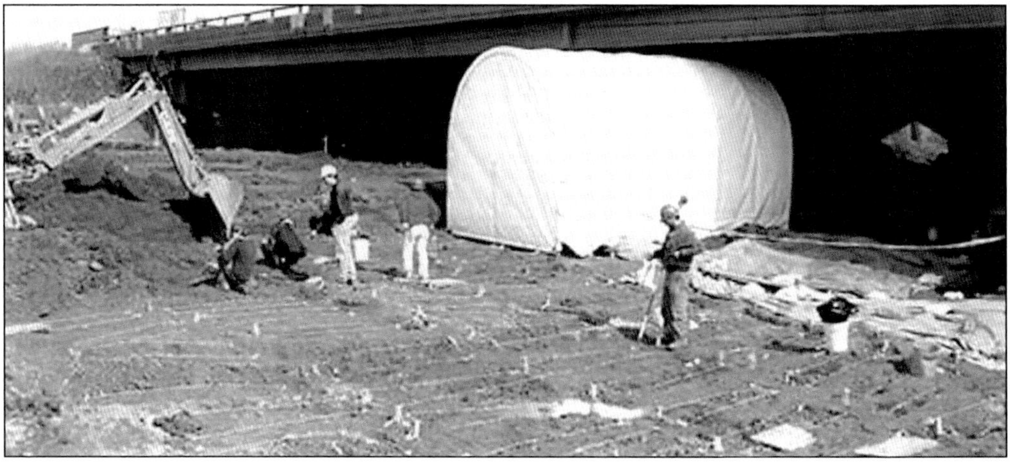

After mechanically removing several feet of soil, archaeologists were able to identify the individual burial shafts. These shafts were each delineated, surveyed, and catalogued. From this point forward the shafts were hand excavated by field archaeologists. It was originally estimated that only a few thousand cubic yards of material would be removed during disinterment activities over the course of the project; however, due to the large amount of debris and soil dumped on the site over the decades of neglect, more than 20,000 cubic yards of material had been removed by project's end.

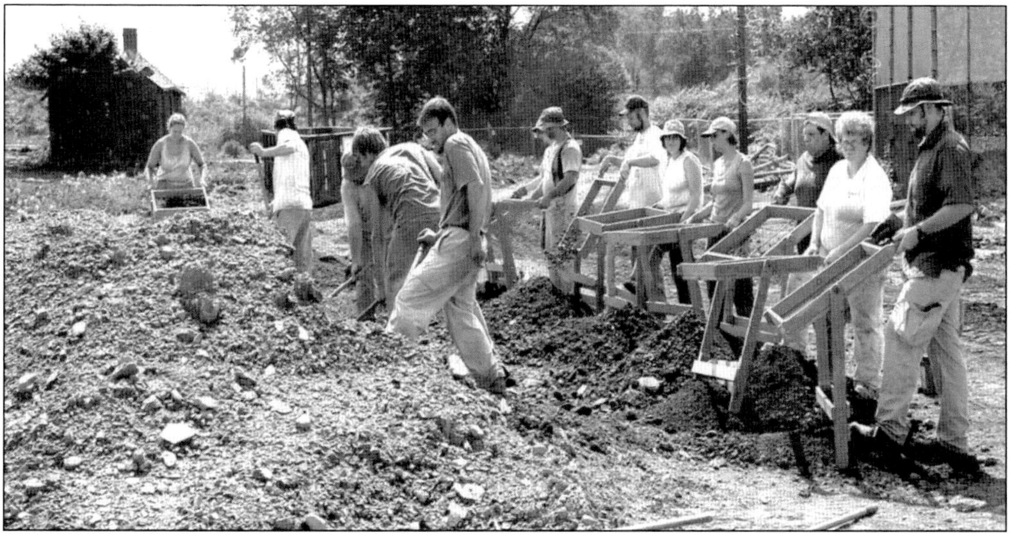

A team of more than 100 field archaeologists, representing 30 states from across the nation, assembled to work on the project. This photograph shows many of the field archaeologists tediously screening through excavated material. In total, 2,686 grave shafts were identified and 4,570 sets of human remains were exhumed, making this project the single largest disinterment ever performed in the United States.

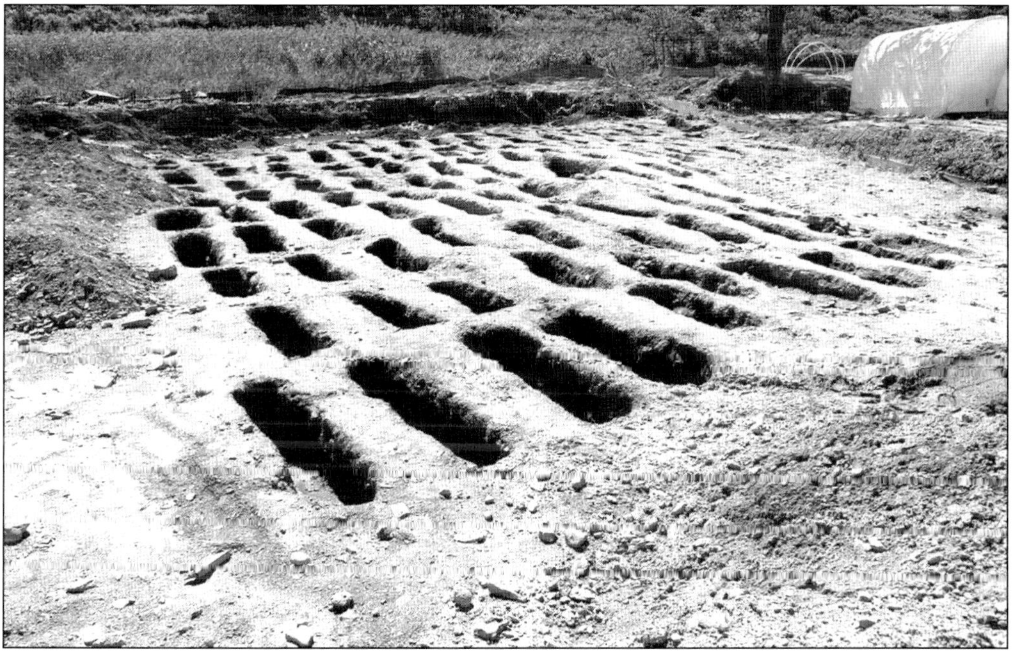

Pictured is a small sample of the 2,686 grave shafts that were disinterred. In general, each grave contained two burials, an upper and lower burial. Individuals were typically buried in simple pine boxes; however, in a few instances, fairly elaborate metal coffins were found.

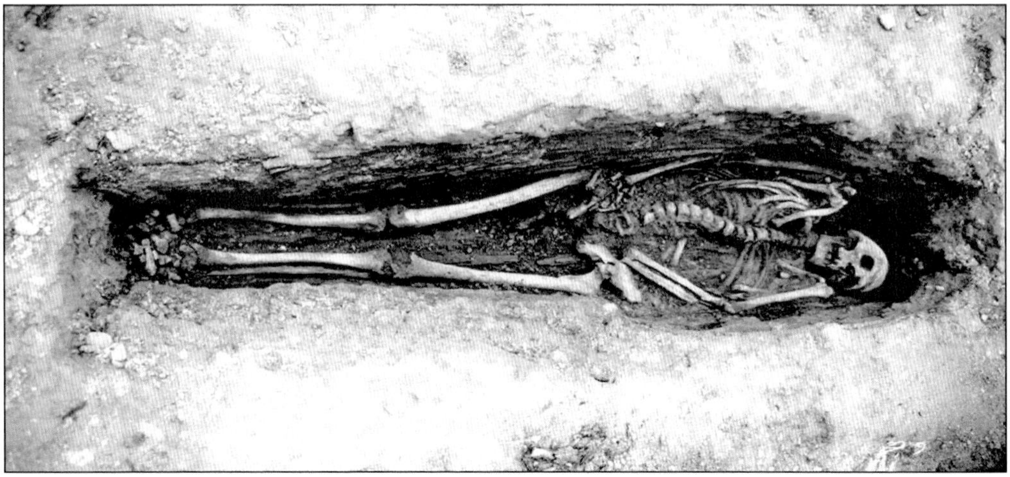

The condition of the remains varied drastically within Potter's Field. Soil permeability and depth of the burial with respect to the water table were greater factors to the condition of the remains than the date of the burial. This photograph shows the remains of a well-preserved individual. Depending on the state of the preservation, archaeologists and osteologists were able to determine the gender and approximate the age at death, the physical stature of the individual, and in some cases, origin, traumas sustained, diseases inflicted with, and cause of death.

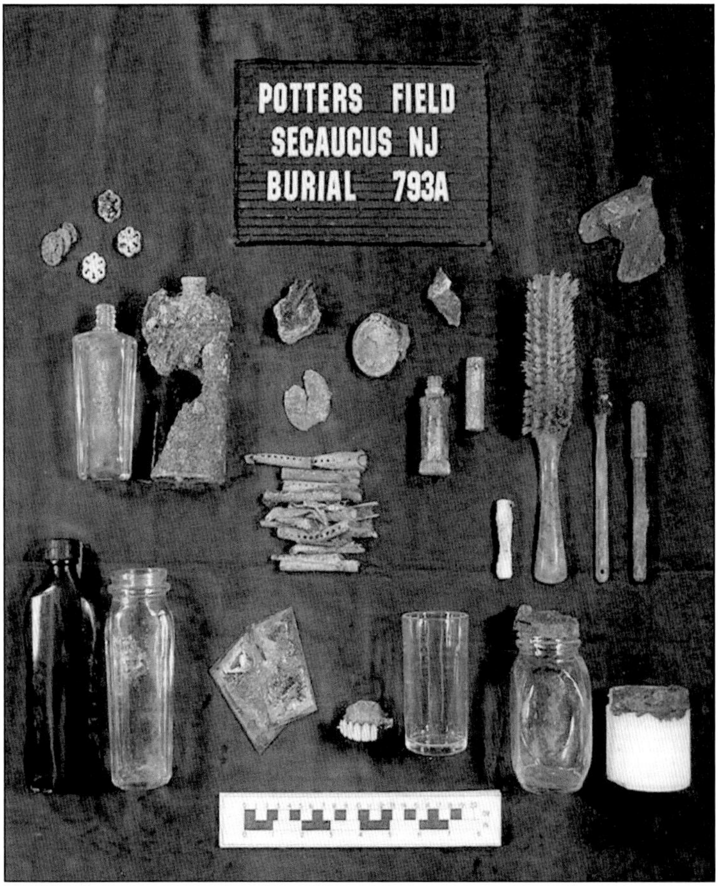

Thousands of artifacts were recovered during the performance of the disinterments. Artifacts included wedding rings; coins dating back as early as 1844; military medals from the Spanish-American War, Civil War, and both World Wars; monogrammed belt buckles; hair brushes; clay pipes; harmonicas; whiskey bottles and religious items, just to name a few. These artifacts were all cleaned, catalogued, and reinterred with the individuals with whom they were found.

During the course of the project, only two families came forward to claim the remains of their loved ones. Remarkably, the archaeologists were able to positively identify these remains, and with the approval of the courts, turn over the remains to the families.

To the right is a photograph of Leonardo Andriani taken in the 1940s. Leonardo's grandson, Patrick, took an active role in the quest to recover the remains of his grandfather, who was believed to be buried at Potter's Field. As a result of Patrick's pursuit, which was well chronicled by the media, the project gained national attention. In the fall of 2003, Turnpike Authority executive director Michael Lapolla informed Patrick Andriani that, based on information provided by the Andriani family, the archaeologists had identified the remains of his grandfather. The courts concurred with the archaeologist's identification, and the remains were turned over to the Andriani family. Following a funeral service held 55 years after Leonardo Andriani's death, the family laid the body to rest in Maple Grove Park Cemetery, just a short distance from the memorial honoring all those buried at Potter's Field.

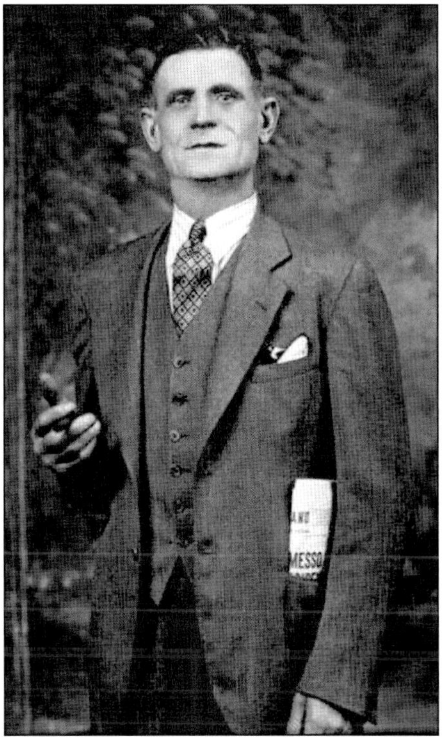

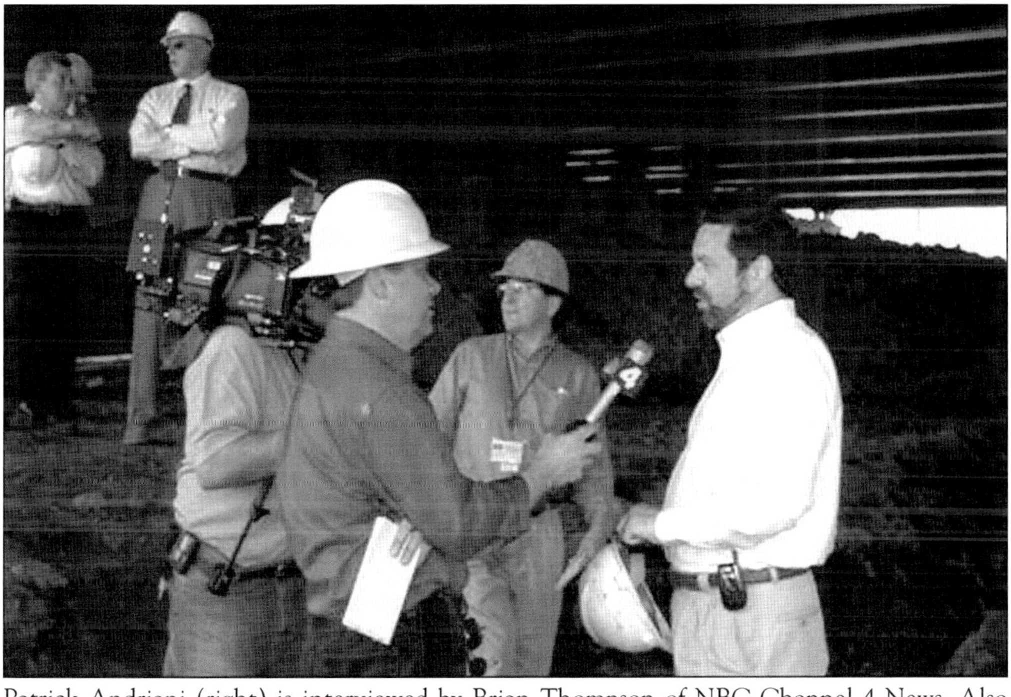

Patrick Andriani (right) is interviewed by Brian Thompson of NBC Channel 4 News. Also at the Potter's Field site for this news conference are Michael Lapolla, executive director of the Turnpike Authority (upper corner, on left), and Richard Raczynski, chief engineer of the Authority (upper corner, on right).

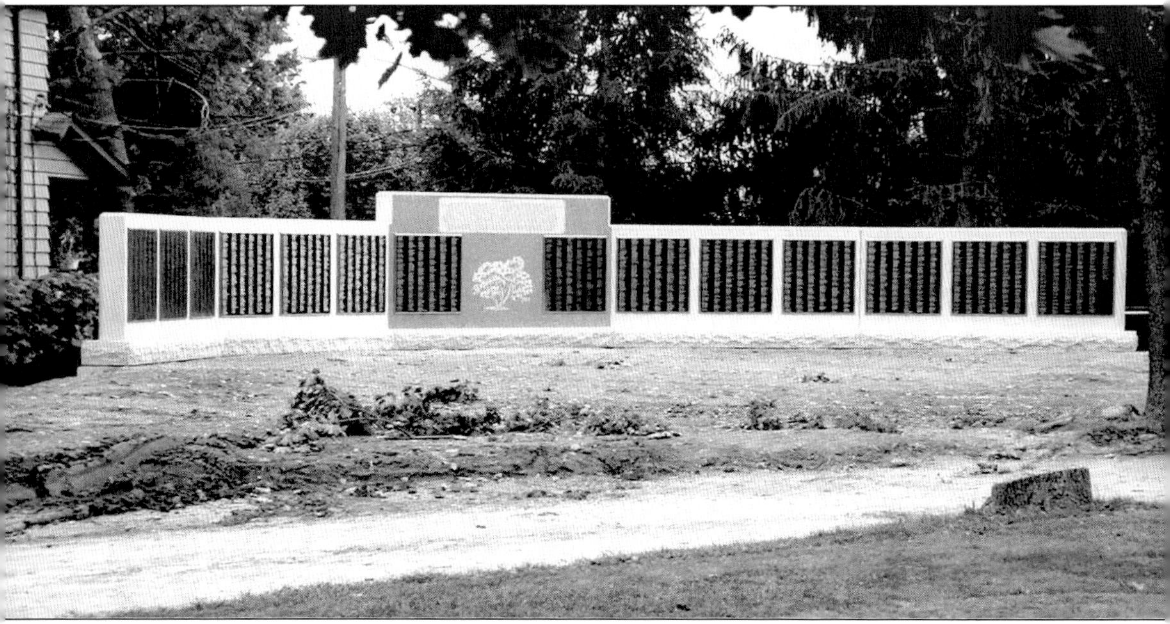

A permanent memorial was erected at Maple Grove Park Cemetery honoring all of the individuals identified in the Hudson County burial ledgers. The inscription on the monument reads: "This memorial has been erected as a tribute to all those men, women, and children who were laid to rest in the former Hudson County Burial Ground, also known as the Snake Hill Cemetery or Potter's Field, in Secaucus. These individuals were buried in the Hudson County Burial Ground because society deemed them poor, medically or mentally unhealthy, criminals, or nameless. This monument stands as a permanent reminder of the 7,496 named individuals and 1,212 unknown souls listed in the burial ledgers from December 1880 to April 1962. We now recognize these people as our mothers and fathers, brothers and sisters, sons and daughters, who were lost but now are found. In 2003, the remains of 4,570 of these individuals were removed from Potter's Field and brought to this spot to be honored and remembered. May this site serve in perpetuity as their final resting place and a sanctuary of peace."

Four

An American Phenomenon

The New Jersey Turnpike

Simon and Garfunkel went looking for America on it. Tony Soprano drives to work on it. Actress Susan Sarandon wants a rest stop named after her on it. Comedian Dennis Miller describes the Earth being like "the Vince Lombardi Service Area on the New Jersey Turnpike" to aliens traveling through space.

Somebody always seems to have something to say about it. But why? How did 148 miles of concrete and asphalt get such an identity all of its own?

There probably is not a rational answer to the question, but a combination of the close proximity to New York City, millions of motorists traveling it every year, and the amount of unusual occurrences that seem to regularly present themselves do a lot to keep the New Jersey Turnpike in the mainstream media.

Throughout its 53 years of existence, the New Jersey Turnpike has seen its share of the unusual that always seems to catch the attention of an audience. From the unexplainable of a still-cold marlin being found at a roadway maintenance yard, to the simply odd of a man hitchhiking with a duck under his arm, to the outrageousness of millions of dollars in cash and coin being spread across the road in an armored car accident, nothing seems to be out of the ordinary on the New Jersey Turnpike.

"Do you guys go looking for this stuff?" asked one reporter recently when talking about the storied history of the turnpike. "No, it generally finds us on its own," is pretty much the standard answer. And it is true, the outlandish and exotic all find their way here—but there is so much more to the New Jersey Turnpike than that.

Over the past few years many people have come to know the New Jersey Turnpike from the opening credits of *The Sopranos* on HBO. Countless people have watched and then looked for the places associated with the hit series. After an episode featuring a turnpike site, it is not uncommon for fans to call the Authority inquiring about the location seen on the television series. But these people all seem to miss the bigger picture of what makes the turnpike an icon.

As discussed earlier, the New Jersey Turnpike has been at the forefront of many technological advances. Very likely it was one of the first roads ever truly marketed to the public. From its initial days of providing travel information to the first motorists via manually changeable roadway signs, to today's overhead electronic message boards, the turnpike has always been ahead of the pack and getting attention for it.

In 2000, the New Jersey Turnpike Authority led the largest initiative in the country to bring electronic toll collection to the roadway with the introduction of E-ZPass. Four years later, the turnpike became one of the leaders of the expansion of that program to Express E-ZPass, which allows motorists to pay tolls electronically while driving at highway speeds.

As a result, word tends to spread. Across the country, turnpike officials are sought out by media and transportation officials and are asked how they accomplished a major initiative by those who are contemplating a similar project or reporting on one.

So, through a combination of a gangster living in New Jersey (only on television of course), some wild animals running loose, and the never-failing effort to keep ahead of the pack and offer motorists some of the most-advanced conveniences in their travel, the New Jersey Turnpike always seems to fit comfortably in any part of the country.

Go ahead, use it in a punch line—someone is going to get the joke.

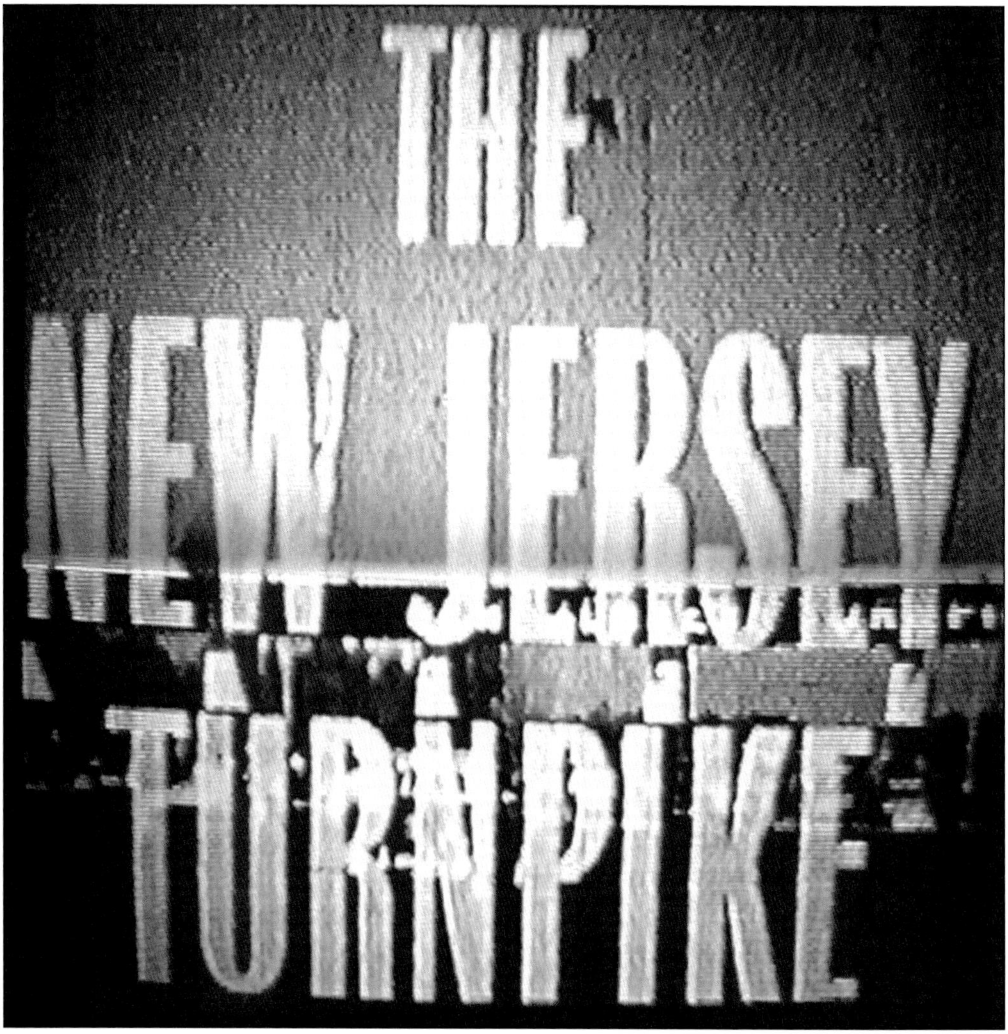

A promotional piece about the New Jersey Turnpike, filmed in the early 1950s, advocated the turnpike as "the most modern, most heavily traveled toll highway in the world . . . a triumph of engineering skills and far-sighted planning . . . planned to meet every need of modern motoring, the New Jersey Turnpike can face any new trial by traffic with confidence that it has paved the way to a new age in road building."

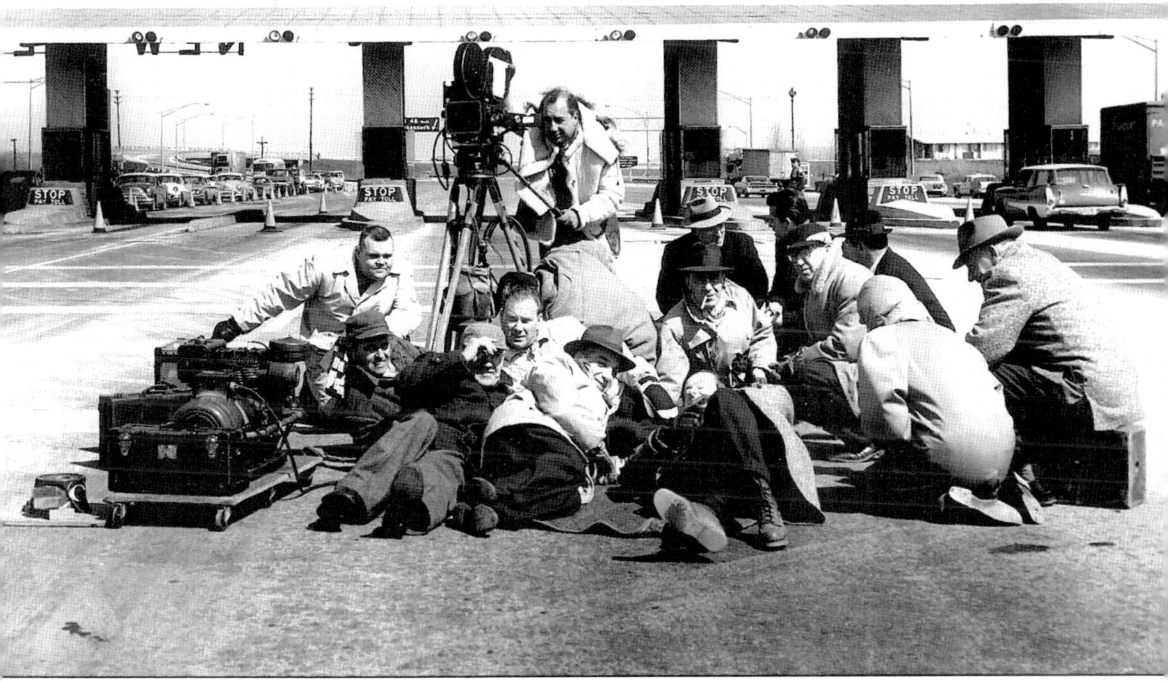

The camera pans around to shoot the fleeing gangsters' car as a television crew ducks to the roadbed to get out of camera range at Interchange 18. The getaway automobile was driven by Ernie Durando.

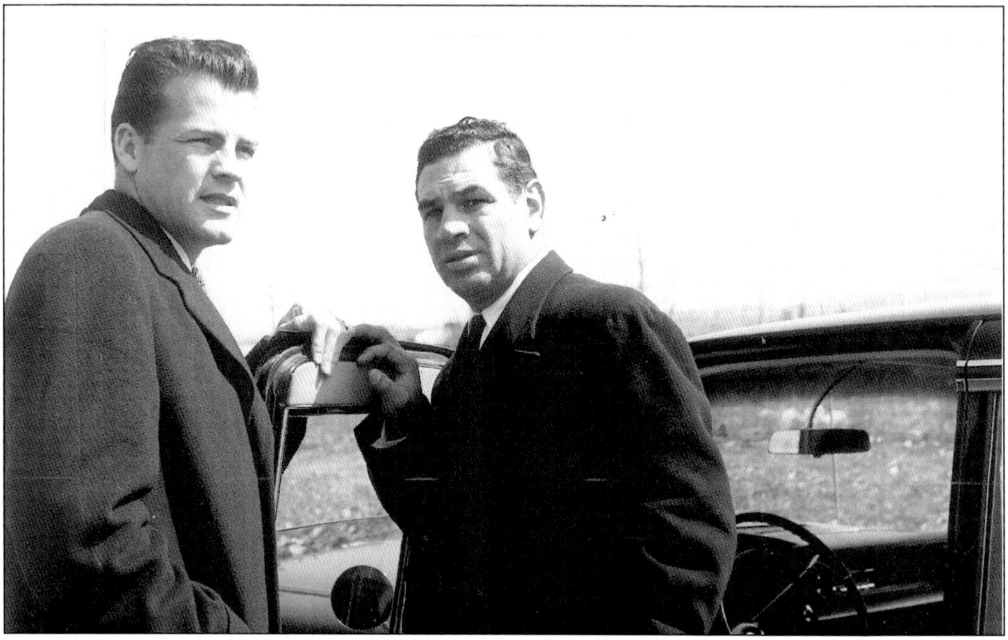

The turnpike's Ernie Durando (right) takes a breather with Frank Gifford, New York Giants' football star, on location during the shooting of the CBS pilot film, *Turnpike*. The film, produced for the Columbia Broadcasting System by Turnpike Television, depicted the role of the pike and state police in combating an underworld plot. Gifford had the lead as a pike sleuth and Durando portrayed a sinister mob henchman. The series also starred New York Giants football stars Alex Webster and Charles Conerly. Filming was completed on March 23, 1960.

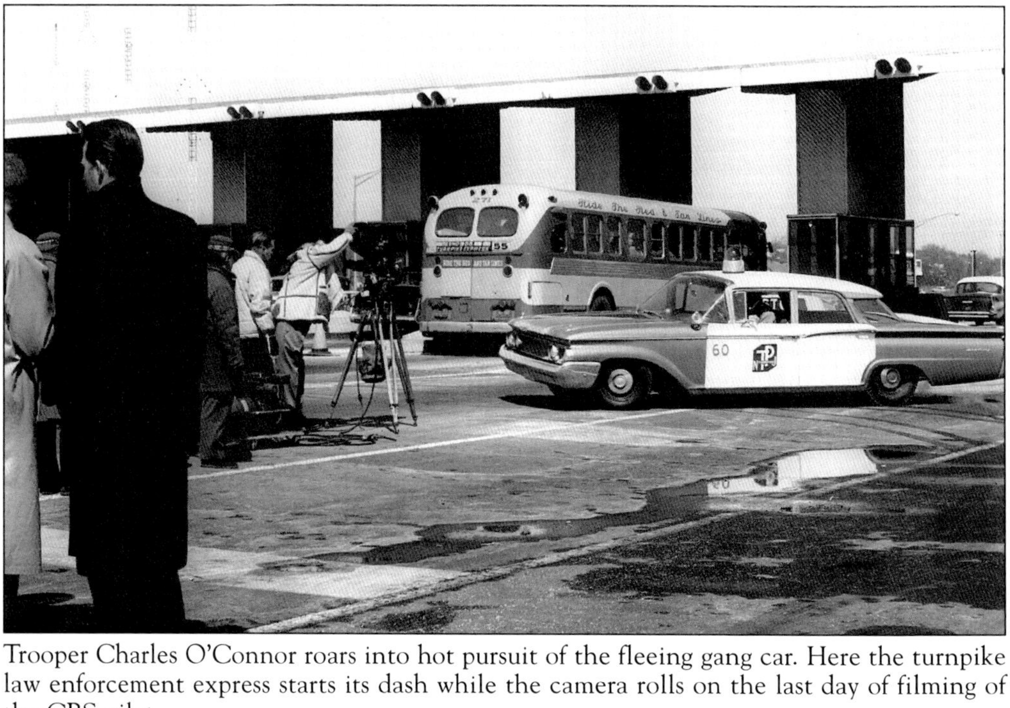

Trooper Charles O'Connor roars into hot pursuit of the fleeing gang car. Here the turnpike law enforcement express starts its dash while the camera rolls on the last day of filming of the CBS pilot.

Turnpike employees at the Lincoln Tunnel Interchange prepare to salute as a motorcade carrying the body of Gen. Douglas MacArthur begins to roll through the exit lane on Sunday, April 5, 1964. From left to right are Toll Collectors William Diehl, Emil Mignone, Joseph Kalter, Walter De Socio, Harry Laderman, and Michael Conte, and Safety Coordinator Ernie Durando. Lt. Clifford Bebout commanded a special state police escort along the turnpike.

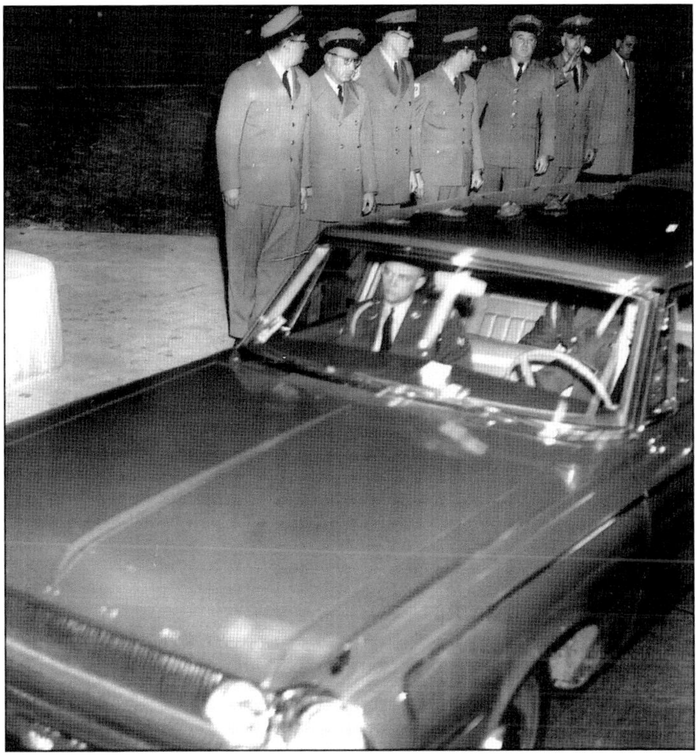

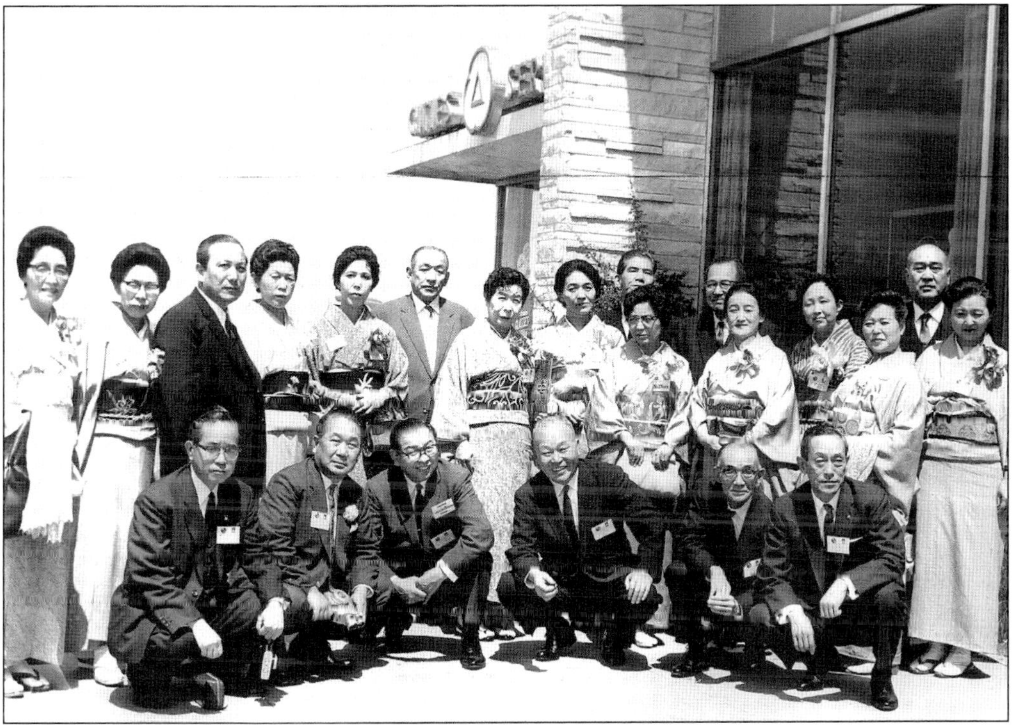

Japanese governors and their wives pose for a group picture while they stop for lunch at the Woodrow Wilson Service Area in Hamilton on May 3, 1964.

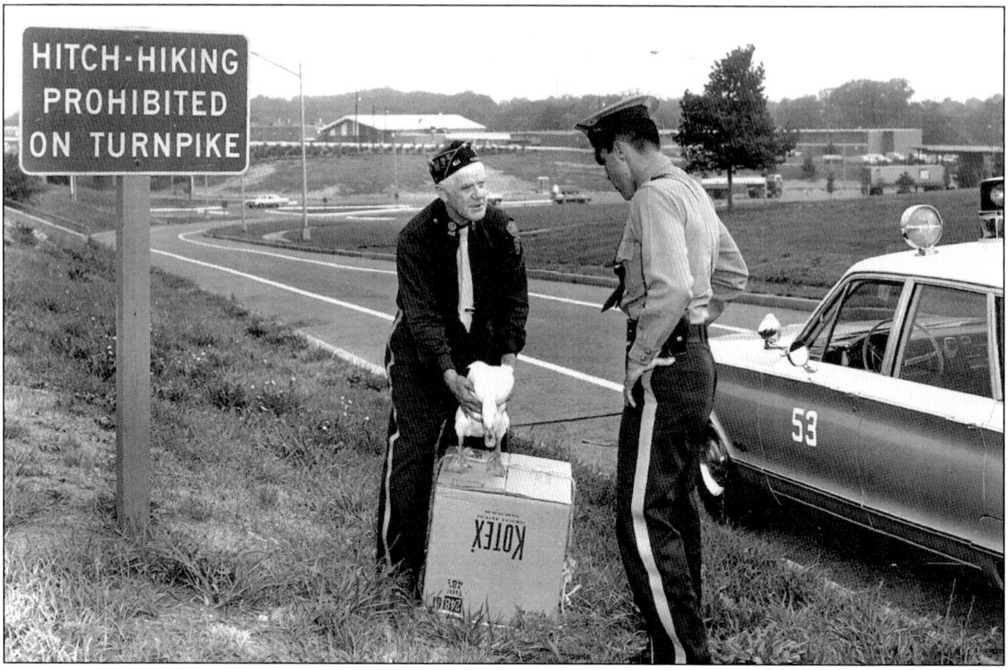

Trooper Richard DeGhetto stops Legionnaire William J. Conway from hitchhiking on the turnpike with a duck. Conway was thumbing his way from his home in Millville, Massachusetts, to the American Legion Convention in Washington, D.C., with the Legion's pet duck, a mascot at all Legion conventions.

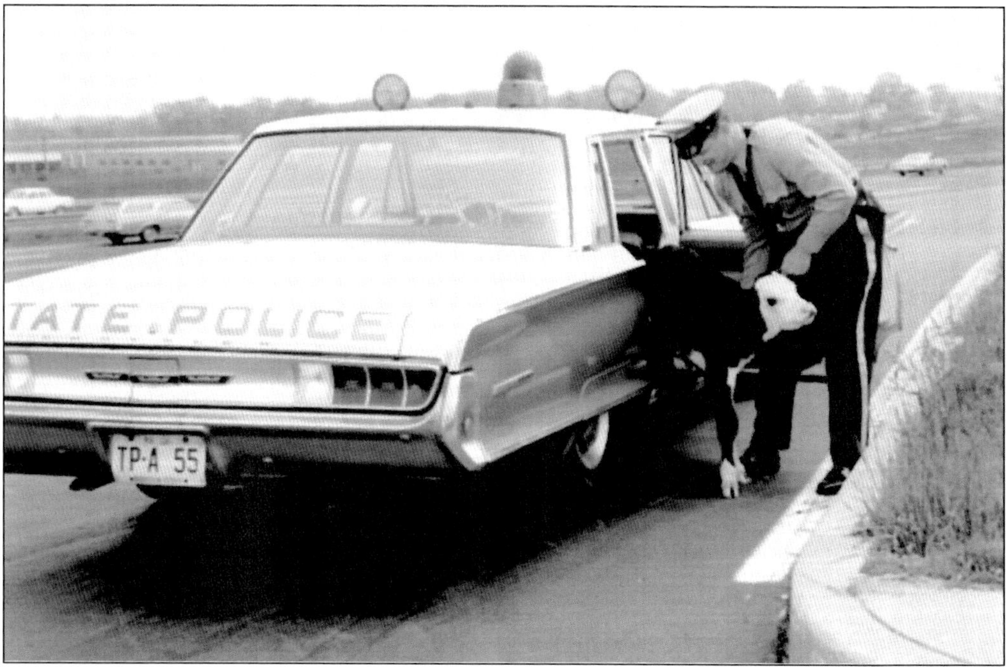

Four calves that had been lost on the turnpike were returned to safety on May 25, 1966. Here, Trooper Stanley Hetman helps the last calf out of a patrol car outside the Turnpike Authority administration building in East Brunswick.

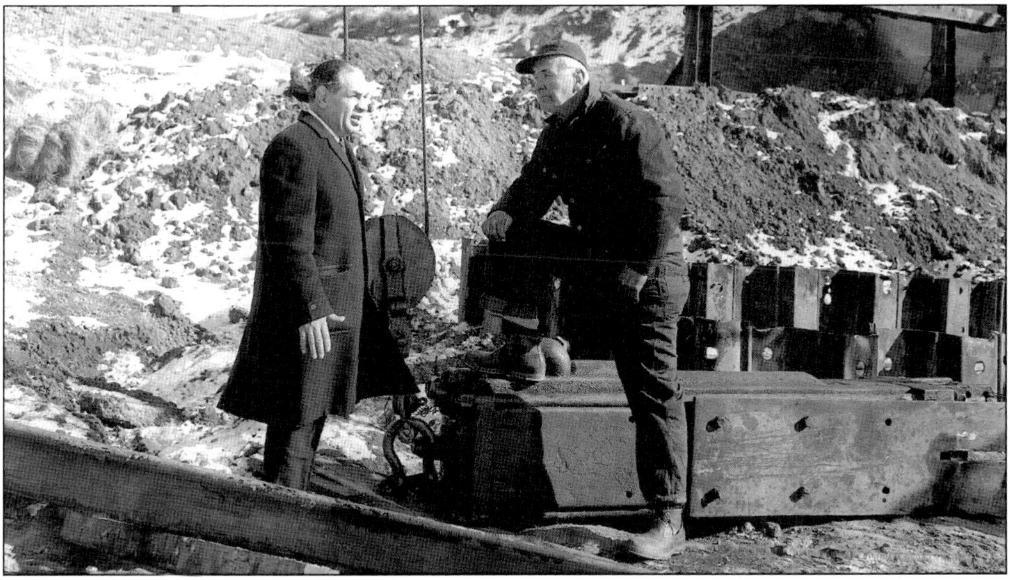

James J. Braddock of North Bergen (right), former world heavyweight champion, now an equipment operator on the New Jersey Turnpike widening project in the Elizabeth area, recalls for Ernie Durando how he defeated Max Baer for the title in 1935. Known as the "Cinderella Man" of boxing, Braddock lost to Joe Louis two years later. Durando, of Bayonne, safety coordinator for the Turnpike Authority, was a middleweight contender who was just one fight away from the title when he was defeated in an elimination tournament by Paddy Young in 1956.

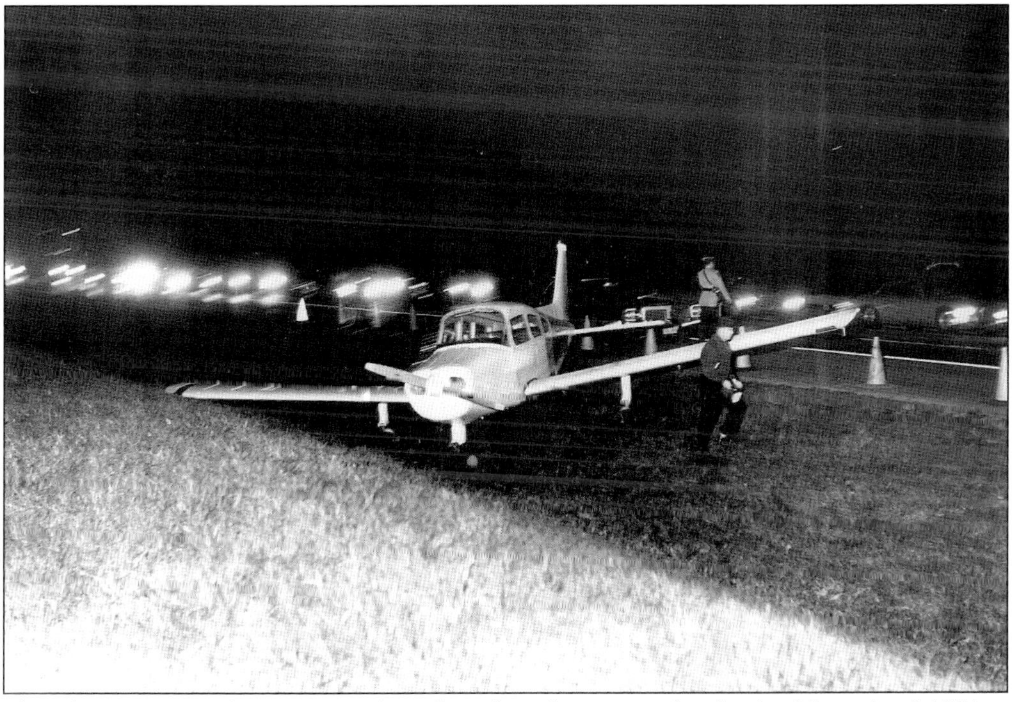

This plane was out of gas at 6,000 feet when the pilot managed to land safely in April 1971 in the northbound lanes near Allentown. The plane was dismantled the following morning and carted off the turnpike.

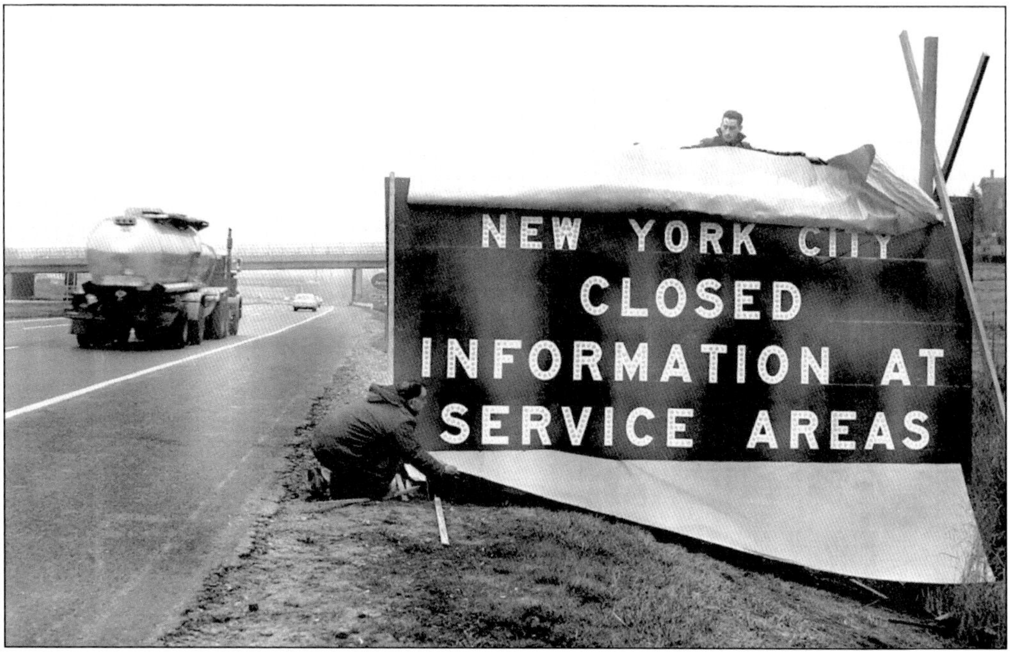

In this photograph, taken just south of the Grover Cleveland Service Area, turnpike maintenance men ready an emergency sign to direct New York City–bound traffic in case of severe weather conditions. The sign was never used.

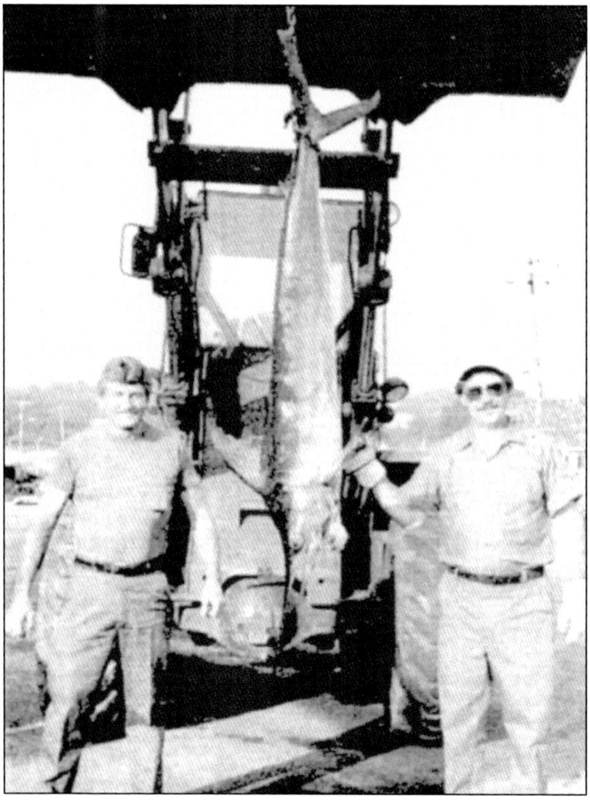

Ninety pounds is the estimated weight of this marlin, believed to be a record catch on the turnpike. The still-cold deep-sea billfish was found one morning in the storage yard at a maintenance district by equipment operators Glen Maindelle (left) and Rudolph Fischer. According to the October 1989 turnpike employee newsletter, "One version of the fish story is that more than one employee had the critter for dinner."

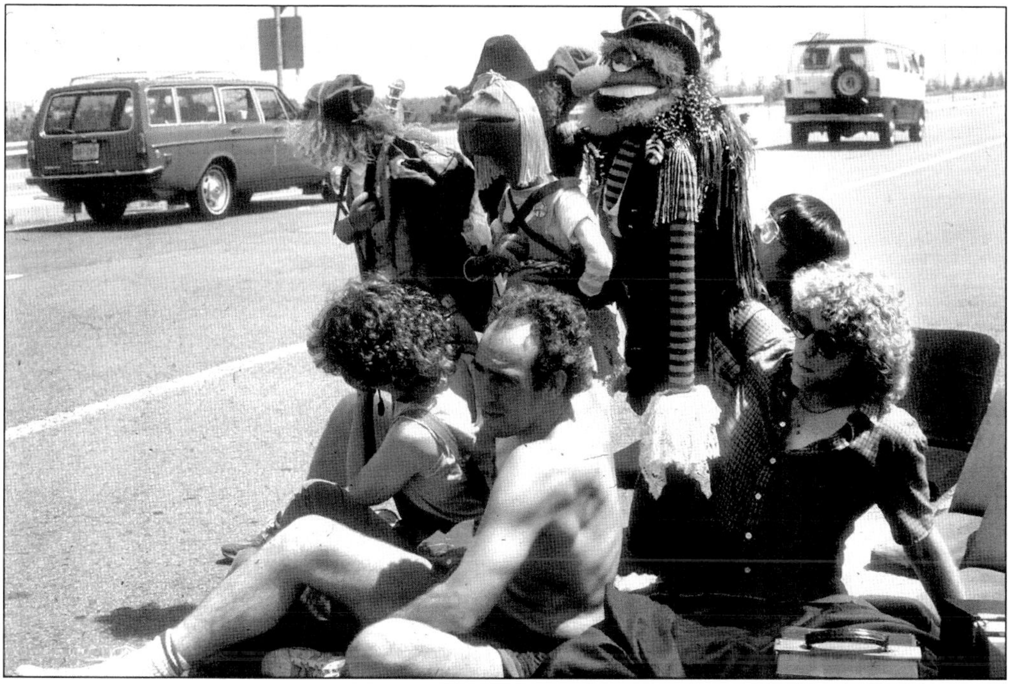

The Muppets Take Manhattan is the last of the traditional Muppet movies made by Jim Henson. This film features Miss Piggy's wedding to Kermit the Frog. Once again, the ramps to the sports complex from the turnpike main line were used for the roadway shots.

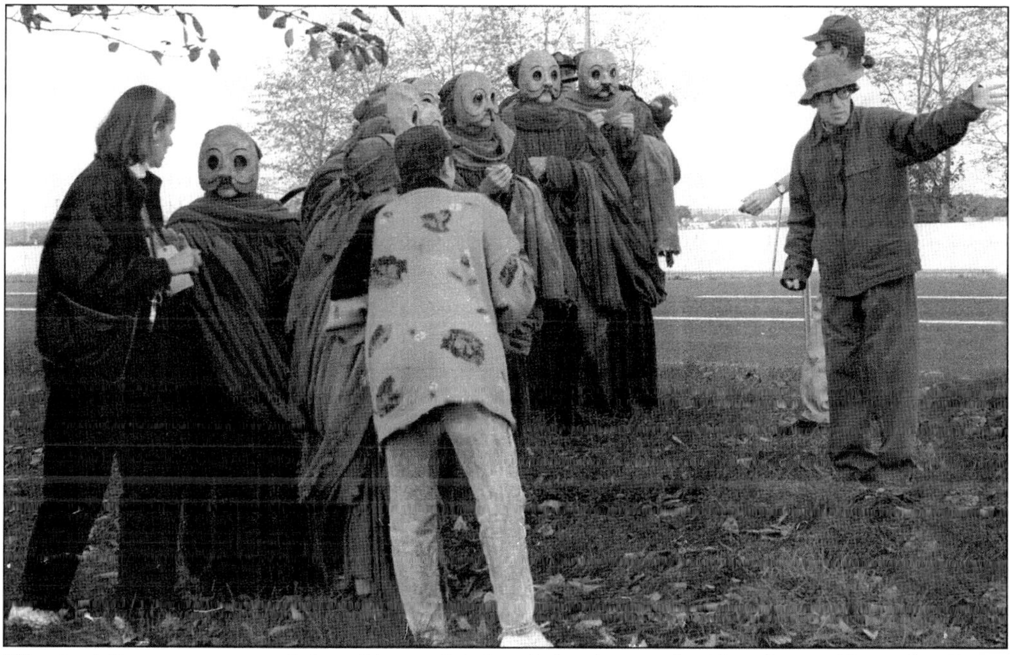

Woody Allen spent several days filming *Mighty Aphrodite* on the New Jersey Turnpike. Here, the director/actor is setting up a scene with a Greek chorus. This segment was filmed on the northbound side of the roadway, near Interchange 18W. The feature is one of seven movies filmed on the turnpike in 1994.

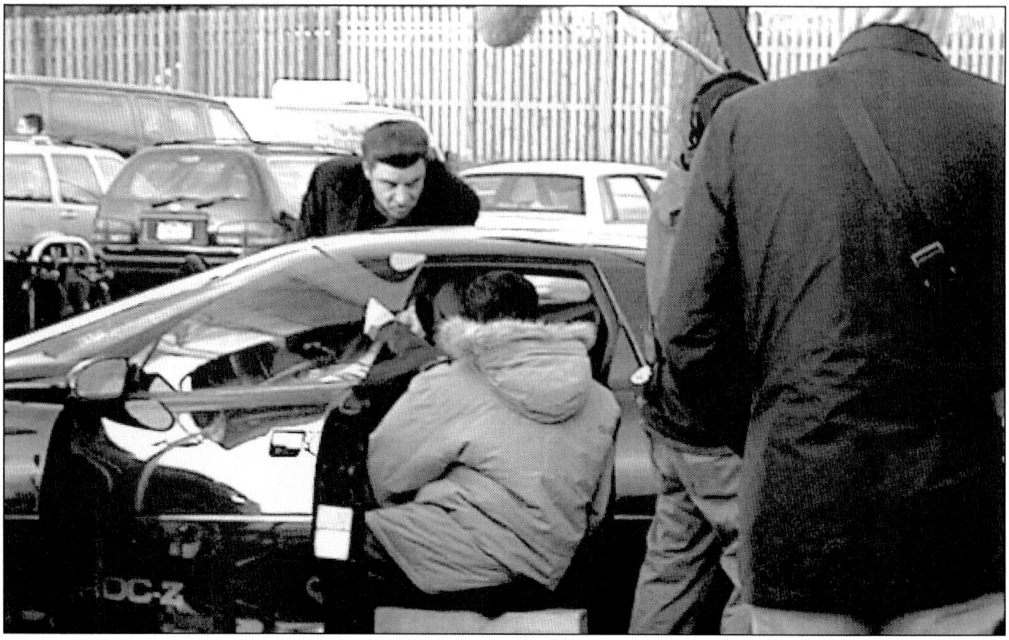

The critically acclaimed award-winning HBO series *The Sopranos*, filmed almost entirely in New Jersey, opens every episode with James Gandolfini as Tony Soprano driving along the northern sections of the New Jersey Turnpike. In this photograph, Steven Van Zandt as Silvio Dante approaches Tony's nephew, Michael Imperioli as Christopher Moltisanti, in the parking lot of the Alexander Hamilton Service Area on the New Jersey Turnpike.

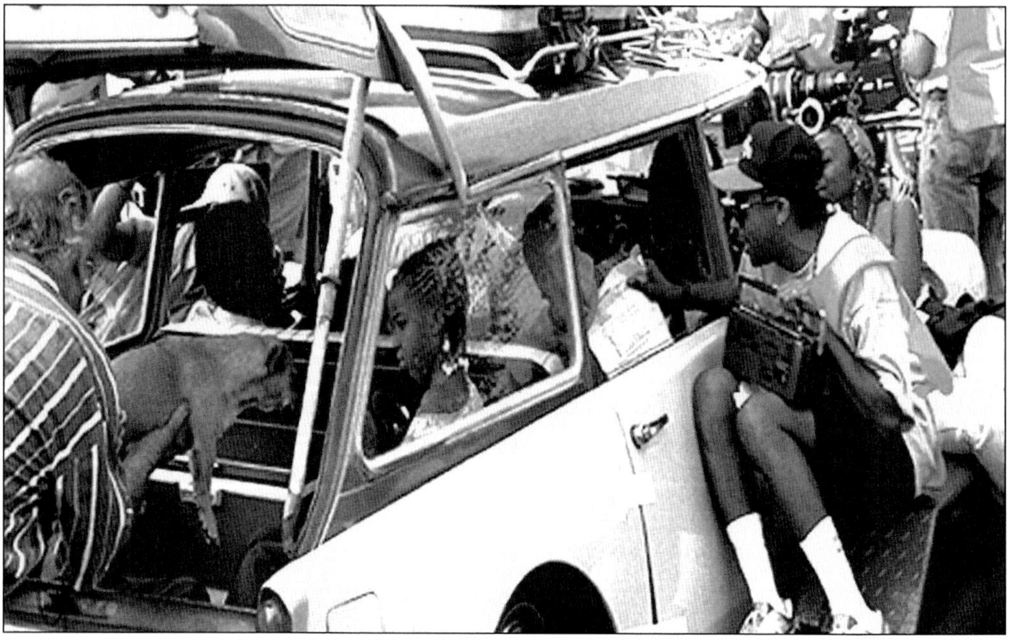

Spike Lee wrote and directed *Crooklyn*, a relatively light seriocomic film based largely on his personal experiences growing up in Brooklyn, New York, during the early 1970s. The story was written in tandem with his sisters Joie and Cinque. The production crew filmed this segment of the film on the ramps leading to the Meadowlands Sports Complex in Rutherford.

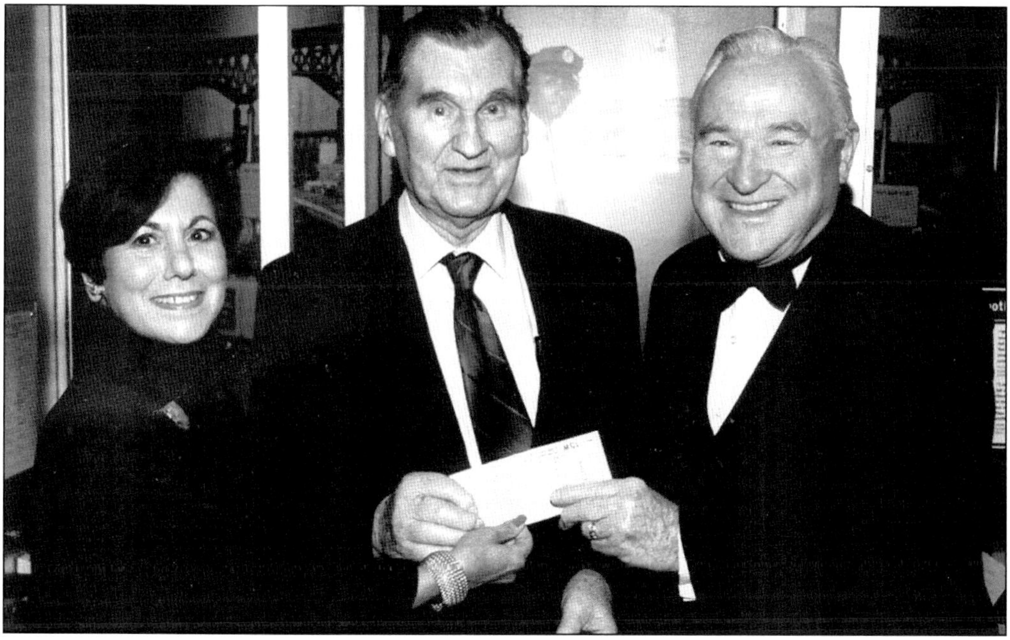

Former vice chairwoman Nancy Becker (left) and former chairman Frank X. McDermott (right) pose with Sam Kostick (center) holding an original toll ticket. Kostick collected the first toll of 15¢ from Omero C. Catan on opening day of the turnpike's initial 53 miles from Deepwater to Bordentown on November 5, 1951.

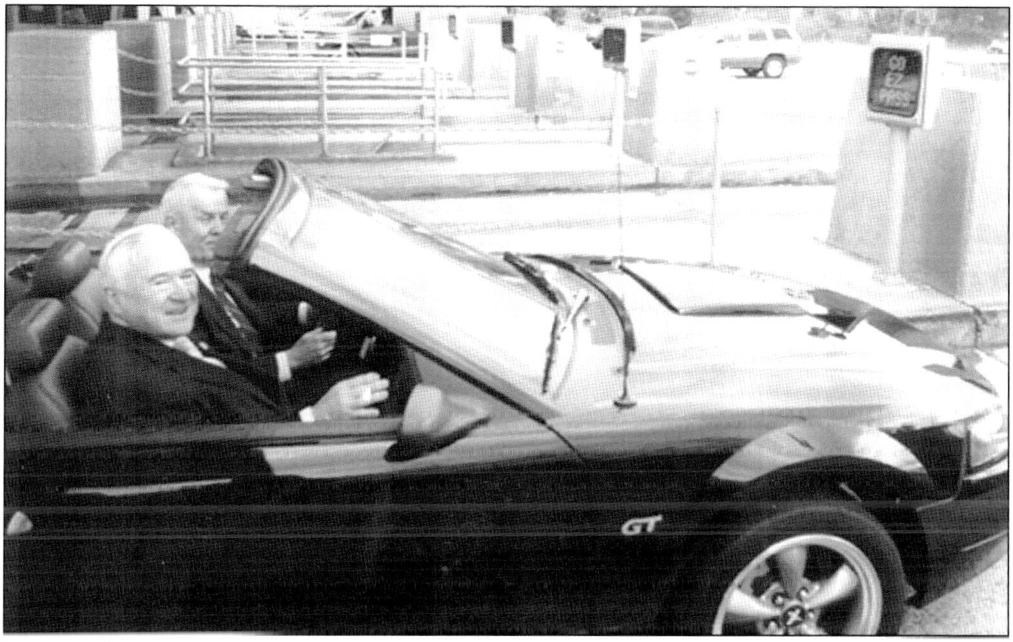

In a grand ceremony on November 5, 2001, former chairman Frank X. McDermott and New Jersey Turnpike Authority employee Richard "Dick" Walley (at the steering wheel) re-created the historical first toll payment of the same day exactly 50 years before, with a twist. Utilizing the modern technology of an E-ZPass lane, the pair honored the past and set in motion the next 50 years of service for the miracle road.

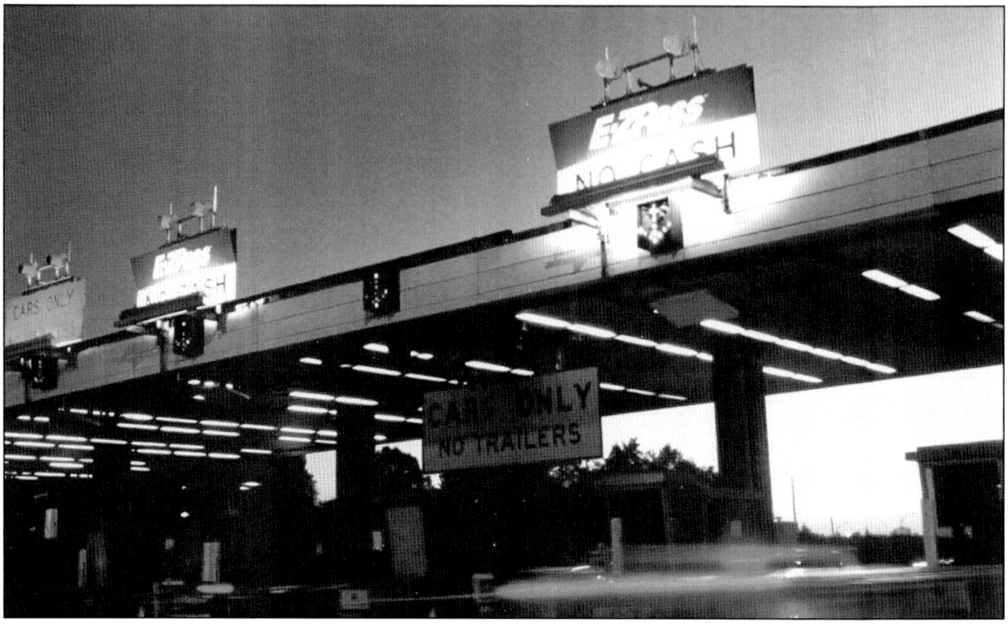

On September 30, 2000, at approximately 4:00 in the morning, the electronic toll collection system debuted in 160 of the turnpike's 341 toll lanes. The New Jersey Turnpike was the lead agency in the largest implementation of electronic toll collection in the United States.

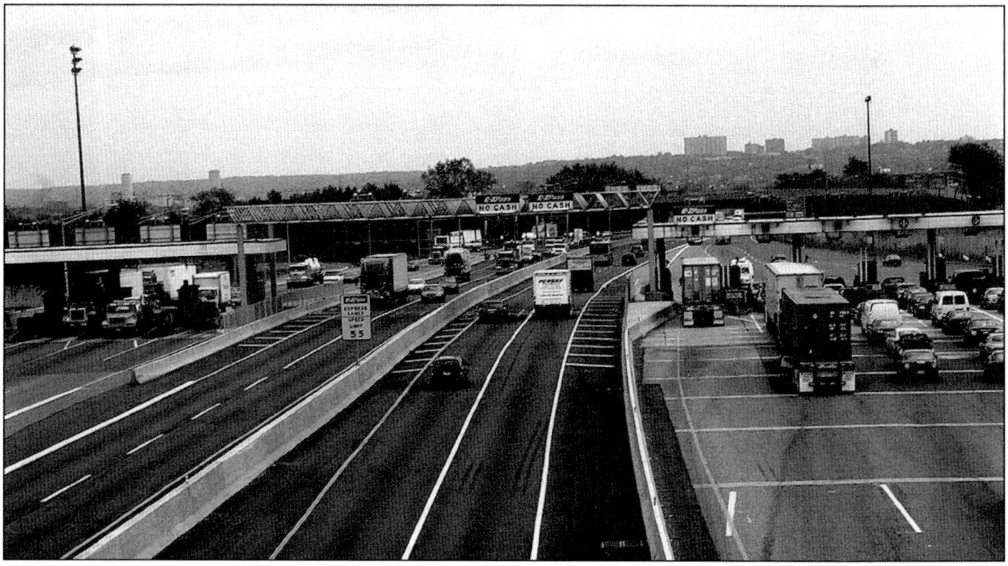

Express E-ZPass removes sections of existing toll plazas and replaces them with overhead gantries with advanced E-ZPass reading equipment. The result for drivers is the ability to travel at posted highway speeds through open lanes without the nuisance of slowing down. In September 2003, the first steps toward the implementation of the Express E-ZPass program were taken as toll booths at the Pascack Valley Toll Plaza on the Garden State Parkway and Interchange 18W on the New Jersey Turnpike were removed to make way for the new high tech lanes. The $45 million program will eventually install Express E-ZPass lanes at Raritan, Asbury Park, and Toms River on the Garden State Parkway, as well as Interchange 1 on the turnpike.

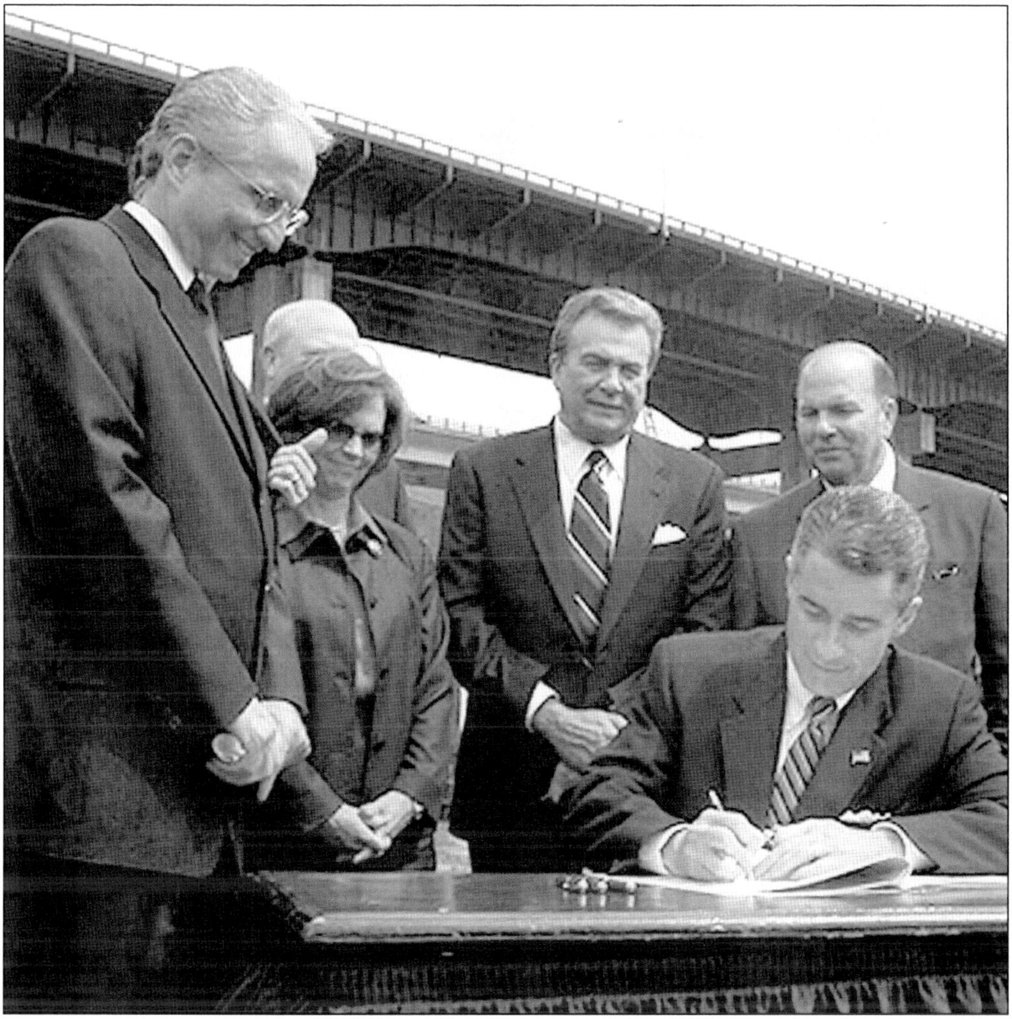

July 9, 2003, marked a groundbreaking day in the history of transportation in New Jersey, as the New Jersey Turnpike Authority assumed operations of the New Jersey Highway Authority to create one agency. With the legislature's ultimate approval in May 2003, Gov. James E. McGreevey (seated) signed the legislation that officially consolidated the New Jersey Turnpike Authority—a $2.5 billion refinancing and debt-restructuring project that created a new model of transportation efficiency and savings. Just as Governor Driscoll, more than 50 years earlier, had selected what he considered the most capable group of individuals to build the roadway, Governor McGreevey selected his team of qualified transportation officials to lead the Turnpike Authority into the next 50 years. "For more than 50 years, the Highway and Turnpike Authorities have operated separately from each other. That means for 50 years, we've had double the bureaucracy, no coordination, and inefficient operations. There is so much more we can accomplish now that we have two agencies working as one." Only six months after consolidation became official, the combined roadways posted an operational savings of $3,858,500—only $150,000 short of the $4 million estimated savings for the entire year. Pictured with the governor at the signing ceremony are, from left to right, New Jersey Department of Transportation commissioner John Lettiere, Assemblywoman Linda Stender, Treasurer John Hibbs (in the background), Chairman Joseph Simunovich, and Vice Chairman Joseph (J. P.) Miele.

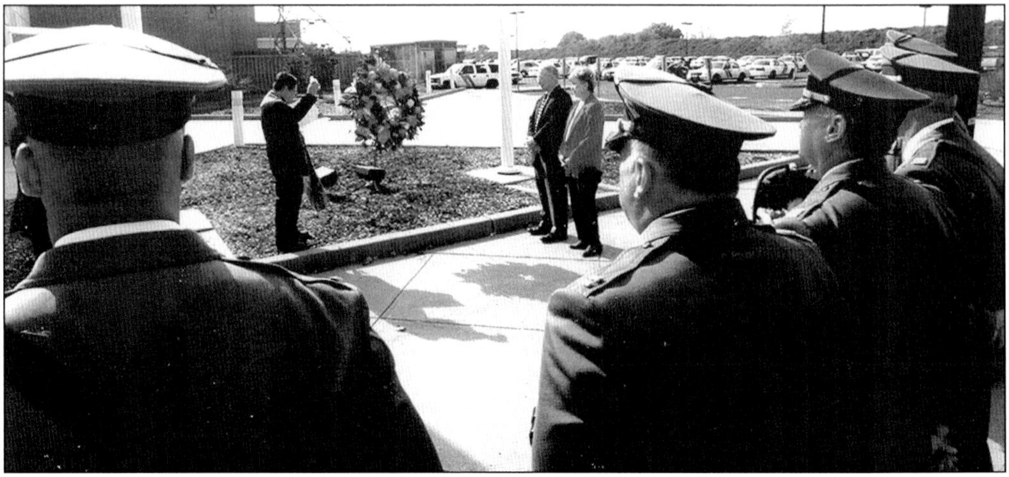

On Friday, November 2, 2001, as part of the 50th anniversary celebration, the New Jersey Turnpike Authority honored the memory of seven of its employees and 13 New Jersey State Police troopers who made the ultimate sacrifice in the performance of their duties. Subsequently, Trooper Christopher S. Scales was killed on December 3, 2002 while performing a routine seatbelt check at Interchange 12, increasing the number of troopers killed in the line of duty to 14.

New Jersey State Police Troop D

Sgt. Frank A. Trainor #682
Trooper Arthur J. Abagnale, Jr. #1671
Trooper William L. Carroll, Jr. #3296
Trooper Joseph P. DeFrino #1605
Trooper Werner Foerster #2608
Trooper Thomas W. Kavula #1809
Trooper Anthony Lukis, Jr. #1754
Trooper John P. McCarthy #3265
Trooper Marvin R. McCloud #4718
Trooper Robert J. Merenda #2393
Trooper Carlos M. Negron #3656
Trooper Christopher S. Scales #4575
Trooper Milan Simcak #999
Trooper Hillary Welenc #1190

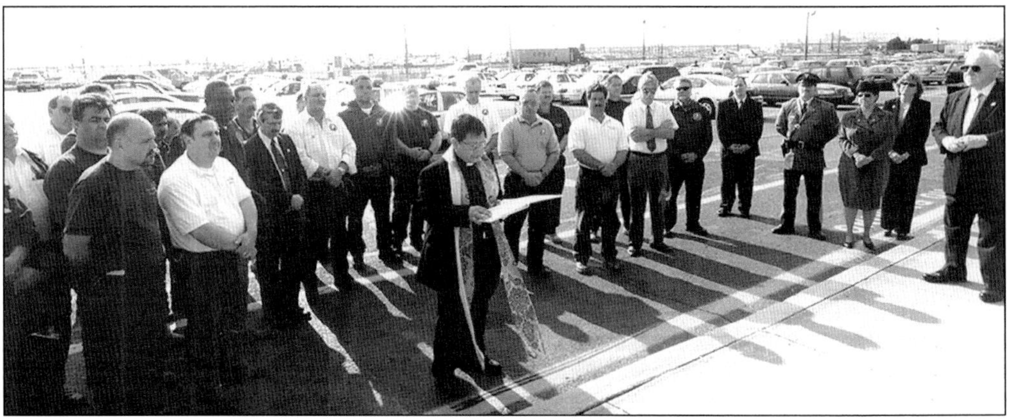

New Jersey Turnpike Authority

Harry Applegate
Robert Baran
Dante Ditillio
Harry Laderman
Dennis Rotonda
Gordon Woodward
Barry Wyckoff